THE DRAGON BOOK

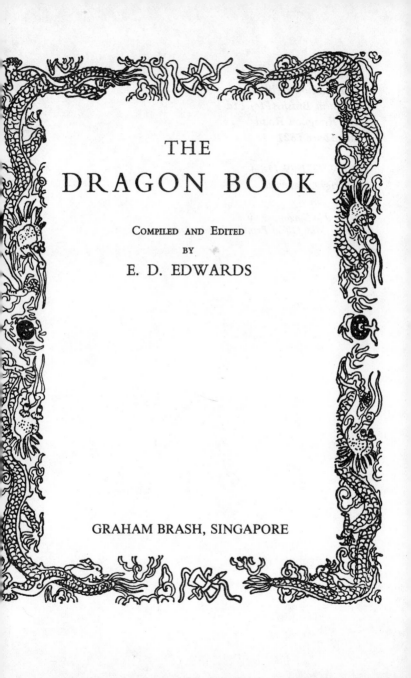

THE
DRAGON BOOK

COMPILED AND EDITED
BY
E. D. EDWARDS

GRAHAM BRASH, SINGAPORE

First published in 1938
This edition published in 1989 by
Graham Brash (Pte) Ltd
227 Rangoon Road
Singapore 0821

ISBN 9971-49-118-4

Printed in Singapore by
Chong Moh Offset Printing Pte Ltd

CONTENTS

PREFACE

" Seek ye knowledge though it be in Cathay."
Week-End Caravan

Dr. LIN YUTANG wrote in *My Country and My People* of ' the calm and beauty and simplicity that distinguished old China.' Those who knew the country before the passing of the Dragon Throne cannot but share his regret at their disappearance. Compensating characteristics have appeared and others will develop, but much of the old beauty and serene detachment is hidden under the ' make-up ' of modern civilization and Western culture. In the hope of recalling something of her ancient spirit this Anthology has been compiled and named *The Dragon Book*.

The first section, Chinese Lore, consists principally of extracts from the writings of Chinese and of early Western observers illustrating Chinese habits, manners, and beliefs from the earliest times.

The Poems which form the second group of extracts have been translated, unless otherwise stated, by the Editor. Many Chinese poems are pictures sketched with a few delicate strokes, and the method of translation employed has been first to visualize the picture suggested by the poet, and then to express it in English, adhering closely to the original and enlarging no more than necessary. Short poems have been used as being best suited to this method.

The longest section of the book consists of anecdotes and tales. Collections of these have been current in China from early times, and those here included are representative of every period and every phase of life. A considerable number of those the source of which is not indicated, are familiar tales retold. The remainder have been translated by the Editor. If the design of the Anthology has been achieved, even the humorous tales will cause more smiles than laughter. Their oddities and abnormalities, arising merely from convention and outlook, amuse without exciting ridicule because they spring spontaneously out of ordinary every-day human experiences and are for the most part far from deliberate *facetiæ*.

The remaining sections—Medical Lore, Flowers and Gardens, and The Epicure—are a medley of translation and miscellaneous knowledge collected in China and in reading Chinese works and books on China. To these it has often been impossible to assign sources. The inclusion of a section on Japanese flower-arrangement in an otherwise all-Chinese Anthology may cause surprise. The original plan of the book included Japanese as well as Chinese extracts, but the Chinese material was so abundant that the original scheme was necessarily curtailed. The section on simplified flower-arrangement was retained however, partly because it had its beginnings in China and partly because its practical as well as its artistic value seemed to justify its inclusion. Like the ' Composite Cookery ' it represents an attempt, based on experiment, to modify Oriental modes to please English tastes.

On the spelling of Chinese names in the Anthology it is only necessary to say that in general this follows the Wade system of romanization. An exception is made in the case of names which occur in the writings of earlier authors, and diacritical marks are only used where their omission would have left the reading of the word doubtful. Yu and Yü are the most frequent example of this.

In order that readers may be able to gain an approximate idea of pronunciation, a table has been prepared setting out the names that occur in the Anthology with an *approximate* English spelling. Where *arn* and *arng* are used for the Wade *an* and *ang* the sound is about half-way between the two. One or two sounds for which no equivalents exist may offer difficulty. In the case of all words beginning with *hsi* it will serve to say *she* with the lips drawn back ; in most other cases a solution is offered.

APPROXIMATE ENGLISH EQUIVALENTS OF THE CHINESE NAMES USED IN THE ANTHOLOGY

Anthology.	Approximate sound in English Spelling.	Anthology.	Approximate sound in English Spelling.
A	are.	Chün	jün.
Ai	eye.	Ch'ung	choong.
An	arn, as in barn.		
		Fa	far.
Chang	jarng.	Fang	farng.
Chen	jun (un as in run).	Fei	fay.
Cheng	jung, as in junk.	feng	fung, as in fungus.
Ch'eng	chun, as in chunk.	Fo	Fore ! (but no r).
Chi	jee.	Fu	foo.
Chia	jee-*are*.		
Chiang	jee-*arng*.		
Chiao	jee-*ow* (ow as in how).	Hai	high.
Chien	jee-*en*.	Han	harn.
Chih	the first syllable of *gi*raffe.	Hang	harng.
		Hao	how.
Chin	gin (and It).	Heng	hung.
Ching	jing (as in jingle).	Ho	her, or hoar.
Ch'ing	ching (as in chink).	Hou	hoe.
Ch'iu	cheeoo.	Hsi	hsee, between see and she.
Cho	jore (as jorum)		
Chou	Joe.	Hsia	hsee-*are*.
Ch'ou	cho, as in choke.	Hsiang	hsee-*arng*.
Chu	joo.	Hsiao	hsee-*ow*.
Ch'u	choo.	Hsieh	hseeh (approx. sheer).
Chü	jü (French u).	Hsin	hsin (approx. shin).
Chuan	jwon.	Hsing	hsing (approx. shing).
Chüan	jüarn.	Hsiu	hsee-*oo*.
Ch'uan	chwon.	Hsü (hsu)	hsü (French u).
Chuang	jwong.	Hu	who.

The Dragon Book

Anthology.	Approximate sound in English Spelling.	Anthology.	Approximate sound in English Spelling.
Hua	wha.	Pei	bay.
Huang	whong.	Pi	bee.
		Ping	bing.
I	ee.	P'ing	ping, as in ping-pong.
		Po	bore.
Jan	ran.	P'o	pore.
Jo	roar.	Pu	boo.
K'ai	ki, as in kite.	San	sarn.
Ko	ger, gor.	Seng	sung.
Ku	goo.	Shan	sharn.
kuai	gwae (Gwydor).	Shen	shun.
Kuan	gwon.	Sheng	shung.
Kuang	gwong.	Shih	Use the first syllable of *che*root.
Kuei	gway.	Shu	shoo.
K'un	kwoon.	Ssu	Use the first syllable of *su*rrender.
Kung	goong.		
Kuo	gwore.	Su	soo.
		Sui	sooee or sway.
Lan	lan, as in land.	Sun	swoon, but lighter.
Lao	lou, as in loud.	Sung	soong.
Li	lee.		
Liang	leearng.	T'ai	tie.
lieh	Lear.	Tan	darn.
Lin	lin, lean.	T'an	tarn.
Liu	leeoo.	Teen	tee-en.
Lo	lore.	Ti	Dee.
Lu	loo.	T'i	tee.
lun	loon.	T'ieh	tier.
		T'ien	tee-en.
Ma	ma.	Ting	ding.
meng	mung (to rhyme with sung).	To	doo.
		T'o	tore.
Mi	mee.	T'ou	toe.
mu	moo.	Tsa	tzar.
		Tz'ai	tseye.
Pao	bow (ow as in bow down).	Tz'ang	tsarng.

Approximate English Equivalents of Chinese Names

Anthology.	Approximate sound in English Spelling.	Anthology.	Approximate sound in English Spelling.
Ts'ao	tsow (ow as in how).	Wen	one.
Tso	dzore.	Weng	wung (w(r)ung).
Tsu	dzoo.	Wu	woo.
Ts'ui	tsooway.		
Tuan	dwon (on as in bon-bon).	Yang	yarng.
		Yao	yow, as in yowl.
Tung	doong.	Yeh	year.
Tzu	dz (as in adze).	yen	yee-en.
Tz'u	tsz.	Yin	yin.
		Ying	ying.
		Yu	yeo, as in yeoman.
Wang	wong.	Yü	yü (French u).
Wei	weigh.	Yung	yoong.

THE decorative illustrations throughout the book have been taken from old Chinese books dating back to the seventeenth century. Although some have no direct connection with the text, their intrinsic merit has been considered sufficient to warrant their inclusion, and thus the anachronism of using modern drawings is avoided.

After three days without reading, talk becomes flavourless.

Proverb

CHINESE

LORE

PROVERBS

When fire burns the old woman's petticoats every one minds his own business.

★

If one son become a priest, all the clan will go to heaven.

★

Better the cold blast of winter than the hot breath of a pursuing elephant.

★

The most important thing in life is to be buried well.

CHINESE LORE

★

AMPUTATION

No Chinese will willingly submit to amputation. It is a fundamental principle of filial piety that the body bequeathed by one's
parents must be treated with respect. For this reason, too, death by
strangling or hanging is regarded as preferable to decapitation.

BAD FORM

IT is bad form
To fall from one's polo pony
To go to bed in one's boots
To sing love-songs in the presence of one's mother-in-law.

LI I-SHAN

BAMBOO

THE uses of the bamboo are innumerable, almost everything in daily
use, from rafts to chopsticks, being made from it. Its young shoots
are eaten salted or fresh, and many of its parts are used in medicine
for their tonic properties.

When the legendary emperor, Shun, was travelling in South
China, he fell ill. His two wives hurried to his relief, but on the
way they learned that he was dead. Turning aside, they wept
pitifully, and their tears fell on the bamboos growing by the road.
To this day the leaves of the ' spotted ' bamboo show dark marks
where the tears of the two empresses fell.

BASIS OF SOCIETY

THE idea of the family is the grand principle which serves as the basis of Chinese society. Filial piety, the constant subject of dissertation for moralists and philosophers, and continually recommended in the proclamations of the emperors and the speeches of mandarins, has become the fundamental root of all other virtues.

HUC

BEAUTY

THE face of a Chinese woman is distinguished by its breadth, and the smallness of the mouth, nose and eyes. . . . The admiration of a white skin is so prevalent that a great many help the defects of nature by the applications of art, which increases the sense of vacancy or at least lack of expression which characterises them when the features are at rest. But no sooner do good or evil nature sparkle in the eye and the lower features melt into a smile, than the deficiency is no longer felt. The smile of a Chinese woman is inexpressibly charming ; we seldom see anything like it, save when the feelings of delight and complacency beam from the eyes of a wife or mistress upon the object of her choice.

In the general outline of the person, the Chinese females differ from those of the Caucasian variety. . . . We miss the expansion of the hip and the graceful flexures of the rising breast—characteristics which both nature and art have conspired to stamp as singularly feminine among those nations where the understanding and the heart have reached the highest pitch of refinement.

LAY

THE ' BURDEN-BEARER '

THE *fu-pan* or ' burden-bearer ' is a little worm with an instinct for carrying things. Whenever it meets anything in its path it bends its head and pushes the burden on to its back. No matter how heavy the load becomes nor how weary the insect is, it cannot stop. Its back is naturally very feeble, and as the weight of the burden increases, the worm becomes unable to move. It sinks flat on its belly and cannot rise. At this point someone may see it and in pity remove its burden. If it is then able to move again, it begins immediately to collect things as before. Moreover it likes travelling upwards, and so it comes at length to the end of its strength, when it falls to the ground and dies.

Nowadays there are acquisitive people who cannot resist anything which they think will enrich them. Engrossed in getting what they want, they never pause to consider the risks they run. They go on accumulating till their greed brings them to dismissal, degradation or exile. If they recover they begin the same process all over again. They think constantly of a higher position, of greater perquisites. They are so covetous that they place themselves in the gravest danger, neglecting the example of those who have perished for the same reason. Such a one, however imposing his rank or famous his name, has no more wit than the little worm—how pitiable is he !

Liu Tsung-yuan

THE CARPENTER'S SONG

A Chinaman has not much idea of home comfort, but he appreciates to the fullest extent the advantages of privacy. He will shut out a fine view rather than expose his dwelling to a curious eye. In towns a two-storied building is the exception. No citizen can overlook his neighbour, and, secure behind the screen before his door, no oyster is more free from observation than he. Just because he is so uncomfortable indoors, he loves to sit at ease under the shade of a summer-house, or sip his tea in the courtyard. On the approach of summer many of the better-class Chinese form this courtyard into a spacious room by a lofty erection of bamboos and matting, which encloses the whole, and during that time the eye is everywhere confronted by the sight of men at work on their airy perch. Farewell for a time then to the much loved seclusion ! Who knows what tales the carpenter might tell of his bird's-eye view of the neighbours' back-garden ! But mark the chivalry of John Chinaman. It is a practice, of which the origin is lost in remote antiquity, that the builders of mat-sheds should play the game of ' I spy ' all the time they are at their work. It takes the form of what may by courtesy be termed a song, and is kept up almost without intermission by one of the apprentices at work on the roof. If any hussy then, forgetting her native modesty, should pop her head out of doors, no one can say the carpenter is to blame.

From *The Chinese Times of* 1887

CATHAY

Of the Kind of Wine made in the Province of Cathay—and of the Stones used there for Burning in the Manner of Charcoal

THE greater part of the inhabitants of the province of Cathay drink a sort of wine made from rice mixed with a variety of spices and drugs. This beverage, or wine as it may be termed, is so good and well flavoured that they do not wish for better. It is clear, bright and pleasant to the taste, and being (made) very hot, has the quality of inebriating sooner than any other.

Throughout this province there is found a sort of black stone, which they dig out of the mountains, where it runs in veins. When lighted, it burns like charcoal, and retains the fire much better than wood ; insomuch that it may be preserved during the night, and in the morning be found still burning. These stones do not flame, except a little when first lighted, but during their ignition give out a considerable heat. It is true that there is no scarcity of wood in

22

the country, but the multitude of inhabitants is so immense, and their stoves and baths, which they are continually heating, so numerous, that the quantity could not supply the demand ; for there is no person that does not frequent the warm bath at least three times in the week, and during the winter daily, if it is in their power. Every man of rank or wealth has one in his house for his own use ; and the stock of wood must soon prove inadequate to such consumption ; whereas these stones may be had in the greatest abundance and at a cheap rate.

MARCO POLO

CATS

CATS are sometimes referred to as protectors of silk-worms, to which rats are very destructive. The picture of a cat on the wall not only wards off harm from silk-worms but also keeps away evil spirits in general.

Early in the eighth century the usurping Empress Wu taught cats and parrots to drink from the same dish, but her belief that she had brought about the millennium was very soon shattered.

CHARMS

CHARMS and amulets are used for almost every conceivable purpose. They generally take the form of characters and symbols written either in black or vermilion on thin paper, the forms depending on the end desired.

To expel demoniacal influences the characters for fire, wind and thunder may be written in red with cabalistic signs in a specific form arranged about them. To ward off calamity it is sufficient to wear them or paste them on door-post or wall ; but to cure sickness the charm must be burned, and the patient must drink the ashes in a draught of water or a cup of tea.

CHINA, A.D. 1710

THE towns, villages, hamlets and roads of China swarm with people. Among the many causes which have contributed to produce such a state of society, I will merely mention these : first, the limited number of bonzes and bonzesses who, like our monks and nuns, profess celibacy ; second, the prevailing custom that each man should marry as many wives as he can support, not caring what may become of the children ; third, the disgrace attached to persons who do not marry ; fourth, the perfect peace that the empire has enjoyed for a long time ; and lastly, early marriages, which generally take place as soon as the parties have attained a suitable age. As an illustration of the numerous progenies of the Chinese, I may add that one day while dining with the steward of the Viceroy, I asked him the number of his children. Not knowing it, he began to reckon them by name ; but when he came to the eighteenth he was puzzled, and called in the servants to help him count the remainder.

Memoirs of Father Ripa

THE CHINESE TABLE

DEER-SINEWS are collected, dried and preserved for a long time in small bundles as an article of food. When they are to be eaten they are first softened in water and then cooked. They form a dish which occupies the second place of honour at a Chinese table, the dish prized beyond all others consisting of swallows' nests, which are found in the rocks and mountains of certain islands near Canton. These nests are not composed of mud, like those in our country, but of a kind of white paste, which, though tasteless in itself, on being prepared with broth and condiments, acquires a taste extremely delightful to the Chinese palate. The flesh of dogs forms the dish held next in estimation by the Chinese, and these animals are therefore kept and fed for their tables.

Ibid.

A CHRYSANTHEMUM GARDEN

FROM the pavilion on the west side of the farm the chrÿsanthemum beds could be seen in full bloom. To the east and west were two lofty summer-houses, of which the eastern was surrounded with young peach trees, for the sake of their blossoms in spring ; while the western, being intended for autumnal visits, was provided in like manner with large collections of the chrysanthemum. It was now autumn, and the abundant richness and beauty of the flowers spread around the base of the building like a variegated carpet of gold.

Their slender shadows fill the enclosure, and a scattered scent pervades the flower-beds, planted in triple rows : the deeper and lighter tints reflect a yellow light, and the leaves shine beneath the drops of dew. Each hungry floweret inhales the passing breeze, as it sheds around its incomparable lustre. The gazer sympathises with the languishing blossoms, bending their heads all faint and delicate : the mournful scene wakes in his mind thoughts suitable to autumn. . . . Such flowers once inspired the poet T'ao Yüan-ming, as he indulged his genius amidst verses and wine.

DAVIS

CLOUDS AND DRAGONS

CLOUDS owe their divine character to dragons ; dragons do not owe their divinity to clouds. Yet the dragon apart from the clouds would have no means of giving form to his divinity. If he lose the thing he is dependent on, is he really without resource ? Strange ! that what he depends on should be something he himself creates. The *Book of Changes* says : ' Clouds emanate from dragons.'

HAN YÜ

COLOURED NAILS

COLOURED finger-nails have long been regarded by the Chinese as attractive ; but instead of painting on a varnish, women tie a petal of the balsam flower on each nail and leave it on until the nails become an exquisite pinky red, which is indelible.

COLOURS

COLOURS in China are symbolic of rank, authority, virtue and vice, joy and sorrow.

Yellow is the imperial colour, assumed only by the emperor and his sons ; purple is prescribed for the grandsons of the emperor ; green or blue for the chairs of princesses. Red is a symbol of virtue, especially of truth and sincerity ; hence, to say a person has a red heart means that he is without guile ; this is also the colour of the button of the first degree of official rank. The emperor writes his decrees in vermilion. Black denotes guilt and vice ; white is used in mourning, and to denote moral purity.

LANGDON

CONVERSATION

UNDER the old regime the Chinese were much given to the use of exaggerated phrases of politeness, especially with strangers. The following conversation gives some idea of this rather difficult but most essential conversational art :

A. Ah ! I have not received instruction. What is your honourable surname, sir ?

B. My cheap name is Li. Your distinguished surname ?

A. My humble name is Lin. From what honourable place do you hail ?

B. My obscure residence is in Shanghai.   What is your honourable age ?

A. This is the twenty-first year of my idiotic existence ; may I presume to ask your great age ?

B. I have already wasted thirty years.   Is that your worthy wife ?

A. That is my contemptible inside (person).

B. (*sententiously*). When there is a good wife in the house the husband never gets into trouble.

MATEER

A CURSE

To avenge the death of one of his chief supporters, the ruler of a certain state called upon every hundred of his soldiers to contribute a pig, and every twenty-five a fowl and a dog, and over the blood of these the whole army cursed the slayer.

Tso Chuan

DAUGHTERS

THE nature of the tiger is most cruel, yet it knows the relation between parent and offspring.   Shall man, who is the superior essence of all things, be surpassed by the tiger ?   I have heard that when female children are killed, the pain inflicted is beyond comparison—long suffering ere they die.   Alas ! the hearts of parents that can endure this !   The disposition of daughters is most tender. They love their parents better than sons do.   Many sons go from home ; daughters cleave to their parents.   Many sons disobey their parents ; daughters are obedient.   Sons have little feeling ; daughters always mourn for their parents.   Daughters love their virtuous husbands, and in many cases increase their parents' honour.   The magistrates sometimes wrote tablets in their praise ; and the Emperor graciously conferred presents on them. Some were made ladies of the palace ; others wives of great men. If you preserve the lives of your daughters, a sure reward will be the consequence.

DAVIS

DE GUSTIBUS NON EST DISPUTANDUM

WITH the Chinese the left takes precedence of the right as the place of honour, and white is the appropriate badge of mourning. Owing to the nature of their compass, which they call 'a chariot pointing towards the south,' they do not number the cardinal points in our order, but always say 'east, west, south, north, west-south, east-north,' and so on.

DIFFERING POINTS OF VIEW

CAN it be said that the arrow-smith is a less humane person than the armourer because the latter desires to save men from being hurt, while the former is anxious that they should be hurt ? Or that the priest is kinder-hearted than the maker of coffins, because the latter would have men die ? It is clear from these examples that the most careful thought is necessary in choosing a profession.

MENCIUS

DIVORCE

The Seven Grounds for the Divorce of Wives

DISOBEDIENCE to parents-in-law ; having no son ; adultery; jealousy of husband's other wives ; leprosy ; thieving ; talkativeness.

Reasons Preventing Divorce

A wife cannot be divorced if she has no family to return to, if she has shared with her husband the three years' mourning for his parents, nor if, having married her when he was poor, the husband becomes rich.

DOING GOOD

YANG CHU said : ' Though you do good without any thought of fame, yet fame will result. If you have fame, though you have no thought of profiting thereby, yet wealth will accrue. If you are rich, though you don't mean to stir up enmity, yet enmity will be unavoidable. Therefore the superior man is cautious about doing good.'

Lieh Tzu

DREAMS

To dream of ascending to heaven, of seeing a fairy, or a well-known person, or of going to a party is considered to indicate good fortune.

It is also good to dream of seeing bats, tortoises or turtles ; to dream of bears denotes the probable birth of a son, and of snakes, of a daughter.

Dreams of eating fruit, or of seeing ants on the matting or of breaking mirrors are all unlucky, while eating pears in a dream is a sure sign of family fights to come.

DENNYS

*

If you dream that you are drinking wine, you will weep when you wake.

If you dream that you are weeping you will begin the day by hunting.

RULES FOR DRINKING

1. GET intoxicated, but don't get helplessly drunk. Drunkenness causes life-long ill-health.

2. Don't lie in a draught when drunk—this brings on fits.

3. Don't lie in the sun when drunk—that way lies madness.

4. Don't lie in the dew when drunk—rheumatism will result.

5. Never force yourself to eat, and never get angry, when you are under the influence of drink or you will break out in boils. Washing the face in cold water has the same effect.

6. Don't drink on an empty stomach or you will certainly be sick.

7. Never take sweet things with wine.

8. Don't eat pork with wine as this causes convulsions.

9. Don't bath when you are affected by wine ; it is bad for the eyes.

10. Don't ride or jump about, or exert yourself in any way when drunk or you will injure your bones and sinews and undermine your strength.

11. When you recover from a bout of drinking, pause before beginning again ; in this way you will avoid adding harm to harm.

12. When drinking don't take too much. When you know you have done so, it is best to vomit it up at once.

13. When drunk don't get so excited that you scare your soul out of your body for good.

14. If you suffer from bad eyes avoid drinking or eating to excess.

15. If you see in your wine the reflection of a person not in your range of vision, don't drink it.

From the *Imperial Cookery Book of the Mongol Dynasty*

DROUGHT

WHEN a drought is prolonged, and occasions any fear for the harvest, it is customary for the Mandarin of the district to make a proclamation, prescribing the most rigorous abstinence. Neither fermented liquors, meat of any kind, fish, eggs, or animal food of any description is allowable ; nothing is to be eaten but vegetables. Every housekeeper has to fasten over his door strips of yellow paper, on which are printed invocations, and the image of the Dragon of Rain. If heaven is dead to this kind of supplication . . . they organise a . . . procession in which an immense dragon, made of wood or paper, is carried about to the sound of music.

If the dragon still will not give rain, prayers are changed to curses ; he who was before surrounded with honours is insulted, reviled and torn to pieces by his rebellious worshippers.

HUC

DWARF TREES

THE dwarfed trees of the Chinese and Japanese have been noticed by every author who has written upon these countries, and all have attempted to give some description of the method by which the effect is produced. The process is a very simple one. . . . We all know that anything which retards in any way the free circulation of the sap also prevents to a certain extent the formation of wood and leaves. . . . This principle is perfectly understood by the Chinese, and they make nature subervient to this whim of theirs.

. . . I have often seen Chinese gardeners selecting suckers and plants for this purpose. . . . Stunted varieties were generally chosen, particularly if they had the side branches opposite or regular, for much depends upon this. The main stem was then twisted in a zig-zag form, which process checked the flow of the sap, and at the same time encouraged the production of side branches at those parts of the stem where they were most desired. When these suckers had formed roots in the open ground . . . the best were taken up for potting. . . . The pots used were narrow and shallow, so that they held but a small quantity of soil compared with the wants of the plants, and no more water was given than was barely sufficient to keep them alive. Whilst the branches were forming, they were tied down and twisted in various ways ; the points of the leaders and strong-growing ones were generally nipped out, and every means was taken to discourage the production of young shoots which were possessed of any degree of vigour. Nature generally struggles against this treatment for a while, until her powers seem in a great measure exhausted, when she quietly yields to the power of art . . . but, should the roots of the plants get through the pots into the ground, or happen to be liberally supplied with moisture, or should the young shoots be allowed to grow in their natural position for a short time, the vigour of the plant which has so long been lost will be restored, and the fairest specimen of Chinese dwarfing destroyed. The plants used in dwarfing are pines, junipers, cypresses, bamboos, peach and plum trees, and a species of small-leaved elm.

FORTUNE

ETIQUETTE *VERSUS* HUMANITY

' TELL me,' said an inquirer to the philosopher, Mencius, ' is it a rule that men and women must avoid touching hands when giving or receiving anything ? '

' It is,' Mencius replied.

'Then,' said his questioner, 'suppose my sister-in-law is drowning, ought I to take hold of her with my hand to rescue her?'

'Only a wolf would let a woman drown on account of such a rule,' Mencius said. 'Not to touch hands with a sister-in-law is a general principle; to touch hands in order to rescue a drowning sister-in-law is a particular case of special emergency.'

THE EYE

No part of the body is more excellent than the pupil of the eye. If the heart is upright the pupil is bright; if not, then it is dull. Hear what a man has to say, and watch the pupil of his eye while he speaks—can he conceal his character from you?

MENCIUS

THE SEEING EYE

On military and trading junks that navigate the 'great sea' a great eye is painted on each side of the bows, so that the vessel may see its way ahead . . . in pidgin English, 'Have eye, can see; can see, can savey; no have eye, no can see; no can see, no can savey.'

LANGDON

FACTORY REGULATIONS

Regulation 2. Neither women, guns, spears nor arms of any kind may be brought into the Factories.

Regulation 5. Foreigners may not row about the river in their own boats for pleasure. On the 8th, 18th and 28th days of the moon they may 'take the air' . . . and may visit the Flower Gardens and the . . . Joss-house, but not in *droves* of more than ten at a time. When they are 'refreshed' they must return to the Factories. They are not allowed to pass the night 'out,' or collect together to carouse. Should they do so, when the next 'holiday' comes, they shall not be permitted to go. If the ten should presume to enter villages, public places or bazaars, punishment will be inflicted on the (Chinese) *Linguist* who accompanies them.

From the *Eight ' Factory ' Regulations of* 1819

FAMILY

THE members of a clan are like a spring of water, which wells up and divides into a number of streams, but the water is still the water from a single source ; or like a tree from which grow countless branches and innumerable leaves, but all proceed from a single root.

Let those who have the means erect ancestral temples where sacrifices may be offered to those members of the clan who have no descendants to sacrifice to them, so that their ' orphan spirits ' may not be left without support ; let them provide schools for those members of the clan who cannot afford to educate their children ; let them set aside some part of their lands for the support of those members of the clan who are poor or too weak to work ; let them compile a clan-register so that distant members and later generations of it may know their place and order in the clan.

Sacred Edict

FATE

A MAN destined to die young will inevitably marry a woman destined to be widowed early ; and the woman doomed to be widowed early will not escape marrying a husband who is to be cut off in youth.

People say of a husband who dies soon after marriage that he robs his wife, and of a wife that she injures her husband. There is no question of their injuring one another ; it is simply destiny working itself out naturally.

WANG CH'UNG

FILIAL PIETY

PARENTS are like Heaven. The ancients had a saying : ' Parents are never in the wrong.'

If your wife dies you can marry again, but where will you find another brother ? Money is like water ; when it is gone, more may come, and so it is with wives. But brothers are different, being the sons of the same parents—and what can wives know about the rights of things ?

If brothers don't agree the bystanders will impose upon them.

Sons or grandsons who disobey their grandparents or parents, or fail to provide for them properly, shall receive one hundred heavy blows and be banished for three years.

Sacred Edict

*

A good son, no matter what his age, does not sit in the presence of his parents.

When his parents call, a son throws down anything he has in his hand, spits out anything he has in his mouth, and flies to answer the call.

When his parents must take medicine a good son tastes it first.

A good son marries a wife in order to have an assistant to share in his service to his parents, and to beget children who will serve his parents and worship his ancestors. If a son is pleased with his wife but his parents are not, he should divorce her, but if his parents are satisfied with her, he should not divorce her even if she does not please him.

*

Among the twenty-four examples of filial sons one lay naked on the ice in mid-winter in order to thaw it and catch carp for his stepmother ; another exposed his body at night to keep mosquitoes away from his parents ; a third fanned his father's bed to cool it in summer and lay in it in winter to warm it. Their piety was not restricted to the living. Wang Ai went out to his mother's grave to comfort her spirit when there was a thunder-storm, and Ting Lan made an image of his dead mother and continued the services and devotional acts which she had been accustomed to perform during her lifetime.

*

When his father or mother is ill, a young man who has been capped should not use his comb, nor walk with his elbows stuck out, nor speak on idle topics, nor take his lute in hand. He should not laugh so as to show his teeth nor be angry till he breaks forth in reviling. When the illness is gone, he may resume his former habits.

Li Chi

*

There are five unfilial acts which must be avoided. It is unfilial to be idle in the use of one's limbs, regardless of the duty of supporting parents ; it is unfilial to gamble, to play chess, or to drink wine, regardless of the duty of supporting parents ; it is unfilial to love goods or money, and to be unduly fond of wife and children, re-gardless of the duty of supporting parents ; it is unfilial to follow the lusts of the eye and the ear, thereby disgracing parents ; and it is unfilial to be addicted to bravery, fighting and quarrelling, thereby endangering parents.

MENCIUS

*

Observe a man's will while his father is alive ; observe his actions when his father is dead. If for three years he does not deviate from his father's way he may be called filial.

CONFUCIUS

FIRE

IN certain parts of China it was the custom for the magistrate to attend outbreaks of fire in person. He was supposed to climb on to the roof of the burning building and buy off the fire-god with offerings of eggs and rice. This he generally commuted by throwing his official hat on to the roof and making the offerings in safety on the ground.

★

So great is the damage that may be caused by fires in the closely-built, flimsy houses in some Chinese cities that ' in case of fires breaking out in the . . . city, when more than ten houses are consumed, the governor is fined nine months' allowances ; if more than thirty houses are burned he forfeits one year's allowances ; if three hundred are burnt, he loses one grade of honorary rank. Fires occurring in the suburbs do not subject him to the same penalties.'

FLOWERS

AMONG flowers most suitable for gifts may be named orchids, plum-blossom and lilies. To intimate friends hibiscus, rhododendron and wild flowers may be offered.

★

The flowers appropriate to baths are as follows :

For a recluse, plum-blossom ; for a man of refinement, begonias ; for a beauty, peonies ; for a beautiful slave, pomegranate ; for a youth of talent, oleander ; for a Taoist, lotus ; for a connoisseur, chrysanthemums ; and for an ascetic priest, the flowers of the wax-plum.

LO CH'IU

FOOTBINDING

CHINESE women who bind their feet generally regard the fact that it is customary as a sufficient reason for the practice. Many parents believe, however, that men admire tiny feet, and that it is impossible to find husbands for girls with large (*i.e.* unbound) feet. The masculine view is that it keeps women from gadding about and from bad company.

FOREIGNERS

I WAS anxious to proceed farther into the country, but the mandarins, who were informed of all my movements by their spies, did everything in their power to dissuade me from making the attempt. They told the consul that . . . the natives were in a state which made it unsafe for a foreigner to trust himself amongst them. . . . When they found that, notwithstanding all their descriptions of the fierce and hostile disposition of the people, I was still determined to go, they declared that no tea was grown in this district ; being fully persuaded that an Englishman could have no other object in exploring the country than to see the cultivation of his favourite beverage. Indeed, every Chinaman believes that we could not continue to exist as a nation were it not for the productions of the celestial empire. It has been stated that his celestial majesty, the emperor himself, during the war recommended his subjects to use every means in their power to prevent the English from getting tea and rhubarb—the one being what they lived upon, and the other their medicine ; without which, his majesty said, they could not continue to exist for any length of time ; and consequently would be more easily conquered in this way than by the sword.

FORTUNE

*

Sand, water, and ants should be avoided in selecting a grave.

Proverb

FORTUNES

ON the night before the seventh day of the seventh month children set a bowl of water in the courtyard to catch the dew. At noon on the seventh day each in turn takes a straw from a broom and drops it into the water. If a boy's straw throws a straight shadow, he will become a successful scholar ; if a girl's straw is like a needle, she is destined to prove a good housewife and needlewoman.

FOXES

FOXES are thought by the Chinese to be possessed of supernatural powers, and many shrines are erected by the roadside in their honour. They often assume the shape of a beautiful girl and charm students from their studies, and many stories of these unions are told. In one of the most charming it is said that the fox-girl could not sew, but in all else she was a pattern to the women of the age.

GENII

A GENIE will live upon air, or even give up breathing the outer air and carry on the process of breathing inwardly . . . for days together as in a catalepsy. He will become invisible ; he will take the form of any beast, bird, fish or insect. He will mount up above the clouds, dive into the deepest sea, or burrow into the centre of the earth. He will command spirits and demons of all sorts and sizes and have them at his beck and call. And finally, after living in the world for perhaps several hundred years, he does not die (for a genie is immortal though a spirit may not be so), but he rides up to heaven on the back of a dragon where he becomes a ruler of spirits.

The Taoist considers genii as the highest class of intelligent beings and places spirits next below them : the strict Confucianist denies their existence.

DENNYS

GEOMANCY

THE dragons and other curious figures seen on Chinese roofs, and the pagodas built on hills are intended to counteract unpropitious influences in the locality in which they are erected. The same purpose may be served by pictures of spirits, or by written characters or stone tablets.

Straight paths, tunnels, railways or canals favour the advance of malignant influences, and this is the reason why China is full of winding roads, crooked furrows, and tall screens preventing direct entrance through doors and gateways.

GHOSTS

WHEN a man has been murdered by another, his ghost will, it is believed, haunt the murderer wherever he goes, and will only be prevented from doing him a mischief by the want of a suitable opportunity. Thus the presence of idols in the same room completely neutralises the ghost's power, and it is moreover believed that in any case no vital injury can be inflicted on the guilty party until the time of his death, as recorded in the Book of Fate, has arrived. The ghosts of suicides (who are distinguished by wearing red silk handkerchiefs) haunt the places in which they committed the fatal deed and endeavour to persuade others to follow their example ; at times even attempting to play executioner by strangling those who reject their advances.

DENNYS

★

To scare away a ghost, rub your hair till it gives off sparks (which it readily does in the dry climate of North China), or bite your middle finger and smear the ghost with the blood. Ghosts seeing themselves will flee in terror, and it is a good thing to hang a mirror over the door to keep them away.

THE GOD OF WEALTH

THE God of Wealth has his favourites, and his worship is universal On the fifth day of the New Year, before business is resumed after the holiday, he must be sacrificed to. The offerings include hens, eggs, fish and game ; and fireworks are let off. The fish used are carp, some of which are returned to the river after the offerings have been made, to ensure that the business may be as prosperous as the spawn of carp is plentiful.

GOOD WISHES

MAY the four seasons be prosperous and the eight feasts peaceful !

May your happiness be full as the eastern ocean and your age as great as the southern hills !

May a hundred joys come all at once and a thousand good omens gather like clouds !

May distinguished friends fill the house, and excellent friends gather like clouds !

May you have wealth, long life and many sons !

May you live to hear the Ode of Longevity sung for you !

May your age compare with that of the stork and the tortoise !

May your old age be like the evergreen pine, and its fragrance like the flower of the red camellia !

DOOLITTLE

GOVERNMENT

THE eight concerns of government are

1. food
2. commodities
3. sacrifices
4. public works
5. education
6. crime
7. the entertainment of guests
8. the army

Shu Ching

HAIR

IN November 1715 I was summoned into the presence of the Emperor, to act as interpretor to two Europeans, a painter and a chemist, who had just arrived. While we were waiting in the ante-room, a eunuch addressed my companions in Chinese, and was angry because they returned no answer. I immediately told him the cause of their silence, upon which he said that we Europeans were all so alike that it was scarcely possible to distinguish one from another. I had often heard the same remark from other persons, our resemblance being generally attributed to the long beards we all wore. The Chinese do not shave ; but their beards are so thin that the hairs might be counted : the few they have, however, they value even to ridicule. The Emperor himself was not exempt from this weakness. He once commanded Father Rod, who acted as his surgeon, to cure him of a boil that had formed upon his face. Father Rod prescribed a plaster, saying that, in order to apply it properly, it would be necessary to cut off a few hairs from his

42

Majesty's beard ; and the Emperor, after a long consultation with his looking-glass, ordered the most dexterous of his eunuchs to cut them. Immediately after the operation he looked at himself again, and, with marks of deep grief, he bitterly reproved the eunuch for having so grossly blundered as to cut off four hairs when three would have been quite enough.

Memoirs of Father Ripa

HORSEMANSHIP

THE good rider is glued to his horse like bark to a tree ; he is swift as lightning, immovable as a rock, and light as a feather.

BALFOUR

HATS

THE customs of the Chinese as to covering the head are the reverse of ours. We consider it a mark of respect to uncover the head ; with them it would be a great violation of decorum, unless among intimates, and with leave asked and given.

DAVIS

HOW TO PROSPER IN BUSINESS

BUY a bag containing a luck-spirit. Take it to your place of business and hide it out of sight. It will cause second-rate goods to appear in the eyes of customers as first-quality goods and so your business will prosper.

Shanghai Folklore

HUMILITY

In the T'ang dynasty lived a man named Lü.

' What would you do if a person spat at you ? ' he asked his brother.

' Wipe it off and leave it at that,' replied his brother.

' If you wiped it off,' said Lü, ' the man would be still more annoyed. It would be better to smile and ignore it and just leave it to dry.'

Now this man, through being so humble, became an officer of state and at last was made Prime Minister. Is not this an example of meekness reaping its reward ?

Sacred Edict

HUNGER AND THIRST

Any food tastes nice when we are hungry, and any drink when we are thirsty. So that when we are hungry and thirsty we do not know the flavour of what we eat and drink, and for this reason we may say that hunger and thirst spoil the palate.

Mencius

ILL-OMENED ACTIONS

To eat lying down
To sigh for nothing
To sing in bed
To eat or write bareheaded
To swear an oath involving one's parents
To perform the toilet or let down the hair by moonlight
To beat the breast while cursing another (because curses light on the
    person pointed at)

Li I-shan

Chinese Lore

ILL-OMENED OCCURRENCES

A DUCK quacking as one passes by

The cawing of crows

Breaking a mirror or an oil-jar foretells separation of husband and
wife

Sit on a chair still warm and you will quarrel with the last sitter

INCONGRUITIES

An illiterate teacher

A pork-butcher reciting Buddhist scriptures

A grandfather visiting courtesans

LI I-SHAN

INTELLIGENCE

THE rich always set aside a small part of the house to form an inner
room, and in this room are stored boxes full of beautiful silks of all
kinds.

In the houses of the poor there is a similar room, but there is
nothing whatever in it, and that is why they are poor.

Now the intelligent are like the rich, and the unintelligent like
the poor. Rich and poor, there is not much difference in stature,
but the intelligent cherish the sayings of all the sages in their hearts,
while the unintelligent, having read nothing whatever, are as bare
as the inner chamber of a poor man's house.

WANG CH'UNG

AN INVITATION TO TEA

' ON the —th day, the spring tea waits for the splendour of your
presence. I most respectfully announce the felicitous season, and
worshipfully invite you at — o'clock.'

LANGDON

THE ISLES OF THE BLEST

THE ' isles of the genii ' were supposed to lie pretty much where Formosa actually exists, and, like the fabled Atlantis of European superstition, they have been the subject of actual search. Su Fu, a necromancer who lived about 219 B.C., announced their existence to the then emperor, and, in accordance with his own request, was placed at the head of a large troop of young men and maidens, and set out on his voyage of discovery ; but the expedition, though it steered within sight of the magic islands, was driven back by contrary winds. It is conjectured by some that this legend has reference to attempts at colonising the Japanese islands.

DENNYS

JUSTICE

FORMS of trial are simple. There is no jury, no pleading. The criminal kneels before the magistrate, who hears the witnesses and passes sentence ; he is then remanded to prison, or sent to the place of execution. Seldom is he acquitted. When witnesses are wanting, he is sometimes tortured until he gives evidence against himself. . . . The jail is commonly called *ti-yü*, hell, or literally, ' earth's prison.' . . . When brought to the execution-ground, the prisoner kneels with his face toward's the emperor's court, and bends forward in the attitude of submission and thanksgiving to expire beneath the sword of the executioner.

THE KITCHEN GOD

IN China, the Kitchen God, to whom an altar is dedicated above the stove, ascends to heaven annually on the 24th day of the 12th month to report the actions of the family. On that day he receives offerings of rice, sugar, fruits and other sweet things to make his lips sticky and his mouth sweet, so that he may be prevented from reporting any bad deeds of the family under his charge.

LAST WILL AND TESTAMENT OF A DYING RULER

I FIRST fell ill from a simple ailment. Other disorders followed, and it became evident that I should not recover. They say that death at fifty cannot be called premature, and as I have passed three score I may not resent the call. But when I think of you, my sons, I cannot but feel regrets. Now I say to you, strive and strive again. Do no evil because it is a small evil ; do not leave undone a small good because it is a small good. Only with wisdom and virtue can men be won. But your father's virtue was but slender, and unequal to the strain.

After my death you are to conduct the affairs of the state with the Prime Minister. You are to treat him as a father, serve him without remissness, and seek instruction from him. This is my final and simple command.

San Kuo Chih Yen I

LEGITIMACY

IF a drop of blood from two persons be allowed to fall into a bowl the two drops will coalesce if they come from close relatives but not if the two persons are strangers. This used to be a not uncommon method of proving legitimacy.

LETTERS

From a Son Abroad to his Parents in China

A WRITING for the information of the two Distinguished Persons. Yesterday I received and read the command from your hands, and learned that your jade bodies were peaceful and happy, and that the family were in health, everyone being blessed by azure heaven.

Since (I), your son, left his parents to live abroad I have accumulated little, for, although it may be said that the goods are easily sold, the accounts are collected with difficulty. Therefore the thoughts of returning which I have long cherished have been impeded. It is not that I am attached to resting in a foreign land, by which I get the imputation of being unfilial. But because I wish my parents to have all the support and ease of heavenly peace, and to add to the number of their days I live in this strange country, and am content to do so. Since I am at peace here, there is no need for you to worry about my being far away.

With my head on the ground I send this to wish you golden happiness.

A respectful statement from your son. . .

A Husband Abroad to his Wife at Home

Since I left my worthy wife half a year has passed swiftly. Every time I think of my family my heart is like the heart of a drunken man ; every night in dreams my spirit travels thousands of miles, and in the morning my thoughts afflict and grieve me. My aged parents in the hall, my tender children at the breast, all depend upon my worthy wife to look after and cherish them, thus preventing my aged parents from repining at my unfilial conduct, and my children from forgetting my rules of careful instruction. Great is my worthy wife's kindness and merit. I am a stranger abroad, exposed to the weather on account of the numerous necessities of my family, doing business and seeking gain solely on account of those two particulars —hunger and cold ; my circumstances allow no other course. How could I willingly on the one hand leave father and mother, and on the other separate from wife and children, dwelling abroad in a strange land ? When I have obtained according to my wishes, I shall immediately return, by no means remaining long in another land. . . . I cannot write all my words, cannot speak all my thoughts. This is sent to Mrs. Wang, my worthy wife, in her own apartment.

Your humble husband's attentive letter. . . .

Chinese Lore

A Wife at Home to her Husband Abroad

Since my honoured husband's departure, the hibiscus has twice opened itself. The multiplied words and innumerable injunctions you gave when you left, your handmaid has remembered with the greatest care, not presuming to contravene them. Those in the high hall have been nourished, I myself waiting on them ; and everything in the house I have myself looked after. Do not make yourself anxious about us at a distance ; but while you, my honoured husband, suffer the inconvenience of a foreign climate, we who are at home do all ardently remember you. As soon as you procure a little overplus of gain, you ought straightway to bring yourself back, respectfully to wait upon your parents, and carefully to teach your children. Your kindred will then all collect together, and laughing converse will fill the hall. Then will those venerable parents not have the longing of those who lean at the village gate, nor your humble handmaid have the sighing of a grey-haired person. The house is near, but its lord is far ;—my little heart flies a thousand miles. This for the information of my honoured husband, offered at the right of his seat.

Your handmaid Wang respectfully states. . . .

To a Friend at a Distance

Your younger brother, the writer, respectfully states that since I parted from you, my exalted elder, imperceptibly the time has slipped away. Twice has the plum-flower blossomed. I remember constantly that we have already been separated for a long time ; there is not a day in which my heart does not look towards you. The other day, while I was thinking of you, your valued favour suddenly arrived ; I am most deeply indebted for your gracious favour. Truly the affairs of life are like the moves of chess. My heart has for a long time been like ashes, or as the torn head of a drum ; how can it be remedied by medicine ? You, benevolent elder brother, have condescended to inquire after me, your younger brother ; but truly I have no mind to look after serious business. I respectfully send this answer, and also wish you present good in every particular.

To —— my worthy and respected elder (brother), at his feet,
His junior —— writes with compliments.

A Note accompanying a Present of Cakes of Ink

Several cakes from the lordly fir-tree, produced by the sombre smoke floating about, or they might be called ' dragon-guests ', are herewith respectfully presented on the right of your seat that they may aid a little your sprinkling pen. Elegant and tasteful compositions, and characters like the cloudy smoke, will of course proceed from them. I beg you will place this trifle by you, and I shall be highly favoured.

To ——, the second brother, respected sir, on the right of his table.
His unworthy junior —— humbly sends compliments.

The Reply

I have received your valued gift of black jade cakes. Although when they come to the ink-pool they are of great value, still I am by no means skilful at composing, and cannot offhand complete an essay to illuminate your bounteous gift. But with drops of dew to rub on the ink-stone, characters like cloudy smoke in curling wreaths will arise from the pool. Your honoured present, placed in a bag of leopard-skin, I thankfully accept, and if you will excuse a short delay I will come and thank you for it in person.

To ——, respected sir, on his writing-table.
His unworthy junior —— respectfully replies.

★

If no money is spent no favour is gained.

Proverb

Chinese Lore

A Request for a Loan

The many times I have received kindness from you are inscribed upon and affect my five inwards. Just now I have suddenly met a pressing emergency, and am without any source from which to most request a loan. Knowing that you, honoured sir, uniformly bestow charity and will undoubtedly commiserate me in the dry rut into which I am fallen, and overflow it with the water of the western river. Therefore, ignoring the sweat of agony produced by my reluctance to trouble you with this request, I beg you to lend me one hundred dollars, by which I shall be relieved from my embarrassment. Looking up I hope you will condescend to accede to my request, and I will then, bowing upon your steps, hasten to receive it. I respectfully send this, at the same time wishing you daily peace. To ——, as if before him.

His junior —— writes with respect.

The Reply

My very good friend, why do you talk of my bestowing charity ? If my worthy brother is in an embarrassed situation, how shall I presume not to accede to his request ? But of late my purse is as clean as if it had been washed. I have been among my neighbours to borrow, yet am unable to get the whole amount ; I can only collect what will be like a patch under the armpit to complete the fur jacket. I beg you will receive it and I shall be satisfied. For this I return an answer, also wishing you happiness and quiet.

To ——, at the right of his seat.

WELLS-WILLIAMS

LIGHTNING

IN the significant phraseology of the Chinese, lightning is called *the thunderer's whip*. If a person has been killed by lightning, he is denied the rites of burial, which he would otherwise have received. They consider it as a mark of the displeasure of God. It is said that Confucius always rose and dressed himself when severe thunderstorms occurred at night, in order to pay respect to . . . ' *the wrath of heaven*.'

LANGDON

LITERARY EXAMINATIONS

THE following is an account of the provincial examination held a Canton about a century ago :

Two examiners are appointed by the emperor himself from among the distinguished officers in Peking ; and they must set out within five days of their appointment. They are allowed the use of post-horses belonging to the government. . . . These are assisted by ten other examiners selected from among the local officials. Besides these there are many inspectors, guards, etc., . . . who, together with the candidates and their attendants, number upwards of ten thousand persons, who assemble in a large ' hall ' especially designed for the purpose. It contains many apartments (or cells) so that each candidate may be seated separate from his companions. . . . The apartments are furnished only with a table and a chair.

The number of candidates who assemble in Canton is between seven and eight thousand. They are generally attended by their friends and they often continue in the city for several months.

The candidates assemble in the eighth month ; but none are allowed to enter the examination except those who have been previously enrolled by the chancellor of the province. The age, features, residence, and lineage of each candidate must be given in the chancellor's list. . . . The examination continues for several days, and comprises several tests. On the first day they write essays on three themes from the ' Four Books ' and compose a poem on a given subject ; the second test is similar, the texts being the ' Five Classics,' while on the third day five questions, referring to the history or political economy of the country, are given. All questions concerning the character and learning of statesmen of the present day, as well as topics relating to its policy, must be carefully avoided.

*

Examination Regulations

1. Candidates must attend the examination held in their native province ; and those who give a false account of their family and lineage shall be expelled and degraded.

2. No candidate can be admitted to the examination at any place unless he can prove that his family has been resident there for three generations.

3. Candidates are required to enter their apartments on the day preceding the examination and are not allowed to leave until the day after it is closed.

4. At the end of each paper the candidate must state clearly how many characters (words) have been blotted out or altered. If the number of altered characters in any paper shall exceed one hundred the candidate shall be deemed to have failed, and he shall at once withdraw from the examination.

5. Candidates are not allowed to get drunk and behave disorderly during the examination.

6. All intercourse between the examiners and the friends and relations of candidates must be discontinued during the course of the examination.

7. On entering the examination-hall each candidate must sign his name in the register. In the case of any error, the officer in charge of

the register shall arrest the candidate at fault and hand him over to a court of inquiry.

8. If a candidate shall employ any person to compose his essays for him, or be found guilty of any other illegal action both he and his accomplices shall be tried and punished.

9. On entering the examination-hall the candidate shall be subjected to a search, and if he is found to have with him any pre-composed essay, or miniature copy of the classics, he shall be punished by wearing the wooden collar, and shall lose his first degrees and be incapacitated from standing as a literary candidate for ever. Moreover both the parents and the tutor of the delinquent shall be prosecuted and punished.

10. All the furniture and utensils (writing desk, ink-stand, etc.) in the candidate's apartment shall be searched ; as also all the attendant officers of whatever grade. Anyone found guilty of conveying papers to the candidates, concealed in their food or in any other way, shall be severely punished.

BRIDGMAN

LOVE

THE state of society is such as entirely to exclude the passion of love. A man marries only from necessity, or for the sake of obtaining an heir to his property, who may sacrifice to his manes, or because the maxims of the government have made it disgraceful to remain in a state of celibacy. The fine sentiments that arise from the mutual endearment of two persons enamoured of each other can therefore have no place in the breast of a Chinese, and it is to the effusions of a heart thus circumstanced that poetry owes some of its greatest charms. Nor can they be considered as a nation of warriors ; and war, next to love, has ever been the favourite theme of the muses.

BARROW

★

A wife is wed for her virtue, a concubine for her looks.

Proverb

LUCKY AND UNLUCKY DAYS

THE Chinese carry out the idea of lucky days to a remarkable extent. While we saddle only one day in the week with ill luck, they have selected a number of days in each month as uncanny for work, or even amusement. On the seventh and other days you must not start on a journey, change your dwelling-place, plant or sow, go to school for the first time, repair your house, purchase landed property, and so on. . . .

New Year's Day is for certain things *the* day of luck. According to Chinese belief you may on this date, in almost any year, present religious offerings or vows to heaven, put on full dress, fine caps and elegant attire ; at noon one should sit with one's face to the south ; may make matrimonial matches, pay calls, get married, set out on a journey, order new clothes, commence repairs to a house, lay foundations, or raise up the frame-work of it ; set sail, enter into business contracts, collect accounts, pound, grind, plant, sow, etc. . . . The most ill-foreboding person it is possible to set eyes on as a ' first-foot ' is a Buddhist priest.

DENNYS

MANNERS

CONFUCIUS was very fastidious about his food. If his rice was not cleaned properly, or was spoiled by heat or damp, or had turned sour, he refused it. If his meat was not finely cut, or properly minced, or if it had turned a bad colour or was out of season, he would not eat it, nor would he touch it unless the appropriate sauce accompanied it. The quantity of meat he ate was always in proportion to the rice, but in drinking he laid down no rules, though he carefully avoided taking too much. He would not touch meat or wine bought in the market; he always took ginger with his meals; and he did not over-eat.

When eating, and when in bed, he was silent. If his mat were crooked he would not sit on it.

Analects of Confucius

MARRIAGE

A MAN must not marry a wife of the same surname as himself, even if she is not related to him. Hence, in buying a concubine, if he does not know her surname, he must consult the tortoise-shell (i.e. divine) about it.

*

Persons whose birthdays fall in years the ruling animals of which do not agree, may not marry; the horse cannot mate with the ox; nor the pig with the monkey; nor the sheep with the rat; nor the dragon with the hare; nor the chicken with the dog; nor the snake with the tiger.

Li Chi

*

If heaven wants to rain, or your mother to marry again, you can't prevent it.

Proverb

MARRYING AGAIN

It being asked : ' Supposing a widow to be very poor and destitute, may she marry again ? ' it was answered : ' The suggestion arises from her being afraid of cold and hunger. It is better to starve to death than to lose respectability.'

A MATTER OF TASTE

' I'M fond of fish,' said the philosopher Mencius, ' and I am fond of bear's paws, too. If I have to go without one or other, I will forego the fish and have the bear's paws. I am fond of life, and fond of virtue. If I must give up one or other I will give up life and keep virtue.'

MEMORIALS

It is the exception rather than the rule for Chinese widows to re-marry, and it is therefore the more remarkable that memorial arches should so often be erected to women who remain faithful to the memory of deceased husbands. Two examples of inscriptions on memorial arches of this character are prefaced by Barrow with a rather severe observation :

' The following are inscriptions on monuments that have been erected to chaste women, a description of ladies whom the Chinese consider to be rarely met with.

I
Honour granted by the Emperor
Icy coldness   Hard frost

II
The Emperor's Order
The sweet fragrance of piety and virginity
Sublime chastity   Pure morals

MORTIFICATIONS

To be penniless when things are cheap
To go for a stroll and run across a creditor
To have a lovely concubine and a jealous wife

Li I-Shan

MOTHERS-IN-LAW

It is the duty of a wife to wait upon her husband's mother ; there is nothing more unreasonable in the world than to expect a mother-in-law to do without in order that a wife may have enough.

Tso Chuan

MUSIC

All music has its rise in the heart of man. The stirrings of the heart are caused by external things. When the heart is moved it finds expression through the voice. Sound calls to sound, and variety results. A variety of sounds artfully combined are called musical notes. When these notes are produced in a manner pleasing to the ear . . . we call it music.

*

The rites serve to direct the people's will ; music to harmonise their voices ; government to unify their conduct ; punishment to prevent them from creating disturbances.

*

Music reflects the harmony which exists between Heaven and Earth . . . its purpose is the fulfilling of the five social relationships, viz. prince and minister ; father and son ; husband and wife ; elder and younger brother ; friend and friend.

In music the sages found pleasure, and saw that it could be used to make the hearts of the people good. Because of the deep influence which it exerts on a man, and the change which it produces in manners and customs, the ancient kings made it one of the subjects of instruction.

Music is joy itself . . . it is the very flowering of virtue.

Li Chi

MY COUNTRY 'TIS OF THEE. . . .

I FELICITATE myself that I was born in China. It constantly occurs to me, what if I had been born beyond the sea, in some remote part of the earth, where the cold freezes or the heat scorches ; where the people are clothed with the leaves of plants, eat wood, dwell in the wilderness, lie in holes of the earth, are far removed from the converting maxims of the ancient kings, and are ignorant of the domestic relations ? Though born as one of the generation of men, I should not have been different from a beast. But how happily I have been born in China ! I have a house to live in, have food and drink, and commodious furniture. I have clothing and caps, and infinite blessings. Truly the highest felicity is mine.

TEEN-KE-SHE—LANGDON

MY LADY

WITH the delicacy of a flower her complexion displays a clear brilliancy which puts to shame the floating light of day ; with the buoyant lightness of the swallow, her movements are ordered with inimitable grace and propriety. The arches of her brows are like the outlines of the vernal hills in the distance, but in their changeful expression they shame the varying tints of even the vernal hills ; the brightness of her eyes equals that of the clear wave in autumn, but the living sentiment which flows from them makes you wonder how the autumnal wave lost its deity. Her waist, like a thread in fineness, seems ready to break ; yet is it straight and erect, and fears not the fanning breeze ; the shadowy graces of her person are as difficult to delineate as the form of the white bird rising from the ground by moonlight. The natural gloss of her hair resembles the bright polish of a mirror, without the false assistance of unguents : her face is perfectly lovely in itself, and needs not paint to adorn it. The native intelligence of her mind seems to have gathered strength from retirement ; and beholding her, you may know that she is of a superior order of beings : the cold and rigid strictness of her manner, severe as she herself is soft and delicate, proves her to be no ordinary inhabitant of the female apartments. Her sweet and feminine disposition, comparable to fragrant flowers, might lead one at first to class her with other fair ones : but the perfection of this pearl, the polish of this gem, discoverable on a longer acquaintance, prove that she possesses qualities not inferior to the most spirited of the opposite sex.

DAVIS

NÜ-WA

ALL mermaids of the deep, all satyrs of the forest, all needle-necked, starving ghosts, the weak and the strong, whatever form they take, whether birds, beasts, fishes or men . . . existed under the rule of the harpy Nü-Wa, who had a human face with the body of a bird. It was she who mended the visible heavens, but unfortunately she left a little hole in the north-west corner, and to this day the wind from that quarter is colder than any other.

DENNYS

OFFICIAL RANK

ALL the officers, civil and military, of the Chinese empire are divided into nine orders, distinguished the one from the other by certain buttons, of the size of a pigeon's egg, which are worn above the official cap. This distinctive ball is of plain red coral for the first order, of carved coral for the second, of a transparent deep blue stone for the third, of pale blue for the fourth, crystal for the fifth, of some opaque white stone for the sixth, and for the seventh, eighth and ninth, of gilt and wrought copper.

HUC

OF THE ANNUAL SELECTION OF YOUNG WOMEN FOR THE GRAND KHAN

THE inhabitants of Ungut, a province in Tartary, are distinguished for beauty of features and fairness of complexion. Thither the grand khan (Kublai), sends his officers every second year or oftener . . . who collect for him to the number of four or five hundred, or more, of the handsomest young women, according to the estimation of beauty communicated to them in their instructions. The mode of their appreciation is as follows. Upon the arrival of these commis-sioners, they give orders for assembling all the young women of the province, and appoint qualified persons to examine them, who upon careful inspection of each of them separately, that is to say, of the hair, the countenance, the eyebrows, the mouth, the lips and other features, as well as the symmetry of these with each other, estimate their value at sixteen, seventeen, eighteen or twenty or more carats, according to the greater or less degree of beauty. The number required by the grand khan, at the rates, perhaps, of twenty or twenty-one carats, to which their commission was limited, is then selected from the rest, and they are conveyed to his court. Upon their arrival in his presence he causes a new examination to be made by a different set of inspectors, and from amongst them a further selection takes place, when thirty or forty are retained for his own chamber at a higher valuation . . . and the duty of waiting upon his majesty's person is exclusively performed by these young females. . . . The remainder of them are assigned to the different lords of the household . . . and upon any person belonging to the court expressing an inclination to take a wife, the grand khan bestows upon him one of these damsels, with a handsome portion. In this manner he provides for them all amongst his nobility.

MARCO POLO

OF THE CEREMONIES OF INTERMENT OF THE GRAND KHANS

It has been an invariable custom, that all the grand khans, and chiefs of the race of Chingis-khan, should be carried for interment to a certain lofty mountain named Altai. It is likewise the custom, during the progress of removing the bodies of these princes, for those who form the escort to sacrifice such persons as they chance to meet on the road, saying to them : ' Depart for the next world, and there attend upon your deceased master,' being impressed with the belief that all whom they thus slay do actually become his servants in the next life. They do the same also with respect to horses, killing the best of the stud, in order that he may have the use of them. When the corpse of Mongu was transported to the mountain, the horsemen who accompanied it . . . slew upwards of twenty thousand persons who fell in their way.

Ibid.

OF THE KIND OF PAPER MONEY ISSUED BY THE GRAND KHAN

IN the city of Khanbalu is the mint of the grand khan, who may truly be said to possess the secret of the alchemists, as he has the art of producing money by the following process. He causes the bark to be stripped from those mulberry-trees the leaves of which are used for feeding silk-worms, and takes from it that thin inner rind which lies between the coarser bark and the wood of the tree. This being steeped, and afterwards pounded in a mortar, until reduced to a pulp, is made into paper, resembling (in substance) that which is manufactured from cotton, but quite black. When ready for use, he has it cut into pieces of money of different sizes, nearly square, but somewhat longer than they are wide [and varying in value according to their size]. The coinage of this paper money is authenticated with as much form and ceremony as if it were actually of pure gold or silver : for to each note a number of officers, specially appointed, not only subscribe their names but affix their signets also ; and when this has been regularly done by the whole of them, the principal officer, deputed by his majesty, having dipped into vermilion the royal seal committed to his custody, stamps with it the piece of paper . . . by which it receives full authenticity as current money, and the act of counterfeiting it is punished as a capital offence.

Ibid.

OF THE PROVINCE NAMED KARAZAN

BEFORE the time of their becoming subject to the dominion of the grand khan the people of this region (Yunnan) were addicted to the following brutal custom. When any stranger of superior quality, who united personal beauty with distinguished valour, happened to take up his abode at the house of one of them, he was murdered during the night ; not for the sake of his money, but in order that the spirit of the deceased, endowed with his accomplishments and intelligence, might remain with the family, and that through the efficacy of such an acquisition, all their concerns might prosper. Accordingly the individual was accounted fortunate who possessed in this manner the soul of any noble personage ; and many lost their lives in consequence.

MARCO POLO

AN OPIUM SMOKER

ONE of my fellow-passengers was an opium-smoker, and the intoxicating drug had made him a perfect slave. . . . He was evidently a man of some standing in society, and had plenty of money. His bed was surrounded with silk curtains, his pillows were beautifully embroidered, and his coverlet was of the richest and softest satin. . . . The curtains were down and drawn close round. . . . He was clothed in the finest silks, and had lain down on his side upon a mat ; his head was resting on one of the embroidered pillows. A small lamp was burning by his side, an opium-pipe was in his mouth, and he was inhaling the intoxicating fumes. After smoking for a few minutes he began to have the appearance which a drunken man presents in the first stage of intoxication ; the fumes had done their work and he was now in his ' third heaven of bliss.'

In a minute or two he jumped up and called for his teapot, from which he took a good draught of tea ; he then walked about the boat evidently a good deal excited, and talked and joked with everyone he met. After spending some time in this manner, he began to smoke tobacco ; he then took another draught out of his teapot and lay down to sleep ; but his slumbers were not of long duration, and were evidently disturbed by strange and frightful dreams. He awoke at last, but it was only to renew the dose as before ; and so on from day to day. . . . Often, during this passage, his little lamp could be seen burning during the night, while the sickening fumes curled about the roof of the boat.

FORTUNE

OPIUM SMOKING

OPIUM prepared for smoking is kept in small cups which are made for the purpose. The smoker lays his head upon a pillow, has a lamp by his side, and with a kind of needle he lifts a small portion of the opium to the candle ; and having ignited it, he puts it into the small aperture of the bowl of the pipe. The candle is applied to the bowl during the process of inhaling, and the smoke is drawn into the lungs in the same manner as an Indian or Chinese swallows tobacco. A whiff or two is all that can be drawn from a single pipe, and, therefore, those who are accustomed to the use of the drug have frequently to renew the dose.

No one who has seen anything of the habits of the Chinese will deny that the use of opium, particularly when taken to excess, has a most pernicious effect both upon the constitution and morals of its victims. From my own experience, however, I have no hesitation in saying that the number of persons who use it to excess has been very much exaggerated ; it is quite true that a very large quantity of the drug is yearly imported from India, but then we must take into consideration the vast extent of the Chinese empire, and its population of 300,000,000 people.

FORTUNE

THE EFFECTS OF OPIUM

LORD JOCELYN, in his *Campaign in China* gives the following account of the effects of opium, which he witnessed, upon the Chinese at Singapore. ' A few days of this fearful luxury, when taken to excess, will give a pallid and haggard look to the face, and a few months, or even weeks, will change the strong and healthy man into little better than an idiot skeleton. The pain they suffer when deprived of the drug after long habit no language can explain ; and it is only when to a certain degree under its influence that their faculties are alive. In the houses devoted to their ruin, these infatuated people may be seen at nine o'clock in the evening at all the different stages ; some entering half distracted to feed the craving appetite they had been obliged to subdue during the day ; others laughing and talking wildly under the effects of a first pipe ; whilst the couches around are filled with their different occupants, who lie languid with an idiot smile upon their countenance, too much under the influence of the drug to care for passing events, and fast merging to the wished-for consummation. The last scene in this tragic play is generally a room in the rear of the building, a species of dead-house, where lie stretched those who have passed into the state of bliss the opium-smoker madly seeks—an emblem of the long sleep to which he is blindly hurrying.'

FORTUNE

THE OPIUM-TRADE

THE statements which have been frequently made in England, both as regards the smuggling and the smoking of opium, are very much exaggerated. . . . The trade is conducted by men of the highest respectability, possessed of immense capital, and who are known and esteemed as merchants of the first class in every part of the civilised world. The trade in opium, although contraband, is so unlike what is generally called smuggling, that people at a distance are deceived by the term. It may be quite true that its introduction and use are prohibited by the Chinese government, but that prohibition is merely an empty sound, which, in fact, means nothing. The whole, or at least the greater part, of the mandarins use it, and it is not at all unlikely that his Celestial Majesty himself makes one of the number of its devotees. It is necessary, however, to publish every now and then strong threatening edicts against it, which are only consigned to oblivion in the pages of the *Peking Gazette*, and have no effect whatever in restraining the Emperor's loyal subjects.

Many instances of the feeble kind of opposition which the Chinese Government employ to stop the opium-trade occurred during my residence in the country. Sometimes an admiral, renowned for his valour, was sent with a number of war-junks to a particular station, where the opium-ships were anchored, for the purpose of compelling them to leave the Chinese shores. Gongs were beat, guns were fired, at a respectful distance, however, and the junks came down with all that pomp and parade which seem to form a principal part of the warlike operations of the Chinese. . . . Presently a message was sent from the admiral, ordering them . . . to stand out to sea and never more to dare to enter the waters of his Celestial Majesty under the penalty of being completely annihilated.

A summons like this in former days might have had some weight, but now . . . the only answer was ' that the foreign vessels were well armed, and that they would not leave their anchorage.' This was quite sufficient to cool the courage of the admiral, who was now in a dilemma ; he durst not fight the ' barbarians,' and if he did not manage to get them out of the way, his character for courage would suffer when the affair was represented at headquarters. He therefore . . . *requested* the captains . . . to move outside for a day or two only, after which time they might return to their old anchorage. This was agreed to . . . and the following morning the opium-vessels got under weigh and went out to sea. The Chinese, who were on the look-out, made a great noise by beating gongs and firing guns. . . . The admiral now sent up a report to his government that he had fought a great battle with the ' barbarians ' and driven them away from the shores. . . . In the meantime, before the report was half-way to Peking, the opium-vessels had quietly taken up their old anchorage, and things were going on in the usual way.

FORTUNE

AN OPTIMIST

AN optimist—one who expects an egg to crow in the morning, and hopes to bring down a bird by looking at a bullet.

CHUANG TZU

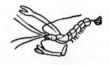

PARENTS

WHEN his parents are in error, the son, with a humble spirit, pleasing countenance, and gentle tone, must point it out to them. If they do not receive his reproof he must strive more and more to be respectful and dutiful towards them until they are pleased, and then he must again point out their error. . . . And if the parents, irritated and displeased, chastise their son until the blood flows, even then he must not dare to harbour resentment ; but on the contrary, should treat them with increased respect and dutifulness.

Li Chi

PERSEVERANCE

A MAN who desires to achieve something is like a person digging a well. If he digs down a hundred feet and then stops before he finds water, he has simply thrown away his labour in digging the well.

MENCIUS

Chinese Lore

THE POWER OF THE PEN

IF the dragon were not accompanied by clouds and rain, it could not rise to heaven. Great writers are the clouds and rain of a state. They carry in their records the virtues of the state, and thus transmit its name and fame through countless generations.

WANG CH'UNG

PUBLIC AFFAIRS

PUBLIC affairs should not be privately discussed.

Officers in their offices should speak only of the official business ; in the treasury, of treasury business ; in the arsenals, of arsenal business ; and in the court, of court business.

At court there should be no talk about dogs and horses. One who keeps looking about him after the business of the court is over may be pronounced uncultivated.

Li Chi

PUNISHMENT

THE favourite Central Asian punishment of tying a man to two horses and riding the animals at great speed in opposite directions is only a pale reflection of a method, apparently not unused in ancient China, known as the division by five chariots, in which the head and limbs of the criminal were attached to five ox-carts facing in different directions, the carts being driven forward at a given signal until the body and members were torn asunder.

Tso Chuan

THE RABBIT

THE moon is inhabited by a hare or rabbit who is said to sit under a tree and pound the drug of immortality. The rabbit has become the friend of unmarried girls, and mothers sometimes secrete a paper rabbit inside the lining of a girl's shoe as a guarantee that the wearer will be married within the year.

REBIRTH

THE extortionate and debtors will be reborn as domestic animals, to repay their creditors by labour ; those who kill are doomed to become pigs and die by the knife ; the licentious will become monkeys ; coquettes become brightly coloured birds ; bullies will find the meaning of fear as timid gazelles ; those who refuse clothing to the naked will be sent into the world again as silkworms ; and gluttonous persons will reappear as flies.

REGULATION OF THE PEOPLE'S LIVELIHOOD

MULBERRY-TREES should be planted round the houses, so that people may have silk clothes to wear from the time they are fifty. Be careful to see that fowls and pigs breed at the proper times, so that everyone may have meat to eat from the age of seventy onwards.

It is impossible for people over fifty to keep warm unless they wear silk, or for people over seventy to feel they are being properly nourished unless they eat meat.

Train the young carefully in their duties to their parents and elders, and no grey-headed people will be seen carrying burdens in the street.

MENCIUS

RESPONSIBILITY

HE who has acted as adviser to another about his army should die if it is defeated. He who has given advice about the country or its capital should perish with it if it is destroyed.

Li Chi

REVENGE

PERSONS who have been wronged and are unable to avenge themselves otherwise, can, by practising certain spells, become invisible necromancers. The most efficacious way is to dig up a coffin, remove the body from it and sleep in it for several nights in succession. At the end of so many days the sleeper becomes invisible till dawn, and can thus gratify his revenge without fear of detection.

DENNYS

RULES FOR MEN AND WOMEN

MALE and female should not sit in the same apartment, nor have the same stand or rack for their clothes, nor use the same towel or comb, nor let their hands touch in giving and receiving.

Li Chi

RULES FOR THE KEEPING OF A SILK-WORM FARM

1. PLANT a hedge all round the farm. During the winter plant twigs of willow and ash mixed, and when they have begun to grow plait them closely together, binding them with fibre of the coir-palm ; outside the hedge plant sour dates, small oranges, thorns and briers. The more prickly the plants are the better.

2. Set up a sign with the words, ' Establishment for the encouragement of silk-cultivation,' and ask the mandarin for a notice forbidding people to tread down the plants.

3. If you can lead the river water to irrigate your field, you will save the expense of digging wells ; while at the same time you can keep fish and breed ducks in your canal, or cultivate the water-lily, water-chestnuts, etc.

4. In the winter months you must nourish the roots of your plants, for which purpose make use of rotten fish preserved in jars, or the juices of decomposed vegetables.

5. In the fourth month plant your mulberries ; in the following year, besides gathering your mulberry-leaves, should there be any vacant ground, you can plant it with arbutus, pomegranates, apricots or pears.

6. Beneath the mulberries you can plant onions, leeks and melons,

or potatoes and yams : in order to prevent the locusts from eating the mulberry-leaves, you may plant the more yams.

7. Withered mulberry-leaves, the parasites of the mulberry, together with white and diseased silk-worms, may all be used as medicine ; but the snails found on the mulberry must be carefully caught, lest they injure the leaves.

8. In the establishment there is need of ladders, tables and sieves, all of which are made of bamboo ; hence it is necessary to cultivate that plant.

9. The leaves of the old mulberries are good for fattening goats, and goats' dung is good for feeding fish. Hence goats may be kept with advantage.

Note.—These directions have been carefully followed by the establishment issuing them, which in two years was already prosperous.

Chinese Miscellany

RULES OF CONDUCT

Do not begin or abandon anything hastily
  Do not take liberties with or weary Spiritual Beings
  Do not try to defend or cover over what was wrong in the past,
    or to fathom what has not yet arrived

Li Chi

SIGNS OF GOOD LUCK

A SINGLE magpie
A swallow flying into the house

SIMILES

LIKE a damp cow's hide—a soft fellow
  Like a cow-hide lantern—a dull fellow
  A pock-marked lady looking in a mirror—the longer she looks
    the more vexed she becomes

A SENSE OF PROPORTION

A CERTAIN man had his fourth finger bent so that he could not straighten it. It did not hurt, nor was it inconvenient in any way. But hearing of a doctor who could straighten it, he thought no distance too great to go to him, simply because his finger looked different from other people's.

A man whose finger is crooked is very conscious of the difference between himself and other people, but if his mind is not like other people's the fact does not bother him at all. This is what is meant by ' having no sense of proportion.'

MENCIUS

STAG-HUNTING, A.D. 1711

IN the month of September the Emperor indulged in stag-hunting. Out of thirty thousand soldiers, which the Emperor had with him at Jehol, only twelve thousand accompanied him to the hunt ; but his retinue was so numerous that the party must have amounted to more than thirty thousand persons. His ladies were in six carriages, three of which were yellow and three black, the former for the queens, the latter for the concubines. Wherever these women passed everybody was obliged to pay them reverence by quickly fleeing away and hiding themselves so that they might neither see them nor be seen : those who were not very active in the performance of this duty never failed to receive a good beating from the mandarins or eunuchs of the escort.

On the afternoon of the 17th began what they call the little hunt, which is for deer, hares and pheasants. Having crossed several hills, we arrived in an open place, skirted by verdant heights ; and in the early morning the stag-hunt was begun. The army consisted of twelve thousand soldiers, divided into two wings, one of which passed on towards the east, then turned northward, whilst the other proceeded to the west, then likewise turned in a northward direction. As they marched on each man halted so as to remain about a bow-shot distant from the next, till at length they surrounded the hills. Then, at a given word, they all advanced slowly towards the centre of the circle, driving the stags before them, and went on in this manner till one was not more than half a bow-shot distant from the other. Every alternate soldier now halted, and the next continuing to advance, two circles were formed. After this they all moved in the same direction till the soldiers of the inner circle being so near as to shake hands, they divided again and formed a third circle. . . . The inner or third circle was less than a bow-shot distant from the second, but the distance from this to the outer circle was much

greater. The three circles having thus taken up their ultimate position, the Emperor entered into the centre, followed by the male part of his family and relatives, and surrounded by the best and most expert hunters, armed for his defence. The signal being given, the Emperor himself opened the chase by killing with his arrows a good number of the multitude of stags thus surrounded ; and when weary he gave permission to his sons and relations to imitate him. The stags . . . attempted to escape by breaking through the circle, but the soldiers drove them back with shouts. Many of the stags, however, leaped over the horses or forced a passage with their horns. The soldiers of the second circle then endeavoured to drive them back to the centre ; but if they did not succeed those of the third were permitted to kill the fugitives.

Memoirs of Father Ripa

STUDY

IF a man does not learn when he is young,
What will he do when he is old ?

*

The need for diligent study is instilled into all Chinese, and many examples are cited of students who overcame poverty or disinclination. One of these tied his head to a beam, so that when he nodded he was sharply reminded of his books. Others studied while they worked, like Li Mi, who rode his buffalo with a book in his hand and the rest of the volumes tied to the beast's horns. Those who could not afford the necessary light devised ways to carry on their studies by means of a bag full of fireflies, or by the light reflected from snow, or by poking a hole through the party-wall and so ' borrowing the light ' of a neighbour.

SUICIDE

THE extreme readiness with which the Chinese are induced to kill themselves is almost inconceivable ; some mere trifle, a word almost, is sufficient to cause them to hang themselves, or throw themselves to the bottom of a well, the two favourite modes of suicide. In other countries if a man wishes to wreak his vengeance on an enemy he tries to kill him ; in China, on the contrary, he kills himself. The reasons for this are two : in the first place Chinese law throws the responsibility of a suicide on those supposed to be the cause of it, and you have only to kill yourself to be sure of getting your enemy into horrible trouble, for he immediately falls into the hands of *justice*, and will certainly be tortured and ruined, if not deprived of life ; and in the second place the family of the deceased is sure to obtain considerable sums by way of compensation and damages.

HUC

SUPERSTITIONS

A TWITCHING eyelid denotes good or bad luck according to the time and to whether it is the right or the left that twitches.

Sneezing—someone is speaking ill of the person sneezing.

A shaking of the second finger indicates an invitation to a banquet.

People whose eyebrows meet can never hope to become ministers of state.

Bearded men will never be beggars.

DENNYS

TABLE MANNERS

Do not roll the rice into a ball ; do not bolt down the various dishes ; do not swill down the soup.

Do not make a noise (in eating) ; do not throw the bones to the dogs ; do not crunch bones with the teeth ; do not put back fish you have begun to eat ; do not snatch.

Do not spread out the rice (to cool) ; do not gulp down soup with vegetables in it, nor add condiments to it ; if the guest add condiments the host will apologise for not having had the soup made better. Do not pick the teeth ; do not bolt roast meat in large pieces.

Li Chi

TABOO

AMONGST all uneducated classes in China there exists a superstitious dread of hearing or using certain words. Thus a boatman is never heard to say the customary word ' to pour out ' tea or water, because the same word also means ' to overturn,' and he fears that if the river-god should overhear, it may ' put ideas into his head ' with regard to the boat of the person so misguided as to use it. Similarly, a thief, fearing that he may find himself ' in ' it, will not call for ' hot water ' in a tea-shop even though, since everyone else does so, he risks revealing his profession by refraining from using the words.

Chinese Lore

TAKING A HINT

WHEN sitting by a person of rank, if he begins to yawn and stretch himself, to turn his tablet round, play with the head of his sword, move his shoes about, or ask about the time of day, one may beg leave to retire.

Li Chi

TANTALISING

HAPPENING upon a tasty dish when the liver is out of order
Making a night of it and the drinks giving out
For one's back to itch while calling upon a superior
For the lights to fail just when the luck begins to favour one at cards

LI I-SHAN

TEA

ABOUT A.D. 519 Bodhidharma arrived in China. His object was to bring the inhabitants of this great country to the knowledge of God. . . . He . . . strove by godly grace to lead an exemplary life, exposing himself to . . . storm and tempest ; chastising and mortifying his body and bringing all his passions under subjection. He lived only on the herbs of the fields ; . . . he denied all rest and recreation to his body, and . . . dedicated his soul wholly to God. . . . After many years of constant watching he was at length so weary . . . that he fell asleep. On awaking next morning he determined to do penance for sleeping, so he cut off his eyelids and threw them on the ground.

. . . On the following day he remarked that each eyelid had become a shrub, the same which we now call tea, but which was then quite unknown. . . . Bodhidharma, eating the leaves of this plant, found that his heart was filled with joy, and that his soul gained new strength and energy to continue his contemplation. . . .

On a slow fire set a tripod, whose colour and texture show its long use ; fill it with clear snow water ; boil it as long as would be necessary to turn fish white, and crayfish red ; throw it upon the delicate leaves of choice tea, in a cup (of porcelain). Let it remain as long as the vapour rises in a cloud, and leaves only a thin mist floating on the surface. At your ease, drink this precious liquor, which will chase away the five causes of trouble. We can taste and feel, but not describe, the state of repose produced by a liquor thus prepared.

Extract from an Ode on Tea, written by
the Emperor Ch'ien Lung (1737–97)

★

Tea-drinking relieves headache and allays swellings better than any physician can do. It is a specific for asthma, grief, thirst, congestion and depression. After a few sips it acts like magic, for it possesses the properties of rich wine or celestial dew.

★

Winged creatures fly ; furry creatures run ; larynxed creatures talk. These all inhabit the space between heaven and earth. They eat and drink that they may live, but with how little comprehension do they drink ! To quench the thirst, drink broth ; to dispel melancholy, drink wine ; to obtain voluptuous sleep, drink tea.

If you want to drink good tea you must first find good water. Boiling water is the arbiter of the fate of tea, for even the finest teas may be ruined by careless boiling. . . . As soon as the water begins to bubble, even though it means a break in conversation or an interruption of business, use it at once, or the very soul of the hot water will be lost. Enquire of any hoary old man whether he can grip the bow, or fit an arrow and hit the mark as he was wont to do in the freshness of his youth.

Su I

Chinese Lore

Lu Yueh was a confirmed woman-hater and a born tea-lover. He used to say, ' Tea needs a slow fire to heat it up and a blazing fire to boil it. To bring out the flavour of tea the bubbles must at first be diffused and the kettle singing gently, then over the whole surface of the water they should well up like a spring, continuous as a string of pearls, and finally there should be rising waves and swelling billows. When guests come do not limit the number of cups ; the tea-things may be handled all day without fatigue.'

CHAO LIN

*

To part her time 'twixt reading and *Bohea*,
To muse and spill her solitary tea.

POPE

*

As some frail cup of China's fairest mould,
The tumults of the boiling *Bohea* braves
And holds secure the coffee's sable waves. . . .

TICKELL

*

For if my pure libations exceed three,
I feel my heart becomes so sympathetic,
That I must have recourse to black *Bohea* ;
'Tis pity wine should be so deleterious,
For tea and coffee leave us much more serious.

BYRON

TEACHERS

IN olden times students must have had teachers. By means of teachers doctrines are propagated, education is instilled, doubts are resolved. Since man is not born with knowledge who can avoid doubts ? And if there are no teachers from whom he may seek enlightenment, his doubts must for ever remain unresolved. He who was born before me and has heard the doctrine is before me, and him I regard as my teacher. He who is born after me and has heard the doctrine is also before me, and him also will I regard as my teacher. What matters it whether my teacher is older or younger than I, so long as I receive instruction in the Way ? Therefore let it not be a question of honour or of seniority, for on the continuance of teachers depends the continuance of the Way.

HAN YÜ

THREE THINGS TO AVOID

I DETEST people who ignore the fundamental rule about putting themselves in the place of others and take advantage of circumstances to act outrageously. Presuming on their authority, they interfere in the concerns of others ; on the strength of their talents, they use force ; and when they find occasion, they become overbearing. But in the end they come to disaster.

Some say these three things are exemplified by the deer, the ass and the rat.

LIU TSUNG-YUAN

TORTURE

ADMITTING that torture was necessary in China to extract confessions from obdurate persons, the kinds permitted by law were probably as unobjectionable as could be devised. Instruments for crushing the ankles, and for squeezing the fingers were considered insufficient for practical purposes. To induce unwilling criminals or witnesses to say what was expected of them, they were often made to kneel on iron chains, their knees being forced down by the weight of men standing on their legs. Other forms of torture were tying up to beams by the thumbs and big toes, destroying the sight by lime or the hearing by piercing the ears.

TRAFFIC REGULATIONS

(THE ruler) does not gallop the horses of his carriage in the capital ; he should bow forward on entering a village.

A charioteer driving a woman should keep his left hand advanced (with the reins in it) and his right hand behind him.

When riding in a carriage one should not cough loudly nor point.

In the streets of the capital touch the horses gently with the brush end of the switch. Do not urge them to speed ; the dust should not fly beyond the ruts.

Li Chi

TRAVELLERS

No one travels by star-light except criminals and those hastening to the funeral of a parent.

Ibid.

TREASON

THE crime of high treason is that committed against the State or against the Sovereign, by destroying the palace in which he resides, the temple where his family is worshipped, or the tombs in which the remains of his ancestors lie buried, or in endeavouring to do so. All persons who shall be convicted of these crimes, or of having intended to commit them, shall suffer death by a slow and painful method, whether they be principals or accessories. All the male relatives in the first degree of the persons convicted of the above-mentioned crimes—the father, grandfather and paternal uncles, as well as their sons, grandsons and sons of their uncles . . . shall be indiscriminately beheaded.

Huc

*

Treason is the gravest of all offences in China, as elsewhere, and simple beheading is considered a punishment too good for a traitor. In olden days the sentence was always death by the slow process, or the ' death by ten thousand cuts,' as it has been called. The criminal is bound to a sort of cross, and receives from the executioner in the soft parts of his body gashes varying in number according to the sentence. When this has been done, a merciful blow of the executioner's sword severs the head from the body.

UNLUCKY

It is unlucky
For a hen to fly on to the roof
To scrape saucepans on the 1st and 15th of the month
To pass under a bridge which a woman is crossing
If thunder is heard while a hen is sitting on eggs. It is wise to
disguise the noise by dragging furniture about the floor

WARNING

With the son of a widow, unless he be of acknowledged distinction, one should not associate oneself as a friend.

Li Chi

WATCHING SPIRITS

A superstition prevails amongst the Chinese regarding ' watching spirits.' Unwillingness to help a drowning man, or anyone in absolute peril of life, is based upon a belief that the ghost of the last man killed always acts as watchman of the purgatory into which, according to Chinese belief, the spirits of the departed first enter, and from which he can only be relieved by the arrival of a fresh defunct· If, therefore, a man's life be saved, the spirit of the person who died last before him is, in a manner, cheated out of his relief, and will assuredly haunt the person whose misplaced humanity has condemned it to a fresh term of dismal servitude.

DENNYS

THE ART OF WAR

Extracts from the Thirteen Articles on the Art of War

ARTICLE I

IF dissensions arise among your enemies, you may profit by them to attract the malcontents to your side.

Never attack if the enemy's strength is greater than yours ; avoid at all cost coming to blows.

ARTICLE II

Those who are thoroughly versed in the art of war will find means to provision their armies at the expense of the enemy.

Lose no opportunity of annoying the enemy and luring him into a trap. Reduce his force as far as possible . . . by kidnapping his convoys, or his baggage trains or anything else that may be of use to you.

Treat prisoners well, as if they were your own men. Let them feel that they are better off with you than with their own army. Treat them as if they were troops who had enlisted of their own accord under your banners.

ARTICLE III

A really able general . . . knows how to humiliate the enemy without giving battle, and how to capture cities without spilling a drop of blood or even drawing his sword. He knows the art of conquering foreign territories without setting foot in them, and adds glory to the ruler whom he serves without having to waste time at the head of his armies.

If your numbers are ten times those of the enemy, surround him completely and leave no loophole of escape ; if five times as many, arrange your army so that it attacks on four sides at once. If the enemy has but half your strength, be content to divide your army in two ; but if your numbers are no more than his, there is nothing for it but to risk a battle. And if, on the other hand, your force is smaller than his, be on your guard and avoid as far as you can any meeting between the two armies. By discretion and resolution a small force may tire out and overthrow even a great one.

ARTICLE IV

In ancient times those experienced in the art of war never undertook a campaign which they knew they could not come out of successfully. . . . Their principle was that if a man were beaten it was always through his own fault, and if he were successful it was through some fault of the enemy. . . . Before going into battle they endeavoured to humiliate, fatigue, and mortify the enemy in a thousand different ways.

ARTICLE XII

There are five methods of fighting with fire—burning men ; burning provisions ; burning baggage ; burning munitions ; burning gear. . . . A general who knows the time to fight with fire is truly enlightened ; a general who knows when to make use of water is an excellent person. However, use water with discretion, and solely for the purpose of preventing the enemy from escaping or receiving help from outside.

ARTICLE XIII

Have spies everywhere; and take it for granted that the enemy has his. When you discover them, be sure not to put them to death, for they can be most useful to you if you see to it that false statements as to your proposed marches, actions, etc., reach their ears, and through them, those of the enemy.

*

A General Outline of the Method of Employing Troops

1. A large army should remain encamped and never change its position, unless obliged; a small army should have no fixed camp but should always be on the move and in action.

2. As far as possible the greater number should attack the less; the strong the weak; and fresh troops should be opposed to those who are weary.

3. In whatever battle, combat or action you may be involved, be sure to have the wind behind you. See to it that there is some defensible place within reach which you can withdraw to and defend if you are defeated. . . .

4. Never go into action in a marshy place, nor fight on ground shaped like a tortoise on its back.

5. What looks like flight on the part of the enemy is not so always; it may be but a discreet withdrawal, or it may be a ruse to draw your army into an ambush already prepared.

*

The *Art of War* says:

'Blunt weapons betray the troops; ill-trained troops betray their general; inexperienced generals betray their master; the ruler who does not carefully select his generals betrays his country.

'Attack before the enemy is prepared; do what he does not expect.

'He who looks down from above easily overcomes the enemy.'

'Memoires Concernant . . . Les Chinois,' vol. vii

WEALTH AND POVERTY

WEALTH is on the way when one
Seeks diligently and uses sparingly
Widens knowledge by practical experience
Takes stock frequently
Is not infatuated by wine and women
Sleeps by night and rises early

POVERTY is on the way when one
Has a lazy wife
Lies long abed
Brings up a boy to be inferior to his father
Runs into debt
Neglects his farm
Maintains many concubines
Is always changing his residence
Frequents the company of the powerful and rich
Insists on buying when things are dear
Does not buy when things are cheap

LI I-SHAN

★

Kind feeling may be repaid with kind feeling, but debts must be
paid with hard cash.

Proverb

WINE

WINE is like a scholar, the older it gets the riper it becomes. It is best from a newly opened jar. The proverb says : ' The first cup of wine, the last cup of tea.'

YUAN MEI—GILES

*

Wine that is clear in colour and strong in flavour is the ' Holy One ' among wines ; that which is golden, clean-tasting and not bitter is the ' Sage ' ; dark wine and sour is the ' Dolt ' among wines.

He who becomes intoxicated on strong, home-made wine is a gentleman ; he who is overcome by millet-spirit is an ordinary fellow ; but the man who gets drunk on stuff from an alley ' pot-shop ' is of the baser sort.

The official who drinks should see to it that he is meticulous in his reports and observant of rules ; the man of refinement should strive to increase the number of rounds he can stand and so add to the number of his conquests and raise his prestige.

HUANG-FU SUNG

WISDOM

THE walls of a city are raised by man's wisdom
But overthrown by woman's subtlety.
The wisest of wise women
Is an owl.
A woman with a long tongue
Is the stairway to disorders,
For these come not down from Heaven
But are begotten of women.
They who can give neither wisdom nor precept
Are women and eunuchs.

Shih Ching

WOMAN

IN accomplishments, it is not necessary that a woman should be remarkable ; in appearance it is not necessary that she should be beautiful ; in conversation it is not necessary that she should be eloquent ; in work it is not necessary that she should excel.

WOMEN AND SERVANTS

OF all people women and servants are the most difficult to manage ; if you are familiar with them they become forward, and if you keep them at a distance they are discontented.

*

A woman should never be heard of outside her own home.

CONFUCIUS

WOMEN AND TREES

THE idea that adopting a girl from another family will increase a woman's own likelihood of bearing children is based on the belief that each living woman is in the unseen world represented by a tree ; and that, just as grafting succeeds with trees, so adoption (which represents the same process in family life) may succeed as regards children.

DENNYS

KUAN P'AN-P'AN, the favourite singing-girl of Chang Chien, was a clever dancer and a fine singer. When her master died she refused to marry and lived alone in the Swallow Tower for ten years.

PAN CHAO, a famous historian of the Han dynasty. She was married in early life to the functionary Ts'ao Shou, but being left a widow she busied herself with literary labours. On her brother's death she was commanded by the emperor to continue and complete the history begun by their father. She was admitted, after her widowhood, into the palace as a lady-in-waiting to the empress.

THE princess Shou-yang, daughter of Wu Ti of the Sung dynasty, was sleeping one day under the eaves of the Han-chang Hall, when plum-blossoms fell on her forehead and remained clustering there. From this originated the practice of wearing flowers in the hair.

In the harem of Yang Ti of the Sui dynasty the women vied with each other in painting 'moth' eyebrows. The officer in charge daily issued for this purpose two pints of Persian black.

THE Empress Wu of the T'ang dynasty, by whom the government of China was usurped during the latter half of the seventh century, was the daughter of a man of low station. She became one of the inferior concubines of the emperor T'ai Tsung of the T'ang dynasty, on whose death in A.D. 639 she retired to a Buddhist nunnery. Here, a few years later, she was observed by the Emperor Kao Tsung, who had already noticed her while an occupant of his father's seraglio. Kao Tsung's empress, anxious to destroy the influence of a favoured concubine, introduced the young nun into the palace, where she speedily contrived to engross the monarch's admiration, and became his prime favourite. In A.D. 655 the empress was deposed to make way for her quondam protégée, and the latter's influence continued to increase. To gratify her vindictive desires, eminent public servants were sent to execution, and changes were introduced in the institutions and ceremonial of the empire. On the death of Kao Tsung in A.D. 683 his successor resigned the government into the hands of the Empress, who relegated him to a state of virtual confinement, and assumed the supreme power, which she continued to wield for nearly twenty years. Her despotic rule was maintained with pitiless cruelty, but she was careful to uphold the external interests of the empire, the boundaries of which she enlarged whilst gaining a fresh hold on the allegiance of the neighbouring nations. Regardless of remonstrance, she introduced sweeping changes in the practice of government, and even sought to signalize her reign by altering the form of some of the most familiar written characters of the language. After many years she threw off all disguise, and having put to death a great number of the Imperial family, she proclaimed herself in A.D. 690 'Emperor' of the Chou dynasty. It was not until age had sapped the commanding intellect of this extraordinary woman that any effectual attempt was made to subvert her power. After some years of threatened revolt, a military conspiracy was at length organized, which in A.D. 705 succeeded in wresting the government from the hands of the empress, and placing the rightful sovereign upon the throne. Even in her downfall the empress retained a portion of the influence and respect she had formerly commanded. Her death took place in the same year as her deposition.

MAYERS

*

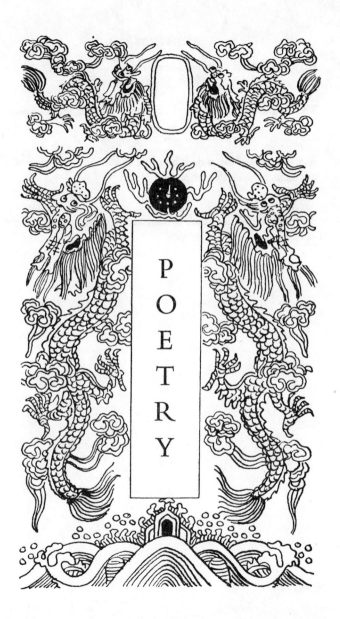

POETRY

PROVERBS

He who can hold a pen need never beg.

*

The enlightened mind is its own heaven ; the unenlightened mind its own hell.

*

As the scream of the eagle is heard when she has passed over, so a man's name remains after he is dead.

*

Better one bite of the peach of immortality than a whole basketful of apricots.

MIDNIGHT THOUGHTS

MIDNIGHT ?—And still I cannot sleep !
I rise and walk, I know not where ;
Then back again, to shut the door
And light the lamp my watch to share.
Chirping within the hollow wall,
What makes that cricket's note so sad ?
It seems to say its life, like mine,
Is robbed of all that made it glad.

Lonely ?—No loneliness like this !
The soldier, held by foreign war
A thousand leagues beyond the pass,
The Buddhist monk, whose vows debar
From ever knowing how they fare,
Think in the night of absent friends,
And see life stretch through weary years
Of wretchedness that never ends.

Anon.

*

When the heart is full, the night is short.

Proverb

WATCHING THE MOON RISE

I RISE and dress and wait to greet the moon,
A waning moon, that rises late to-night.
Slowly she creeps above the rugged hill,
And touches first the tree-tops with her light ;
Then golden wavelets shiver in their sleep ;
Faint and more tenuous flows heaven's silver stream.[1]
I linger till Orion's stars have set,
Then sleep again, and see it still, in dream.

Anon.

CONTENT

When the sun comes forth we work ;
When the sun goes down we rest :
We dig a well and we drink ;
We plough a field and we eat.
What is the emperor's power to us ?

Anon.

THE COMING OF SPRING

UNTO these immemorial hills
Imperial Spring returns again ;
Around these immemorial hills
The herald showers proclaim his reign.
Peach-trees and plum array themselves
To form his genial company,
While white-and-golden orioles
Accord their rapturous symphony.

Anon.

---

[1] The Milky Way.

ASCENDING A MOUNTAIN PEAK AT SUNSET

HERE a cascade falls sheer, three thousand feet ;
There the hibiscus forms a nine-fold screen ;
The thrusting peak now severs sun and moon,
And thunders roll amid the flying snows.

Like a white crane that soars among the clouds,
Mocking the winds, I mount into the void,
And looking down upon the world below,
I see the evening smoke in wisps of blue.

Anon.

LINES ON A GIRL IN THE PALACE SCHOOL OF MUSIC

WHEN the moon lights the trees in the courtyard
Her bright eyes discover a bird on its nest ;
Leaning forward from the shadows, with her jade hairpin
She rescues a moth from the flame.

CHANG HU

THE MOON IN THE MOUNTAINS

HERE in the mountains the moon I love,
Hanging alight in a distant grove ;
Pitying me in my loneliness,
She reaches a finger and touches my dress.

My heart resembles the moon ;
The moon resembles my heart.
My heart and the moon in each other delight,
Each watching the other throughout the long night.

CHEN SHAN-MIN

THE HERD-BOY'S SONG

SPLASHING water,
Luscious grass ;
Somebody's child is herding an ox,
Riding his ox by the river-side.
Browsing ox,
Happy youth ;
Somebody's child is singing a song,
Shouting his song to a little white cloud :

Away at morn my ox I ride,
And back again at eventide.

My two feet never touch the dust ;
In wealth and fame who puts his trust ?

My rush hat shelters me from rain ;
In silk and sables what's to gain ?

I quench my thirst at a mountain rill ;
Who'd spend a fortune his belly to fill ?

When the sun on his golden horse rides high
Down by the river go ox and I ;

When the sinking sun makes shadows creep
He carries me home on his back, asleep.

CHEN SHAN-MIN

GRASS

GRASS withers ; its roots don't wither ;
When spring comes they revive.
Sorrow's roots, if present,
Don't wait for spring to thrive.

Ibid.

NIGHT SONG

A CROW caws on the wall ;
From a window in the darkened street
Lights shine ;
Within a girl still plays her lute
To one whose sorrows are twice drowned,
In sleep and wine.

CHU CHU-T'O

SNOW AND PLUM-BLOSSOM

PLUM-BLOSSOM without snow
Loses its rarity ;
Snow without verses—
Shocking vulgarity !
Verses at dusk completed,
And snow falling
With plum-blossom for company—
Spring is calling.

FANG CH'IU-YAI

TYRANNY

As clouds disperse when a strong wind blows,
The people scatter when a fierce king rules :
The man of wrath breaks up his empire.

EMPEROR KAO OF THE HAN DYNASTY

LOVE REMEMBERED

THEN—

A streak of cloud
Like a shuttle of jade ;
A pale, pale robe
Of thin, thin gauze ;
Delicately knitted moth-eyebrows.

Now—

An autumn wind,
A steady rain ;
A plantain tree,
A nest or two,
Long nights of bleak endurance.

LI HOU-CHU

ABSENCE

RANGE beyond range, the hills lie between us—
High hills, wide skies, cold, misty water.
The leaves of the maples have reddened and faded.
I'm longing.

Chrysanthemums bloom ; chrysanthemums wither ;
High in the sky wheels a hawk from the border.
The wind through the curtain comes cold with the moonlight.
I'm waiting.

Ibid.

A MORNING PICTURE

THE shrinking moon withdraws before the dawn ;
Night mists grow thinner and disperse.
Propped on my elbow, silently I watch,
But now recalled from fragrant dreams
By fragrant grasses. A hawk's thin cry
Falls from invisible heaven.

The frightened orioles scatter in alarm,
Tumbling late blossoms on the garden paths,
Or under the pavilion's painted eaves
Seeking a sanctuary. In vain the petals, white and red,
Are swept away ; for others, following, weave
A vivid carpet for the homing dancers' feet.

Ibid.

FISHING

A LIGHT spring breeze,
A tiny boat ;
A silken line,
A bobbing float.
A carpet of flowers,
A jar of wine ;
For a moment in a lifetime
Liberty's mine.

LI HOU-CHU

LINES WRITTEN ON SEEING PLUM-TREES
IN BLOOM BY THE RIVER

IN a dream I am back in the far, warm South, drowsing in scented
    Spring ;
Music of flute and poignant strings is wafted from boats on the river.
But the breath and dust of the city streets close in on me again ;
Stifling the dream the flowers brought, and choking me with tears.

Ibid.

THE HERMIT

Lines on a painting by Wang An-chieh

His home is on a mountain-side
Where passers-by are rare ;
In a grove all wind and rain
He dreams of endless youth.
His Taoist exercises
His only real care,
From lute to book he alternates
His pleasant search for truth.

LI LI-WENG

THE SOLDIER'S FAREWELL

A SOLDIER, bound for war, said to his wife,
' Death, my dear, we cannot know, nor life ;
I dead, you living, must depend, I fear,
For comfort on the new-born child you bear.'

LIN CHI

ALONE

HEAVY with wine, I drowse away the day
Till dusk creeps softly.   When I wake
White drifts of fallen petals heap my gown.
I rise and shake them off, then by the stream
I wander with the moon.
Birds hurry to their nests, men to their homes.

LI PO

SUMMER DAY IN THE HILLS

My white feather fan is idle in my fingers ;
My cap hangs on a rock ; my gown is laid aside ;
And while I drowse in comfort, in the green shade of the forest,
A faint, pine-scented breeze plays on my brow.

Li Po

LINES TO ONE FAR AWAY

My love was here. My house was filled
With spring's rare essences.
My love is gone. To me remains
Her sweet bed's emptiness.

Her empty bed her fragrance holds
In every silken flower ;
My empty arms are empty still—
My love will come no more.

My love is gone. Her fragrance stays
To haunt my heavy years
Till yellow autumn's leaves are laid
By winter's whitening breath.

Ibid.

RIVER SONG

By the river Lu, when the moon is bright
In a cloudless sky,
And paddy-birds fly,
The water-chestnut gatherers go by,
Homeward singing in the night.

Ibid.

THE WHITE EGRET

A SOLITARY egret, left behind
In the swift southward flight,
Sinks like a falling snowflake on the river ;
Not ready yet to fly, it rests awhile
Beside a sandbank, motionless.
No fears ruffle its white breast, smooth as the water
From which the ripple of its coming has withdrawn.

Ibid.

UNSEEN MUSIC ON A NIGHT IN SPRING

A FLUTE of jade in unseen hands,
Played in an unknown house. . . .
The air is filled with flying drifts of sound ;
Rising and falling on a fitful breeze,
They stir the silent city with breaking waves of music.
The scattered theme of this night song is *Broken Willows* ;
Memories of old gardens touch a thousand hearts.

Ibid.

FRAGMENT

I WAIT the moon's rising ;
The moon does not hasten.
I watch the river ;
The river flows on.

Ibid.

THE REBEL

Leviathan
Dwells in the northern sea.
From his throat a hundred rivers pour ;
He blows—the hills are white with snow ;
He tosses the fretted foam,
And tempests follow his wake ;
The throne of heaven totters as he leaps,
But still unsatisfied,
He rushes on.

LI PO

DRINKING ALONE IN THE MOONLIGHT

IF wine were not favoured by Heaven
No Wine Star would shine in the sky ;
If wine were not loved by the Earth
No Wine Spring would gush from her breast.
The blessing of Heaven, Earth's cordial stream
No man in his senses denies.

The wine which is golden and clear
Is instinct with the soul of a sage ;
The wine which is heady and strong
Is wisdom's best gift to the wise.
The pattern of sages, and wisdom's behest,
No man, but a monster, defies.

Three cups are the gateway to bliss ;
A jar, and the world is all yours.
The rapture of drinking, and wine's dizzy joy,
No man who is sober deserves.

Ibid.

GROWING OLD

BEAUTY's a lightning-flash ;
Time's like a whirlwind.
On grass still green the frost falls white ;
The moon's in the east ere the sun has set.

Greying temples—autumn's here,
Its havoc complete in a moment.
Not even holy men of old
Had time to achieve their purpose.

The great will change to bird or ape ;
The small to sand or insect.
Nor shall we ride as Immortals ride,
With a bird-drawn cloud for chariot.

Ibid.

COMPLAINT OF A NEGLECTED WIFE

NEW love delights the heart like flowers ;
Old love is jade of rarity.
The flowers dread the wind's cold touch ;
Pure jade holds fast its purity.

The old to-day was lately new ;
To-morrow's old is new to-day.
Should jade be laid aside for flowers
That live an hour and pass away ?

Ibid.

SOLITUDE

For me, the pine-tree, gaunt and lone,
Not the fair grace of peach or plum.

Old minister Yen, when he fell from favour
Like a falling star, retired afar
To his native mountains.   There by a brook,
His mind soared high—as he dangled his hook—
With the clouds that scurried across the sky.

My spirit, too, from unscaled heights
The wind invites to share its lair,
And leave for ever earth's dusty delights.

Li Po

RETREAT

You ask me why on this green hill
   A home I find.
I laugh in answer ; should I say,
   For peace of mind ?
Here, dim 'neath flowering peach-trees,
   The rivers flow—
A world remote, original,
   Where peace I know.

Ibid.

TIME

In youth how easy, but in age how hard
It is to learn.
A single golden inch of time, they say,
You should not spurn.
    If spring be drowsed away
    On the edge of life's green pool,
    Before you realise
    Red leaves begin to fall,
    Autumn's brief day grows cool,
    Mist dims the eyes.

LU FANG-WENG

HOME TO OUR MOUNTAINS

Up and up winds the mountain road—
    Where does it end ?
Down and down runs a chattering brook
    As I ascend.
Through leaves' crisp rustle in the wind
    A dog barks loud ;
I see the smoke of a pine-wood fire
    Against a cloud.

LU LUN

FRIENDSHIP

IN planting trees you must select a spot ;
A soil ill-chosen will mis-shape the root.
In making friendships, if the choice is bad
It is a cause of scandal in the way.

A good man's heart is like a cassia tree,
Fragrant in spring, by adverse winds unchanged ;
Hibiscus blossoms are the mean man's heart,
Blooming at dawn but fading in a day.

Don't step on winter ice till it is firm,
Beneath the surface waits the treacherous flood ;
On tried and solid rock your friendships found ;
Let all your converse be with saint and sage.

MENG CHIAO

THE DANCERS

SUBTLY from slender hips they swing,
Swaying, slanting delicately up and down.
And like the crimson mallow's flower
Glows their beauty, shedding flames afar.
They lift languid glances,
Peep distrustfully, till of a sudden
Ablaze with liquid light
Their soft eyes kindle.   So dance to dance
Endlessly they weave, break off and dance again.
Now flutter their cuffs like a great bird in flight,
Now toss their long white sleeves like whirling snow.
So the hours go by, till now at last
The powder has blown from their cheeks, the black from their brows,
Flustered now are the fair faces, pins of pearl
Torn away, tangled the black tresses.

With comb they catch and gather in
The straying locks, put on the gossamer gown
That trailing winds about them, and in unison
Of body, song and dress, obedient
Each shadows each, as they glide softly to and fro.

CHANG HÊNG—WALEY

LAZY MAN'S SONG

I HAVE got patronage, but am too lazy to use it ;
I have got land, but am too lazy to farm it.
My house leaks ; I am too lazy to mend it.
My clothes are torn ; I am too lazy to darn them.
I have got wine, but I am too lazy to drink ;
So it's just the same as if my cellar were empty.
I have got a harp, but am too lazy to play ;
So it's just the same as if it had no strings.
My wife tells me there is no more bread in the house ;
I want to bake, but am too lazy to grind.
My friends and relatives write me long letters ;
I should like to read them, but they're such a bother to open.
I have always been told that Chi Shu-yeh
Passed his whole life in absolute idleness.
But he played the harp, and sometimes transmuted metals.
So even *he* was not so lazy as I.

PO CHÜ-I—WALEY

AFTER LUNCH

AFTER lunch—one short nap :
On waking up—two cups of tea.
Raising my head, I see the sun's light
Once again slanting to the south-west.
Those who are happy regret the shortness of the day ;
Those who are sad tire of the year's sloth.
But those whose hearts are devoid of joy or sadness
Just go on living, regardless of ' short ' or ' long.'

PO CHÜ-I—WALEY

ON HIS BALDNESS

AT dawn I sighed to see my hairs fall ;
At dusk I sighed to see my hairs fall.
For I dreaded the time when the last lock should go . . .
They are all gone and I do not mind at all !
I have done with that cumbrous washing and getting dry ;
My tiresome comb is for ever laid aside.
Best of all, when the weather is hot and wet,
To have no top-knot weighing down on one's head !
I put aside my dusty conical cap ;
And loose my collar-fringe.
In a silver jar I have stored a cold cream ;
On my bald pate I trickle a ladle-full.
Like one baptized with the water of Buddha's Law,
I sit and receive this cool, cleansing joy.
Now I know why the priest who seeks Repose
Frees his heart by first shaving his head.

Ibid.

A RUSTIC SWAIN

How lovely she is, my bashful girl !
She said she'd be here at the corner of the wall.
Hopelessly in love and not finding her here,
I scratch my head, bewildered.

How bonny she is, my bashful girl !
She made me a present of this red tube.
How bright and shining my pretty red tube,
And how I adore my girl's beauty !

She brought these grasses from the fields,
To give me, white and rare.
Your beauty means nothing to me, my grasses,
But the beauty whose gift you are.

Shih Ching

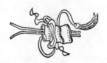

A BEAUTY

Her soft fingers are young white-grass ;
Her skin is smooth as ointment.
A sinuous tree-grub is her neck ;
Her teeth are seeds of melon.
Head, like cicada's, broad ; eyebrows
Like silkworm-moth's antennae.
Her dimples wait on artful smiles ;
How black and white her eye !

Ibid.

THOUGHTS ON PASSING AN OLD HERMIT'S HOUSE IN THE MOUNTAINS

A ROAD that winds along a rocky shore ;
Trees that are ancient springing from the walls ;
Rivulets meeting in a mountain stream ;
Peach-flowers that mark a village ;
A clucking hen that flies across the fence ;
Grandsons as well as sons to serve the wine.
 I too am old, and I too will retire
 To that same peak, just opposite his door.

SHIH YÜ-SHAN

THE PICTURE

(Lines on a picture of a recluse fishing)

WHAT trouble drives that weak old man on the Five Lakes to wander ?
From his lonely boat at the mountain-foot his slender line he throws ;
A white cloud floats towards me, shadowing the quiet water ;
By a corner of the house, just visible, a green hill shows.

Ibid.

HOT CAKE

WINTER has come ; fierce is the cold ;
In the sharp morning air new-risen we meet.
Rheum freezes in the nose ;
Frost hangs about the chin.
For hollow bellies, for chattering teeth and shivering knees
What better than hot cake ?
Soft as the down of spring,
Whiter than autumn wool :
Dense and swift the steam
Rises, swells and spreads.
Fragrance flies through the air,
Is scattered far and wide,
Steals down along the wind and wets
The covetous mouth of passer-by.
Servants and grooms
Throw sidelong glances, munch the empty air.
They lick their lips who serve ;
While lines of envious lackeys by the wall
Stand dryly swallowing.

SHU HSI—WALEY

*

Veil your ambition with the appearance of humility.

Proverb

COMPLAINT

THE Great Bear points to the north-east ;
How white the fields stretch, and how vast,
Lying a foot deep in crisp snow !
It's cold and I have no cloak ;
In the night the candle dies ;
Ghost-fires flicker in the dark ;
Sprites show a foot,
And then jump, groaning, to my side.
Though not afraid,
I loathe their malformed ugliness,
And when the dawn breeze comes to help
I'll yoke my horse and make for home.

SUNG LI-SHANG

A PLUM-TREE IN A POT

A FEW bent branches throwing crooked shadows
Stir in the wanderer distant dreams of home ;
The thousand trees that border the West River
With snow-white bloom are imaged in this pot.

SUNG LI-T'IEN

ON THE BIRTH OF HIS SON

FAMILIES, when a child is born,
Want it to be intelligent.
I, through intelligence,
Having wrecked my whole life,
Only hope the baby will prove
Ignorant and stupid.
Then he will crown a tranquil life
By becoming a Cabinet Minister.

SU TUNG-P'O—WALEY

PEAR-TREES BY THE FENCE

PEAR-TREES translucent white ;
  (My heart is sad to-night).
Willows brilliant green ;
  (Against the rail I lean).
Catkins and pearly blossoms fill the air.

The pear-tree by the fence
  (How soon we must go hence !)
Is a pillar of snow.
  (A man may never know
How few springs such as this will be his share !)

SU TUNG-P'O

PLANTING FLOWERS

DARK and pale,
Red and white,
Let colours be properly mingled.
Season by season,
Early and late,
Look well to the order of planting.
    Better a year with no wine to drink
    Than a day with no flower unfolding.

TS'AI HSIANG

AN OLD FAN

FOUR years ago I gave you that fan with a verse on it ;
Thank you, Pretty One, for taking care of it.
How would Hsiang-ju's lute-song have become famous
If a contemporary's genius had not preserved it ?

YUAN TS'ANG-SHAN

BEANS

BEANS may be boiled for brose,
Or salted and sieved to make sauce.
　　Some beans in a pot cried out
　　To the stalks burning under the pot,
　　' Say ! You are the stalk of the root
　　Of which we are the fruit. Pray,
　　Why must you make us so hot ? '

TS'AO CHIH

FLUTE MUSIC

WHITE moonshine on the autumn hills,
Strange music all around ;
Whose is the skill which can create
That soul-disturbing sound ?
A bamboo pipe and a grieving wind
In harmonious, mystic union joined,
To-night are eerily married.

TU FU

SORROW ON SORROW

STILL over-run on all sides by the rebels
(I wonder what my garden looks like now !),
How few of my acquaintance are returning !
On scattered fields of battle they lie low.

Ibid.

APPROACHING DEATH

My failing breath re-enters Space ;
My warm heart soon will cease to beat.
Those things on earth which I have left
Another must complete.

Our Royal Master, wise and good,
Controls and orders all our day.
Mercies for which I gave no thanks
My spirit shall repay.

YANG CHI-SHENG

DYING

A soul recedes into the Void ; a heart
Into the past that has no end ;
A life's unfinished and imperfect tasks
New ages must complete and mend.

Ibid.

*

A LETTER FROM HOME

THE river is a thousand miles long ;
This letter took fifteen days to come.
And after all that, it simply says,
' Do, please, hurry home.'

YUAN K'AI

SPRING SONG

I WAKE from wine-flushed sleep to see
A cold moon shining.
Outside the window flowers have bloomed ;
The room is sweet within.
The blossoms, sentient as it seems,
Are here to say good-bye ;
Their souls are leaving with the breeze,
Their forms stay here with me.

YUAN SUI-YUAN

LATE AWAKENING

FOR forty years I have idled,
Sleeping in drowsy content ;
But now I am really waking,
And my eyes see only too well
The sun which shows me already
That half my day is spent
Ere I rise and go to the watch-tower
To ring the morning bell.

WANG YANG-MING

NEWS

STRAIGHT from my village, Sir, you come ;
Pray give me news of my old home.
The day you left, as you passed by,
Outside my nursery window did you spy
My early plum-tree blooming ?

WANG WEI

ENFIN SEUL

THE guests have gone ; the house is still at last.
Roll up the screen ; let in the evening breeze.
Shadows are long ; we sat late over wine,
And a bright sickle shows above the trees.

WEN CHIH

ON A MOUNTAIN ROAD

CLOUDS on the mountain
Are hanging low ;
The path, winding upward,
Is lost to view.
Cold autumn breezes
Blow through my gown ;
Monkeys call sadly ;
The sun goes down.

WU CH'ING-JEN

PROVERBS

WHEN one wears green glasses everything is green.
If we pinch ourselves, we understand another's pain.
Diseases may be cured, but not destiny.
The torment of envy is like a grain of sand in the eye.
Given the father there must be the son.
Don't invite a man of seventy to spend the night or a man of eighty to sit down.
It is unlucky and impolite to step on a person's shadow.
Long robes may hide large feet.
Better to suffer in the world than to lie beneath the sod.
When the lips are gone the teeth are cold.
Measure your throat before you swallow the bone.
Let the liver be large and the heart small—blend courage with caution.

EXCELSIOR !

THE following poem, in pidgin English, is quoted by Professor H. A. Giles from an anonymous author. It is given here as an example of the most difficult of all the forms of speech spoken in China for the reason that, being familiar with the original, readers will have no difficulty in discovering the meaning of the phrases.

> THAT nighty time begin chop-chop,
> One young man walkey—no can stop.
> Maskee snow ! maskee ice !
> He carry flag wid chop so nice—
>   Topside-galow !

> He too muchey sorry, one piecee eye
> Look-see sharp—so—all same my,
> Him talkey largee, talkey strong,
> Too muchey curio—all same gong—
>   Topside-galow !

> Inside that house he look-see light,
> And every room got fire all right,
> He look-see plenty ice more high,
> Inside he mouth he plenty cry—
>   Topside-galow !

> Olo man talkey, ' No can walk !
> By'mby rain come—welly dark,
> Have got water, welly vide.
> Maskee ! My wantchey go topside.
>   Topside-galow !

'Man-man !' one girley talkey he ;
'What for you go topside look-see ?'
And one time more he plenty cry,
But all time walkey plenty high.
   Topside-galow !

'Take care that spoil'um tree, young man,
Take care that ice—he want man-man !'
That coolie chin-chin he good night,
He talkey, 'My can go all right.'
   Topside-galow !

Joss-pidgin man he soon begin,
Morning-time that Joss chin-chin ;
He no man see—he plenty fear,
Cos some man talkey—he can hear !
   Topside-galow !

That young man die, one large dog see,
Too muchey bobbery findee he ;
He hand b'long colo—all same ice,
Have got that flag, wid chop so nice,
   Topside-galow.

Moral

You too muchey laugh ! What for sing ?
I think-so you no savey what thing !
Supposey you no b'long clever inside,
More better *you* go walk topside !
   Topside-galow !

THE SMALL-FOOTED MAID

THE Anglo-Chinese phraseology of the following verses, which I
believe were written by Mr. E. C. Baber, but for which I have to
thank Mr. C. H. Brewitt-Taylor, may be puzzling to readers who do
not know China, but for the sake of those to whom they will bring
memories of an old and different age, they are included. (A glossary
is appended.)

> In Yüan-ming-yüan, all gaily arrayed
> In malachite kirtles and slippers of jade,
> 'Neath the wide-spreading tea-tree, fair damsels are seen
> All singing to Joss on the soft candareen.

> But fairer by far was the small-footed maid
> Who sat by my side in the sandal-wood shade,
> A-sipping the vintage of sparkling Lychee,
> And warbling the songs of the poet Maskee.

> Oh fair are the flowers in her tresses that glow,
> The sweet-scented cumshaw, the blue pummelow,
> And dearest I thought her of maids in Pekin,
> As from the pagoda she bade me chin-chin.

> One eve, in the twilight, to sing she began,
> As I touched the light notes of a jewelled sampan,
> While her own jetty finger-nails, taper and long,
> Swept softly the chords of a tremulous gong.

> She sang how ' a princess of fair Pechelee
> Was carried away by the cruel Sycee,
> And married by force to that tyrant accursed,
> That Portuguese caitiff, Pyjamah the First.

' Though her eyes were more bright than the yaconin's glow,
And whiter than bucksheesh her bosom of snow,
Yet alas for the maid ! she is captive, and now
Lies caged in thy fortress, detested Macao !

' But she muffled her face with her sohotzu's fold,
And the jailor she bribed with a tao-t'ai of gold,
And away she is fled from the traitor's harem,
Tho' the punkahs may flash and the compradores gleam.'

Thus she ceased ;—and a bumper of opium we took,
And we smoked the ginseng from a coral chebouque,
And we daintily supped upon birds' nests and snails,
And catties, and maces, and piculs, and taels.

Then we slew a joss-pigeon in honour of Fo,
And in praise of Fêng-shui we made a kotow ;
And soon the most beautiful girl in Pekin
Fell asleep in the arms of her own mandarin.

GLOSSARY.

Yüan-ming-yüan	.	The old summer palace of the emperors.
Joss .	.	A Chinese idol.
Candareen .	.	$\frac{1}{100}$ of an ounce of silver.
Lychee	.	A fruit.
Maskee	.	Never mind : no matter.
Cumshaw	.	Gratuity.
Pummelow .	.	Like a large grape-fruit.
Sampan	.	Small boat.
Pechelee	.	Pei (northern) Chih-li, the region in which Pekin (Pei-p'ing) is situated.
Sycee	.	' Shoes,' or ingots of Chinese silver.
Yaconin	.	Any Japanese official servant.
Macao	.	A place.
Sohotzu	.	Wheelbarrow.
Tao-t'ai	.	A high official.

Compradore	.	.	Buyer to a commercial firm.
Ginseng	.	.	A medicine.
Catties	.	.	A catty is a weight, something over an English pound.
Mace	.	.	$\frac{1}{10}$ of an ounce of silver.
Picul	.	.	A measure.
Tael	.	.	An ounce of silver.
Fo	.	.	Buddha.
Fêng-shui	.	.	' Wind and water ' ; Chinese ' geomancy.'

THE BONZE

READERS unacquainted with the street literature of the Chinese may be amused by the following free rendering of a popular native comic song, which, like many others, turns upon the contemptuous idea entertained of the Buddhist priesthood.

A Bonze with a shaven pate,
     And tearful watery e'e,
Went into the joss-house gate'
     And joss-stick burnèd he.

The bell and gong did ring,
     Their sound it was ding-dong,
And the priest began to sing,
     Chanting the following song.

Oh Buddha, who cam'st from the west,
     But now sitt'st in the centre of heaven,
To Chia-lan and Chia-shan, of saints the best,
     To squat on each side is given.

I pray you, oh Buddha, protect your son,
     Though I have made a sort of *faux pas* ;
I have broken a vow, and my soul is undone,
     Having married an aged mamma.

My vows that I vowed I've not properly kept :
  I'm a family man with a boy ;
My name from the list of the saints must be swept,
  The priesthood I must not enjoy.

Ten years as a bonze is, I'm quite sure, enough,
  'Tis enough for the holiest saint ;
If I still stay a priest, I should prove what a muff
  Was this ' beauty without any paint.'

G. T. GARDNER

FOLK SONGS

1.

Now the Sun has risen in the East.
As a mountain-tree fears twining creepers,
As a foreign vessel dreads the pirates,
So a young girl fears a handsome lover.

2.

Now the Sun has reached the zenith.
Days incessant I continued wooing,
By the Heavens we swore to love each other,
Should she false be, may the lightning strike her !

3.

Now the Sun shines forth with scorching heat.
At her gate a girl is planting onions,
Every day she sighs, ' There are no onions ' ;
Every night she sighs, ' I have no husband.'

4.

Blazing is the Sun, one hopes for clouds ;
Parched are the fields, they hope for water ;
Cloudless is the sky, one hopes for showers ;
Single is that girl, she hopes for—whom ?

5.

Bright the Sun may be and bad the weather,
Trees and flowers gay, the garden dreary ;
Good the plant may be and bad the crop,
Fine a girl may be and die a spinster.

6.

Don't blame Heaven for sending rain in torrents ;
Mind that fearful drought some years ago,
When for rice were paid cents six-and-thirty,
And to death were starved the fairest maidens.

7.

Incense burned leaves embers in the censer ;
Is the lampwick burned, there are but ashes.
If you want to woo, then woo two Sisters :
Is the one at work, you have the other.

8.

If your sweetheart jilts you, never mind,
Every mountain sends some creeklet forth,
Every valley has some little water,
If you fail on one side try the other.

9.

Ah ! the world is worse than ever it was,
Finger-rings are worn as large as door-rings ;
Once a lover wanted but one ring,
Now a lover wants a lot of dollars.

10.

Twice I met my sweetheart in the dusk,
And this night we met behind her house.
When somebody passed and looked askant,
She seized a twig and called her pigs.

E. J. EITEL

LINES TO AN OLD CHIT-BOOK

MOULDY thou art,—thou has suffered much
   From mildew and damp and age,
But many a vanished hand's soft touch
   Rests on each faded page.

Six years I have used thee, and till now
   Thy cover has lasted well ;
Thou knowest far more of that time, I trow,
   Than ever myself could tell.

For as I look over the chits sent out,
   And their marginal short replies,
I can't recollect what 'twas all about ;
   Thus Time with fleet Memory flies !

Who was this Mrs. Smith, and why
   In pencil record her grief ?
Had she asked me to tiffin, and then had I
   Refused—to her great relief ?

And here, De Tompkins, who puts, I see,
   ' With pleasure ' in violet ink.
Had I asked him to dinner, and who was he ?
   Stay ! when I come to think—

De T. was a stranger in the land,
 Travelling from town to town ;
See here, I notice his bold free hand
 A few lines further down.

This time, however, he puts ' Will send '—
 What was it he sent to me ?
Had he held bad cards—or did he but lend
 A novel I'd asked to see ?

Yet there are some I remember well,
 Remember each line I wrote,
Yes ! and the smile of the ' boy ' when I'd tell
 Where he should take the note.

I know that I sent a chit each day,
 With something—a book or flower—
Something to give me a chance to say
 I thought of her every hour.

'Twas long ago—and yet now, in dreams,
 Often I see sweet Kate ;
But when I think of those days it seems,
 'Twas idleness all—*not* Fate.

Ah ! idle moments and far between,
 Idle, yet happy too !
Their sum is not in one's life, I ween,
 More than a week or two.

. . . . .

Ah well ! go back to thy shelf to-day,
 Rest, since thy labour's o'er ;
Some day, when my hair is turning grey,
 I'll study my youth once more !

TUNG CHIA (Master of the House)

MY TEACHER

WHO looked so very spick-and-span,
So Oriental with his fan,
When first afar I did him scan ?
    My teacher.

Who, as I got to know him more,
Became a most decided bore
When daily he tapped at the door ?
    My teacher.

Who sipped his tea the whole day long,
As I droned through the Tone sing-song,
And never cared if I read wrong ?
    My teacher.

Who when the sounds I failed to catch,
With me had quite a shrieking match,
Which made me ache beneath my ' thatch ' ?
    My teacher.

Who fanned himself and looked serene,
And preached the ' Doctrine of the Mean '
(Which meant not much for me, I ween) ?
    My teacher.

Who had a face of aspect lean,
Which long with soap or things that clean
On speaking terms had never been ?
    My teacher.

Who on cold rice and garlic fed ?
Who had an oven for a bed ?
Who wore a tail upon his head ?
    My teacher.

Who begged me of a meal to take
Of rotten eggs and sea-slug cake,
Which gave me such a stomach-ache ?
    My teacher.

Who sweets me brought to give relief
(Which smelt much more like ' lofty ' beef),
Wrapped in his dirty handkerchief ?
    My teacher.

Who likes to snore, or in dull speech
To mutter low, or else to screech ?
Who teacher is, but doesn't teach ?
    My teacher.

HSÜEH SHÊNG (Pupil)

VOX ET PRAETEREA ?

(AN interesting debate took place at the last meeting of the Peking Literary and Debating Society, the subject being ' Truth ; not advisable under all circumstances.' To those who were present the following lines are respectfully dedicated, with apologies and thanks to Mr. Lewis Carroll.)

Our learned young Society
Doth strive with all its might
To make the paths of wisdom seem
Accessible and bright,
And round itself a halo spreads
Of literary light.

They quote as well as well can be,
Their facts are dry as dry,
Their wordy warfare often runs
Most dangerously high ;
For one strong point about them is
That none of them are shy.

A youth and eke a sinologue
(Both of them close at hand)
Were very grieved indeed to see
The ignorance of the land ;
' If this could only be dispelled,'
They said, ' it would be grand.'

' If we our wisdom could expound,
During the coming year,
Do you suppose,' the young man said,
' That we should make things clear ? '
' I doubt it,' said the sinologue,
And shed a bitter tear.

' Good people, come and talk with us ! '
The youth he did beseech,
' And when we've finished our remarks
Each one can make his speech ;
Draw it but mild, and we will lend
A willing ear to each.'

Our ancient cynic looked at him,
But never a word he said,
That ancient cynic winked his eye
And shook his hairless head.
Meaning to say he'd rather seek
His comfortable bed.

But many people did attend
And took their seats in turn,
Each one was eager, and to speak
Right earnestly did yearn ;
Now this was odd, because, you know,
They should have come to learn.

' The time has come,' the young man said,
' To talk of many things :
Of Jesuits—of casuists—
Of cabbages—and Kings ;
Also if truth be good for trade
And whether pigs have wings ?

.   .   .   .   .

' I hold the right ' (he wandered on),
' Though Truth I dearly prize,
That we should sometimes have recourse
To well-selected lies.'
At this the worthy sinologue
Did wipe his streaming eyes ;

But, gulping his emotion, he
Right eloquently said,
That though such lies might useful be
Truth must come in ahead ;
And then he quoted learned books
Which nobody had read.

The young man and the sinologue
Talked for an hour or so,
Until the information tide
All sluggishly did flow ;

Around them folks sat patiently
And none got up to go.

.   .   .   .   .

' Oh audience,' said the sinologue,
' Now that we're really done
Shall we be going home again ? '
But answer came there none.
And this was scarcely odd, because
They slumbered every one.

' Biddy,' in the ' Chinese Times,' 1882

THE WOOSUNG BAR

ADAPTED from Mr. Kingsley's celebrated song, and respectfully dedicated, in spite of themselves, to the enterprising navigators who discovered the New Old Channel at Woosung.

Three genii went sailing a-down the Wangpoo,
To the Woosung Bar, when the tide was low,
For the ships were small and the steamers were few,
That over the Bar at low tide could go.
    And skippers would rave and pilots would swear,
    And the vessels would stick in the mud down there ;
    While the Woosung Bar was moaning.

Three feet more deep a channel they found,
Where the vessels could float when the tide was low,
So that inward or outward, where'er they were bound,
They never need wait for the ebb or flow,
    So no more need skippers to rave and swear ;
    No vessels need stick in the mud down there ;
    While the Woosung Bar is moaning.

Three naval commanders went down to see,
And surveyed the channel all o'er and o'er,
And they found the others correct to a T.
The pilots all said they knew it before.
> So no more need skippers to rave and swear ;
> No vessels need stick in the mud down there ;
> While the Woosung Bar is moaning.

Three vessels came sailing up into Woosung,
To cross the bar when the tide was low ;
But they stuck in the mud, and there they hung,
The three feet of water had vanished—Heigho !
> And skippers may rave and pilots may swear,
> The channel, alas, is no deeper there,
> And the Woosung Bar is moaning.

From ' Puck,' or the ' Shanghai Charivari '

THE TREE

OF KNOWLEDGE

PROVERBS

When the white dog gets the bone the black dog must go without.

*

A horse's back is not as safe as a water-buffalo's.

*

When there are no fish in the pond a shrimp is great.

*

The tiger cares nothing that the sow is lean.

*

You can't have a horse that will run fast but won't want grass.

*

The water can do without the fish ; the fish cannot do without the water.

ANIMAL WORLD

Of zoology as a science the Chinese know very little. . . . An old and popular arrangement of the whole animal world is into five divisions : feathered, hairy, naked, shelly and scaly animals ; at the head of each of these divisions stands a type. The phoenix, unicorn, man, tortoise and dragon are the respective types of these divisions, and in themselves comprise all the good qualities of all the other 360 species found in it.

LANGDON

THE BIRD OF PARADISE

This bird is found in Amboyna ; its appearance is like a variegated pheasant ; it remains among the clouds, drinking fog and eating mist, and never sets foot on the earth until it dies, when it falls to the ground. Its feathers are very light and loose, soft and pliable ; at the ends of the wings are two beautiful feathers, more than a foot long ; its tail is like that of the swallow, which it trails in a graceful manner, and when borne along by the wind, it soars irresistibly away.

WANG TA-HAI

THE CHIANG-LIANG

The *chiang-liang* has the head of a tiger, the face of a man, four hoofs, long arms, and a snake between its teeth.

THE CH'OU-T'I

In the region west of the Red Water lives a beast called the *ch'ou-t'i*, which has a head growing out of each side.

THE CH'UAN-T'OU PEOPLE

The denizens of the Ch'uan-t'ou country have human heads, bat-like wings, and birds' beaks. They live entirely on raw fish.

THE HSIAO

The *hsiao* is like the owl but has a human face, the body of a monkey, and the tail of a dog. Its appearance portends severe drought.

THE HSING-HSING

The *hsing-hsing* are like monkeys. They have white faces and pointed ears. They walk upright like men, and can climb trees.

THE HSING-T'IEN

THE *hsing-t'ien* is a headless being who, having fought against the gods, was decapitated and condemned to continue without a head for ever. Its eyes are in its breast and its navel is its mouth. It leaps and prances in the wilds, brandishing its shield and hatchet.

THE HUA-FISH

THE *hua-fish* or flying-snake fish, looks like a fish, but has the wings of a bird. Its appearance portends drought.

THE HUI

THE *hui* of the hills looks like a dog with a human face. It is a very fine jumper, and can move with the swiftness of an arrow, for which reason its appearance is regarded as presaging typhoons. It laughs derisively at the sight of man.

THE LONG-ARM PEOPLE

THE natives of the long-arm country have arms so long that their hands touch the ground. They support themselves by catching fish on the sea-shore.

THE MERMAN

THE mermen have human heads and arms, with the body and tail of a fish. They appear on the surface of the Strong Waters.

THE MUSICAL SERPENT

THE Musical Serpent has the head of a snake and four wings. It makes a noise like the musical stone.

THE PING-FENG

THE *ping-feng*, which inhabits the Magic Water country, looks like a black pig, but has a head at each end.

THE SKY-HORSE

THE sky-horse looks like a white dog with a black head. It has fleshy wings and is able to fly.

THE STRANGE-ARM PEOPLE

IN the strange-arm region the people have all one arm and three eyes. They are remarkably ingenious and know how to make flying-carriages, in which they travel on the wind.

THE TI-CHIANG

THE *ti-chiang* is a supernatural bird found in the Heavenly Mountains. It is as red as vermilion, has six feet and four wings, but neither face nor eyes.

Shan Hai Ching

FOXES

FOXES, at the age of fifty, have power to change themselves into women; at one hundred they can take on the appearance of a beautiful girl, or a medium, or they can become men and marry human wives. They know what is happening hundreds of miles away, and are familiar with all the arts of misleading and betraying. At a thousand years they become transcendent.

T'ai P'ing Kuang Chi

THE BOA CONSTRICTOR
OR ELEPHANT-SUSPENDING SNAKE

IN the country of Palembang there are many white elephants, which are used in war. Formerly an old elephant was killed by a snake, and the elephant-keeper, having traced him into the jungle, found him suspended to a tree, with several folds of a snake twined round his body. The keeper attempted to sever these with his sword, but the weapon made no impression. An old woodman, hearing the circumstances, said : ' This is the elephant-suspending snake ; in the interior of Siam there are many such ; but I did not expect to find them here. Neither axes nor saws will affect them ; but they are afraid of fire.' On applying fire, therefore, the snake fell to pieces and died. Having collected the joints and measured them, they found the animal to be upwards of a hundred feet in length.

WANG TA-HAI

CRANES

THE favourite bird of Chinese poets is the crane. In legends it ranks second only to the phoenix. Its plumage is usually white, but blue, black and yellow cranes are mentioned in Chinese literature. The crane, the pine-tree and the tortoise are emblems of longevity, and for this reason bronze cranes are often used as ornaments in rock-gardens and stone-paved courtyards.

Cranes are also regarded as birds of wisdom. It was supposed that they could be taught to pick out words and understand orders, and for this reason as well as because they typify long life, they are the chosen bird of the immortals, who ride through the air on the back of a crane or change themselves into one at will.

CREATION

IN the beginning the earth and the heavens were floating about in the water. Then appeared P'an Ku, who spent eighteen thousand years forming the sun, moon and stars, the heaven and the earth, and finally died in order that the works of his hands might receive life. His head became the mountains, his breath the wind and the clouds, his voice the thunder, his limbs the four quarters of the earth, his blood the rivers, his flesh the soil, his beard the constellations, his skin and hair the herbs and trees, his teeth, bones and marrow, the metals, rocks and precious stones, his sweat the rain, and the insects creeping over his body became human beings.

DRAGONS

ACCORDING to Chinese belief the authentic species of dragon or *lung* has a camel's head, a deer's horns, a rabbit's eyes, a cow's ears, a snake's neck, a frog's belly, a carp's scales, a hawk's claws and a tiger's palms.

DENNYS

THE INK-MONKEY

THIS creature is common in the northern regions and is about four or five inches long ; it is endowed with an unusual instinct ; its eyes are like cornelian stones, and its hair is jet black, sleek and flexible, as soft as a pillow. It is very fond of eating thick Chinese ink, and whenever people write, it sits with folded hands and crossed legs, waiting till the writing is finished, when it drinks up the remainder of the ink ; which done, it squats down as before, and does not frisk about unnecessarily.

WANG TA-HAI

K'UN-LUN MOUNTAIN

THE celebrated mountain K'un-lun (usually identified with the Hindu Kush) is said to be peopled with fairies who cultivate upon its terraces the ' fields of sesamum and gardens of coriander seed ' which are eaten as ordinary food by those who possess the gift of longevity. Here too is the 'Lake of Gems' on whose borders dwells the fairy mother Hsi Wang Mu, and beside whose waters flourishes the tree of life, which bears fruit once in three thousand years. This fruit is bestowed by the fairies on their favourites, who thus become immortal.

DENNYS

ORANG-OUTAN OR MOUNTAIN STRANGERS

THESE are wild men, of the ape species, found in the deep forest jungle. The face resembles the human countenance, but the body approaches nearer to that of the ape; they have hair one or two inches long, and are in stature about two or three feet high; their bellies are like drums; they are not fond of sporting about; whenever they look up or down they strike on their bellies, and on meeting people cover themselves as though they had some sense of shame. How strange! that even the orang-outan should display a degree of modesty.

WANG TA-HAI

THE SOUTH-POINTING CARRIAGE
OR MARINER'S COMPASS

IN a European mariner's compass the card is attached to the needle, and in a Chinese compass the needle is free, so that the compass must be continually turned to accommodate it to the play of the needle. A Chinese traveller in the eighteenth century, on first observing this difference, wrote thus : ' When Chinese mariners wish to proceed anywhere they turn the characters of the compass, to accommodate it to the position of the vessel; but when European sailors want to go towards any quarter, they turn the vessel in the direction of the compass. Still, it is one and the same principle; only the instrument is of a different construction.'

Ibid.

THE SEA-HORSE

THIS animal is found in Macassar, where it frequently comes on shore to seek after its mate ; on which occasions it is sometimes caught. Its hair is of a fine black colour and very sleek ; its tail is long and sweeps the ground ; on shore it walks about like other horses, is very tractable, and will go several hundred miles in a day ; but you must not attempt to bathe it in the river, for no sooner does it see water than its former nature revives, and darting into the stream it swims away.

Ibid

THE SEA-MAN

THE sea-man is found on the shores of the southern ocean ; its body is about three or four cubits long, in appearance not very unlike that of a man ; its colour is yellow, and from the navel proceeds a stalk several hundred feet in length, which is attached to the rocks at the bottom of the sea. Whenever it is produced, male and female appear together, so that there are no solitary persons among them. The Dutch, who are very desirous of collecting all sorts of curious things, pay the fishermen to catch these, but when the root is severed they die ; they are, however, put into spirits and preserved.

Ibid.

TRIPANG OR BÊCHE-DE-MER

TRIPANG is a slug found in the sea, of an oblong shape ; when first caught it is nearly a foot long, and as soft as cotton ; but boiled in a solution of alum, and afterwards dried in the sun, it contracts to about two or three inches in length. It is found in deep water, among rocks, and the deeper the water the finer and more plentiful the tripang. There is a large variety of the species but the best are the prickly tripang and the crêpe tripang.

Ibid.

TORTOISE-SHELL

THE form of the animal whence this substance is taken is like that of the common tortoise, having on its back twelve plates ; which are detached in the following manner. The tortoise is suspended with its head downwards, its back is moistened with vinegar, and fire is applied, when the plates of the tortoise-shell fall off. The plates first detached fetch a high price. Should the animal now be let go into the sea, in a year's time the shell will be reproduced, when, if taken, it must be scorched again, but the plates will be thinner and softer, and fetch a lower price in the market.

WANG TA-HAI

WATER-SPOUTS OR THE DRAGON INHALING WATER

ON the wide ocean, when storms occur in the dusk of evening, a line of black clouds, like a needle, is sometimes seen to descend, gradually coming lower and lower, until it reaches the sea ; when the water, thereby thrown into commotion, forms a violent eddy. Those who are at a distance experience no injury ; but should the phenomenon approach, then it is necessary to burn fowl's feathers, and let off crackers to disperse it ; while great care must be taken to cover the water-casks and reservoirs on board with cotton or cloths, otherwise the water in them would be drawn up into the clouds. The taste of the sea-water is naturally salt, but when thus drawn up and formed into rain it becomes fresh. This is one of the inscrutable ways of Heaven, whereby human life is preserved.

Ibid.

The Tree of Knowledge

A NATURE CALENDAR

In the first month of spring the vapours of heaven descend and those of the earth ascend. Heaven and earth are in harmonious co-operation. All plants bud and grow.

In the second month of spring the rain begins to fall. The peach-tree begins to blossom. The oriole sings. Hawks are transformed into doves.

In the last month of spring the influences of life and growth are fully developed ; and the warm and genial airs diffuse themselves. The crooked shoots are all put forth and the buds are unfolded.

In the first month of summer the green frogs croak. Earth-worms come forth. The royal melons grow. The sow-thistle is in seed.

In the second month of summer the period of slighter heat arrives. The praying mantis is produced. The shrike begins to call. The mocking-bird ceases to sing.

In the last month of summer gentle winds begin to blow. The cricket takes its place in the walls. Young hawks learn the ways of their parents. Decaying grass becomes fireflies.

In the first month of autumn cool winds come. The white dew descends. The cicada of the cold chirps.

In the second month of autumn sudden and violent winds come. The wild geese arrive. The swallows depart. Tribes of birds store up provision.

In the last month of autumn the wild geese come like guests. Small birds enter the great water and become molluscs. Chrysanthemums show their yellow flowers.

In the first month of winter water begins to congeal. The earth begins to be penetrated by the cold. Pheasants enter the great water and become large molluscs. Rainbows are hidden and do not appear.

In the second month of winter the ice becomes more strong. The earth begins to crack. The night-bird ceases to sing. Tigers begin to mate. . . . Rice begins to grow. Worms curl. The moose-deer shed their horns.

In the third month of winter the wild geese go northwards. The magpie begins to build. The cock-pheasant crows. Hens hatch. The ice is now abundant. Orders are given to collect it and it is carried to the ice-houses.

Li Chi

THE TWENTY-FOUR SEASONS

In addition to the division of the year into months the Chinese calendar was subdivided into periods of fifteen days, chiefly, it would seem, for the convenience of farmers. Beginning approximately in the first week of February according to the Western calendar, the divisions were as follows :

> Beginning of spring
> Rain water
> Awakening of insects
> Spring equinox
> Pure brightness
> Great rain
> Beginning of summer
> Slight filling (of grain in the ear)
> Grain in the ear
> Summer solstice
> Slight heat
> Great heat
> Beginning of autumn
> End of heat
> White dew
> Autumn equinox
> Cold dew
> Frost descends
> Beginning of winter
> Slight snow

Great snow
Winter solstice
Slight cold
Great cold

BARBARIANS

FAR to the east of the Middle Kingdom is a country where the inhabitants eat their first-born. When a man dies his wife is carried out of the house and abandoned. Widows are called ' demon wives,' and may not live with other people.

To the south of the kingdom of Ch'u is another strange country where they remove and throw away the flesh from the bodies of their dead parents and bury the bones. This is regarded as truly filial.

In the far west, beyond the country of Ch'in, is a land where men burn their dead parents and are considered unfilial if they fail to do so.

Po Wu Chih

*

The *Man* tribe in the south wore their hair loose and went barefoot. Their weapons were bows and crossbows and long spears and swords and axes. And they had shields to ward off blows. In the middle was the king, who advanced to the front. He wore a golden inlaid headdress ; his belt bore a lion's face with a clasp ; his boots had pointed toes and were green ; he rode a frizzy-haired horse the colour of a hare ; and he carried at his waist a pair of swords chased with the pine-tree device.

The *Mans* are brave, but prone to doubts and hesitations, and they will not advance in the face of the unknown. They all assembled on the appointed day—ten legions of them—massing like clouds and sweeping in like mists gathering on the mountains, each and all of them obeying the commands of the king.

San Kuo Chih Yen I

IN a place known as Silver Pit Ravine the *Man* barbarians, who inhabit the region south of the Yangste River, had built a palace, and there was an ancestral temple, which they called the ' Family Devil,' where they solemnised sacrifices of bulls and horses at the four seasons. They called these sacrifices ' enquiring of the Demons.' Human sacrifices were offered also, men of the region or of their own people belonging to other villages. Sick persons swallowed no drugs, but prayed to a chief sorcerer, called Drug Demon. There was no legal code, the only punishment for every transgression being death.

When girls are grown they bathe in the stream that flows through the ravine. Men and women are kept apart and they marry whom they will, their parents having no control in that particular. They call this Learning the Trade. In good seasons the country produces grain, but if the harvest fails they make soup out of serpents and eat boiled elephant flesh.

San Kuo Chih Yen I

*

The people of Wu-ch'i live in caves and eat earth ; they bury their dead. Their hearts do not decay, but after a century are changed into men.

In the land of Lu it is the knee-caps of the dead which survive and these become men after a lapse of one hundred and twenty years.

In Hsi the process is more rapid, and the unchanged liver of dead persons takes human form at the end of only eight years.

Yu Yang Tsa Tsu

THE TOOTH-EXTRACTING TRIBE

THERE is a tribe of people at Benjarmasin, who are much addicted to praying every evening. They worship towards the setting sun, and recite charms till the sun goes down. They do not eat the flesh of dogs or pigs, and when their friends die, they pull out their hair, draw their teeth, and strip them of their clothes ; saying, that as they did not bring these things into the world with them, so when they die they should not carry them away. This is one of the cruelties of false religions.

WANG TA-HAI

FOREIGN DEVILS

MANY strange peoples were believed by the Chinese to reside beyond the civilised borders of the Middle Kingdom. Among these few were stranger than those who were said to be provided with a hole through their chests so that all that was required to transport a person of rank from one place to another was a long bamboo, which was passed through the hole, and on which he was carried along by bearers in the manner of a sedan-chair.

Shan Hai Ching

A TRAVELLER'S TALE

' ONCE when I was returning to Fukien by sea,' says Chou Yü, ' the ship met adverse winds which blew for five days and nights, and drove us no one knew how many thousand *li* off our course. On that journey I saw six countries.

The first of these was the Dog Country. The inhabitants, who wear no clothes, came out carrying dogs, but ran away in terror when they saw the ship.

We next passed the Country of the Hairy People. They are small in stature and wear their hair long and have hair on their bodies, rather like gibbons.

Thereafter we came to the Country of *Yakchas*. The ship struck a hidden rock and sprang a leak, so the passengers and cargo were landed to wait till the tide fell, and the ship could be repaired. At first we did not know where we were, and many of the people went into the woods to gather wild herbs. Suddenly they were set upon by *yakchas* and one caught, while the rest fled in terror. Looking back they saw the unfortunate captive being devoured by the ravenous beings. Everyone was terrified and did not know what to do. In a little while we saw approaching about a hundred of the creatures, with ferocious eyes, red hair and teeth like tigers. They were armed with sticks and spears, and some fifty of the passengers seized bows, spears and swords to withstand their attack. Two of the *yakchas* were shot down and the rest fled. Preparations were made to ward off another rush, but the *yakchas* were afraid of the bows and arrows and did not return, and in two days the ship was repaired and we again set sail.

Driving with the wind, we came next to the Country of Giants. The inhabitants are huge men and wild. Seeing the ship they ran out with great clamour, then turned tail and fled.

We next came to a country where the people wore hemp and were civilised. They brought us food, and asked for nails and iron in exchange. Some of the passengers who were able to make out a little of their speech, gave it as their opinion that the inhabitants were the descendants of Chinese who had been driven ashore there by tempests, and advised us to hasten our departure, as they feared some misfortune might befall us there.

So we went on the Country of Dwarfs, where the men are of the size of children of five or six years. Our food by this time was exhausted, and, while looking for the dwarfs in their holes and caves, we came upon some fruit which we divided and ate.

The Tree of Knowledge

After sailing two more days we came to an island and hoped to get water there. A herd of goats appeared, quite tame, and very sleek and fat. At first we thought that there must be people on the island to whom they belonged, but we could find no trace of human life, so we captured a hundred of the animals and ate them.'

Liu Hsun

EUROPEANS

(As seen by a Chinese merchant in the early 19th century)

. . . They make use of no formality in their most extensive bargains more solemn than a mere shake of the hand. . . . When a guest arrives, the host helps him with his own hand to the juice of the grape, for they welcome visitors with wine, not with tea. To touch glasses in drinking is a mark of friendship. In winter evenings they sit by the fire and pour out *cold* wine, careless of the snow lying deep outside the door. . . . They make light of their lives on occasions of personal contest, and when two of them quarrel, the consequences may be very serious. They stand face to face and discharge fire-arms at each other on a given signal. If one fall, the survivor is not punished ; if neither fall, there is an end of the quarrel. They do this to show that they are not afraid. . . . Their distant voyages abroad keep them long from home, and it is not until they have accumulated a fortune that they return to take a wife. Many do not marry before fifty years of age ; and if the bride be very young on these occasions, it is no scandal. . . . In the regulation of the annual period, they have no intercalary month, but the new year always commences ten days after the winter solstice. On this occasion they used to powder their heads with white dust, and all get tipsy. . . . The foreigners have all been fighting one another for the last twenty years, but it is to be hoped that they will soon make peace with one another, and all have an opportunity of improving themselves by intercourse with China.

Davis

In their manners Europeans aim to be polite, and affect an elegant air. They seem delighted at meeting their friends, and are lavish in their compliments to one another. When young people see a stranger, they compliment him with a bow, and when menials meet their masters, they honour them by kneeling ; this is according to the liberality of human feeling displayed in ancient times, and is truly praiseworthy. . . . But there are no writings of philosophers and poets among them, wherewith to beguile the time ; nor any friends of like mind, to soothe one's feelings ; no deep caverns or lofty towers to which one could resort for an excursion ; all of which is much to be lamented.

THE DUTCH

THE Dutch inhabit the north-west corner of the ocean ; they have high noses and red hair, white faces and grey eyes ; they do not allow their beards to grow ; their coats are clean and neat, with short bodies and narrow sleeves ; while their gait is light and nimble. They share the sovereignty of Europe with the English.

The Dutch say that their country is very cold ; that in the month of October they have frost and snow, when the leaves all fall from the trees. Many of their people, they affirm, attain to a hundred years of age. . . . But in the climate of Batavia they do not attain great longevity ; and fifty or sixty years are looked on as the maximum. Those who are born in Batavia have not red hair, and their eyes are dark, which is perhaps to be ascribed to the climate.

THE ENGLISH

THE English nation is poor but powerful, and being situated at a most important point, frequently attacks the other (nations). . . . The English are denominated by the Chinese, the red-haired people ;

they also dwell in the north-west corner of the ocean, very near to the Dutch, whom they resemble in person and dress, but their language and writing are different. English manufactures are very superior, while their swords and guns, and other implements, are the best in all countries to the north-west.

THE FRENCH

THE French also reside in the north-west corner of the ocean, very near the English and Dutch. Their appearance, apparel and household furniture are all similar to those of the Dutch, but their language and literature are different. Their dispositions are violent and boisterous ; their country is poor and contains but few merchants. Whenever the Dutch are insulted by the English, they depend on the French for assistance. The kingdom of France is large, and the population numerous, so that the English are somewhat afraid of them.

THE PORTUGUESE

THE Portuguese are called by the Chinese black demons. There is no account of their forefathers, but they belong to Batavia, in which city they have a church. In their reckoning of time, as well as in their language and mode of writing they follow the Dutch. Their men are slenderly formed, but their women are beautiful, and contract marriages with the Dutch, who seem to prefer them. This class is principally employed as clerks or soldiers ; they are of an artful disposition, and the Dutch, out of jealousy, will not allow them to rise in office.

EUROPEAN BALLS CALLED TANDAK

WHEN Europeans make an entertainment, they set out a long table, at which scores of people sit down, which is called a feast, or *festa*, and when the stringed instruments play up, men and women stand opposite each other and dance, which is called dancing or *tandak*. When a young woman is marriageable, she is allowed to select her own partner, who is called her lover or *Sooka* (suitor ?). If they are fond of each other, they dance together, in order to settle the match.

Supplementary Remarks

The dependent countries of Europe are intermixed and connected without end ; some of these places can be visited by ships, when they become a little known ; and some are held in subjection by the Dutch, and governed by them. The rest live in hollow trees and caves of the earth, not knowing the use of fire, and wander about naked, or in strange and uncouth attire ; they cannot all be fully known, nor are there any means of inquiring about them.

JAVA

In Java they look upon wind as a demon, and on water as a medicine ; all who are exposed to the wind, and consequently get fevers, have only to bathe in the river and they get well. Women immediately after labour, and young children afflicted with the small-pox, all bathe in the river. . . . If the weather be ever so hot and sultry, they never take off their clothes, nor fan themselves, but always sleep in close rooms with curtains spread over them ; the least exposure to the wind brings on sickness, hence in their rooms they use glass for doors and windows, because it keeps out the wind but admits the light. In our tales it is said that ' in the luxurious lands of the genii they have flowers all the year round, and glass windows, and tortoise-shell bridges ' ; now in the western regions these are common things, so that it is not worth while making any wonder about it.

BATAVIA

Batavia is a fertile country on the sea-shore, an extensive region in the extreme south-west. It is calculated that the voyage from China is about 280 ship's watches, each watch comprising 50 *li* (*i.e.* $16\frac{2}{3}$ miles), making altogether 14,000 *li*, after sailing over which we arrive at Batavia.

The Tree of Knowledge

The city faces north. Its gates are strong, and the walls high ; the territory is extensive and the streets are wide ; merchandise is abundant, and all the tribes of foreigners assemble there. . . .

The virtuous influence of our (Chinese) Government extending far, all the foreigners have submitted, and thus mercantile intercourse is not prohibited. . . .

Batavia originally belonged to the Javanese, but the Dutch, having by stratagem and artifice got possession of the revenues, proceeded to give orders and enact laws until, squatting down all along the sea coast, they have . . . brought the natives under their entire control. The Hollanders have long noses and red hair, they are deep-schemed and thoughtful, and hence they acquire such an influence over the natives. . . .

Our rich merchants and great traders give bribes to the Hollanders, and are elevated to the ranks of Captain, Lieutenant, Commissioner of Insolvent and Intestate Estates, Secretary and such-like appellations ; but all of them take the title of Captain. When the Chinese quarrel or fight, they represent their cause to the Captain, before whom they make a low bow, calling themselves ' juniors.' The rights and wrongs, with the crookeds and straights of the matter, are all immediately settled, without giving the affair a second thought. . . .

With respect to the Dutch, they are very much like the man who stopped his ears while stealing a bell. Measuring them by the rules of reason, they scarcely possess one of the five cardinal virtues : the great oppress the small . . . thus they have no benevolence ; husbands and wives separate, with permission to marry again, and before a man is dead a month his widow is allowed to go to another, thus they have no rectitude ; there is no distinction between superiors and inferiors, men and women are mingled together, thus they are without propriety. . . . Of the single quality of sincerity, however, they possess a little. As it respects the manners of the natives, with their uncouth forms, their singular appearances, dwelling in hollow trees, and residing in caverns, with their woolly hair and tattooed bodies, their naked persons and uncooked food, and all such monstrous and unheard-of matters, it is scarcely worth while wasting one's breath upon them.

Every seven days the Hollanders keep a ceremony-day, when from nine to eleven in the morning, they go to the place of worship, to recite prayers and mumble charms ; the hearers hanging down their heads and weeping, as if there were something very affecting in it all ; but after half an hour's jabber they are allowed to disperse, and away they go to feast in their garden-houses and spend the whole day in delight. . . . Then you may see the dust of the carriages and the footsteps of the horses all along the road in unbroken succession. . . .

BANTAM

BANTAM lies to the west of Batavia, and is inhabited by Javanese. The Hollanders collect the revenues, and hold the lands on the sea-coast in possession, in order to keep in order the various foreigners who come and go for purposes of trade. . . . The Javanese . . . are very much afraid of the Hollanders . . . not daring to treat them with the least neglect. . . . Outside the palace of the Sultan there is a small fort, where 12 Hollanders and 100 native troops are stationed under the name of guards of honour, but really to control the Sultan. . . . The Javanese are dull and stupid by nature, thinking that the Hollanders reverence them, and therefore take the trouble to collect their revenues ; they imagine also that the Hollanders respect them, and have therefore built them a fort, and personally act as their guards of honour. . . . The Hollanders cannot muster one for their thousand . . . but the Hollanders are courageous and scheming, whereby they form plans for entrapping the people, and then overawe them by majesty and allure them by gain, till they have sufficiently subdued their minds. . . . Rightly therefore did the ancients esteem wisdom above force.

The Tree of Knowledge

SAMARANG

SAMARANG is a district subject to Batavia . . . the country is rich and well-watered, and the people rich and affluent. . . . According to the custom of the place, those who come originally from China are preferred as sons-in-law, while those born in the country are not esteemed. In the former case a pair of wax candles may serve for a marriage-portion, which is most delightfully cheap. The servants and slave-girls each attend to some particular business. The distinction between masters and servants is very strictly observed. . . . Wives are called ' mistress,' and the men are very much afraid of them ; the affairs of the family are all under their control ; they keep everything shut up very closely and their jealousy is insupportable. . . . Men and women walk about hand in hand, and sit down shoulder to shoulder, while some of them proceed so far as to go arm in arm, or to take one another round the waist ; so little do they know of the decencies of public morals. Female slaves carry umbrellas, to screen their mistresses from the sun, or fans to agitate the wind for them ; or they hold the spitting-dish, or carry the betel-box. Throughout the whole country the practice is the same, and has therefore ceased to excite wonder.

MANILLA

BAPTISMAL CEREMONY

IT is the custom in Manilla highly to venerate the foreign priests, setting up monasteries for the padris and keeping up the ceremony day (Sunday). These padris or paleys are foreigners. They lay great stress on the sprinkling of water, and in their service turn night into day. Every monastery strikes its bell in order to fix the time. At mid-day and midnight they commence reckoning their hours, going on to twelve respectively. They venerate the cross and do not sacrifice to their ancestors, while they worship no other spiritual being than Deus. There is something still more extraordinary : the padris forgive people's sins, and are very much honoured. The ordinance of baptism is thus administered : the corpse of the chief padri having been boiled down to an ointment, one of the instructors takes charge of it, and when any wish to enter their religion, they make them swear that their whole persons are derived from Deus, after which the padri takes the ointment with water, and drops it on the head, hence it is called water-sprinkling.

MARRIAGE CEREMONY

The ceremony of marriage is performed by holding each other's hands ; in addition to which, on the day of the nuptials, the minister throws a garland round the neck of the bride and bridegroom. Every seventh day they go to church and ask the padri to forgive their sins ; old and young attend to this.

There are also nunneries, where they collect monies for the public service ; the nunnery is locked up very closely, all the males being excluded ; the building is high and imposing ; daily necessaries are hoisted in by a basket over the wall.

When the chief padri meets the abbot, the usual ceremony is to smell his hands ; but when common people pay their respects to him, it is done by smelling his foot.

MECCA, CALLED ALSO THE RESIDENCE OF BUDDHA

On the shores of the western sea is the residence of the true Buddha : the hills are extremely high, and the whole ground is replenished with real gold and beautiful gems, which are guarded by a hundred genii, so that the treasures cannot be taken away. The true culti- vators of virtue may ascend to Mecca, and worship the real Buddha, when after several years' fasting they return and receive the title of dukun, or doctor ; they can then bring down spirits, and subdue monsters, drive away noxious influences, and behead demons.

' Our author,' says the anonymous translator, ' has here confounded the birthplace of Mohammed with the residence of Buddha, and fails to speak according to his usual good sense when misled by superstition.'

WANG TA-HAI

THE EIGHT IMMORTALS

1. CHUNG-LI CH'ÜAN, whom some legends call the first of the Eight Immortals, is said to have lived in the Chou (or perhaps the Han) dynasty and met the patriarch of the Genii, who instructed him in the mysteries of alchemy and gave him the magic formula of the elixir of life and the secret of transmutation. Being admitted among the genii he has appeared from time to time on earth as the messenger of Heaven. He is usually depicted as a fat man carrying a fan with a horse-hair tail attached, and sometimes holding a peach of immortality in his other hand. He represents the military type and in some pictures is shown riding on a dragon. He is by some said

to be the hero of the incident of the woman fanning the grave. (See p. 207.)

2. Chang Kuo-lao lived in the 7th and 8th centuries A.D. One of the Eight Immortals who gained fame by performing wonderful feats of necromancy. His constant companion was a white mule, which carried him thousands of miles in a day, and which, when he halted, he folded up and hid away in his wallet. When he again

required its services he spirted water upon the packet from his mouth, and the beast at once resumed its proper shape. According to Taoist tradition, the Emperor Ming Huang repeatedly invited him to his Court, but he spurned every tempting offer. About A.D. 740 the Emperor once more summoned him, but the message had scarcely reached the sage when he expired, or, as the Taoists assert, entered on immortality without suffering bodily dissolution. His emblem is a musical instrument shaped like a piece of hollow bamboo with two sticks to beat it.

3. Lu Tung-pin. Born A.D. 755. One of the most prominent among the later patriarchs of the Taoist sect, of whose doctrines he was an ardent votary. While holding office as magistrate of a district in modern Kiang-si he encountered, it is said, the immortal-ized Chung-li Ch'üan, and was instructed by him in the mysteries of alchemy and the magic formula of the elixir of life. It is related (in a legend borrowed from a Buddhist prototype), that when the mystic

being declared to him who he was, Lu Tung-pin expressed an ardent desire to convert his fellow-men to the true belief. After having been exposed to a series of temptations, all of which he successfully overcame, he was invested with the formulas of magic and given a sword of supernatural power, with which he traversed the empire for more than four centuries slaying dragons and ridding the earth of divers kinds of evil. In the 12th century, temples were erected in his honour and dedicated to his worship. For some obscure reason he is the patron of the fraternity of barbers. He carries a fly-whisk in his hand or a sword slung across his back.

4. Li T'ieh-kuai. One of the legendary patriarchs included in the category of the Eight Immortals. No precise period is assigned to his existence upon earth. He is said to have been named Li and to have been of commanding stature and dignified mien, devoting himself wholly to the study of Taoist lore. In this he was instructed by Lao Tzu himself, who at times descended to earth and at times summoned his pupil to the celestial spheres. On one occasion, when about to mount on high at his patron's bidding, the pupil left

a disciple of his own to watch over his material soul with the command that if his spirit did not return within seven days the material essence should be dismissed into space. Unfortunately, on the sixth day the watcher was called away to the death-bed of his mother, and when the disembodied spirit returned on the evening of the seventh day, it found its earthly habitation no longer vitalized. It therefore entered the first available refuge, which was the body of a lame and crooked beggar, whose spirit had at that moment been exhaled, and in this shape the philosopher continued his existence, supporting his halting footsteps with an iron staff.

His symbol is the gourd of the pilgrim, out of which floats a scroll showing that his spirit has power to escape from his body.

*

5. Han Hsiang-tzu. One of the Eight Immortals. According to the legends, he was a grand-nephew of Han Yü, and an ardent votary of transcendental study. Lu Tung-pin, himself one of the immortals,

appeared to him in the body, and made him his pupil. Having been carried up to the supernatural peach-tree of the genii he fell from its branches, and, in descending, entered upon the state of immortality. His symbol being the flute, he is the chosen patron of musicians.

*

If you're sure there is a tiger on the mountain, avoid the mountain.

One word to a wise man is as good as a touch of the whip to a fast horse.

Don't go hunting for your donkey when you are astride it.

He who hunts the stag despises the rabbit.

Proverbs

6. Ho Hsien-ku. The maiden immortal, named Ho, one of the Eight Genii. At the instant of her birth, six hairs were seen growing on the crown of her head. When fourteen years old, she dreamed that a spirit gave her instruction in the art of obtaining immortality, to achieve which she was to eat the powder of mother-of-pearl. She complied with this injunction, and vowed herself to a life of virginity. Her days were thenceforth passed in solitary wanderings among the hills, where she passed to and fro as though endowed with wings,

returning to her home at night with the herbs she gathered during her lonely pilgrimages. She gradually renounced the use of the ordinary food of mortals, and the fame of her wondrous mode of life having reached the Empress Wu, that sovereign summoned her to Court, but while journeying thither she suddenly disappeared from mortal view. She is said to have been seen once more in A.D. 750, floating upon a cloud of many colours, at the temple of Ma Ku, and again, some years later, she was revealed to human sight in the city of Canton. She may be recognised by her lotus-stalk and is the patroness of housewives.

7. Lan Ts'ai-ho.   A legendary being, one of the Eight Immortals. Of uncertain sex, but usually a female.   She wandered abroad clad in a tattered blue gown, with one foot shoeless and the other shod, wearing in summer an inner garment of wadded stuff, and in winter choosing snow and ice for a sleeping place.   In this guise the weird being begged a livelihood in the streets, waving a wand aloft and

chanting a doggerel verse denunciatory of fleeting life and its delusive pleasures.   She carries a basket of flowers and is the favourite genie of flower-sellers.

★

Misfortune and happiness alike we bring upon ourselves. If Heaven sends a misfortune, we may possibly be fortunate enough to escape, but when we bring down a misfortune on ourselves our fate is sealed.

A bird can roost but on one branch ; a mouse can drink no more than its fill from a river.

You cannot strip two skins off one cow.

Before you hit the dog look at his master.

Proverbs

8. Ts'ao Kuo-chin (11th century A.D.) is said to be a brother of the empress Ts'ao Hou of the Sung dynasty. For this reason he appears in court dress and cap, and holds in one hand his official tablets (or perhaps a pair of castanets).

PROVERBS

Time passes like a white colt passing a crack in a wall.

Riding a tiger—can't get down.

With money, a dragon ; without, a worm.

Don't look for a phoenix in a hen's nest.

In a wind horses and cows are not of the same mind ; the horse runs against the wind, the cow with it.

A discontented man is like a snake swallowing an elephant.

A stone lion is not afraid of rain.

When the tiger roars the wind rises.

Lightning in the east—fine weather ; lightning in the west—shower after shower ; lightning in the south—continuous rain ; lightning in the north—a gale from the south.

The Tree of Knowledge

A scholar does not quit his books, nor the poor man his pigs.

Even those who won't burn incense in times of prosperity clasp the feet of Buddha in the day of misfortune.

When you paint a tiger you paint his skin, not his bones ; when you know a man you know his face, not his heart.

Let the law be severe but the judge merciful.

Man corresponds to the firmness of heaven ; woman to the complaisance of earth.

Among the blind the one-eyed man is king.

Virtue is light as a hair, but few are they who can raise it.

The heart of a worthless man is as unfixed and changeable as a mountain stream.

In making a candle we seek for light, in reading a book we seek for reason : light to illumine a dark room ; reason to enlighten a man's heart.

Inadvertent wrongs, however great, should be pardoned ; intentional wrongs, however small, should be punished.

She who is happy dies before her husband.

A long journey tests a horse's strength ; a long life proves a man's heart.

Two persons should not look into a well together.

Even the genii sometimes drop their swords.

Sweep the snow from your own doorstep and leave alone the frost on your neighbour's tiles.

If you don't scale the mountains you can't see the plain.

STORIES SHORT AND TALL

PROVERBS

Frugality is not difficult for the poor nor humility for the lowly.

*

The way to glory is through the palace ; to fortune through the market ; to virtue through the desert.

*

It is better to lose life than to lose face.

*

Virtue is the surest road to longevity, but vice meets with an early doom.

*

If a man be not enlightened from within, what lamp shall he light ? If his intentions are not upright, what prayers shall he say ?

THE ACID TEST

A CERTAIN man married a woman whose age was given on the marriage-certificate as thirty-nine.

When he was able to get a good look at her after the wedding he suspected from the wrinkled appearance of her skin that she was a good deal older.

' How old did you say you were, my dear ? ' he asked.

' Still young,' she replied. ' Only forty-five.'

' Then how did you come to say thirty-nine on the certificate ? ' her husband demanded. ' Now that I see you, I should say you were more than forty-five. Tell me the truth.'

' Well,' answered his wife reluctantly, ' I won't deceive you any longer ; I'm fifty-four.'

Still unsatisfied, though he felt it would be a lack of tact to press the matter, the husband thought it over in silence for a while. Then getting to his feet, he remarked, ' Well, I suppose I had better go and put the cover on the salt-jar to keep the rats out.'

His wife burst out laughing. ' Well, I never ! ' she cried, ' that's the first time I ever heard that rats would eat salt in all my sixty-eight years."

THE ADVANTAGES OF HAVING NO MEMORY

WHEN Hua Tzu reached middle age he suddenly lost his memory. If he received anything in the morning, he forgot all about it by the evening ; if he gave anything away overnight, he forgot all about it by next day. He would forget to walk, or to sit down. He would forget to-day the events of yesterday ; and by to-morrow he would have forgotten all about to-day. Hoping for a cure, his family engaged in turn the services of a soothsayer, a magician and a doctor ; but their attempts proved equally futile.

In a neighbouring state lived a scholar, who volunteered to effect a cure, the sick man's wife and son offering him half their fortune.

' This disease cannot be cured by divination or prayer, or medicine,' the scholar declared. ' I shall address myself to his *mind*. His mind must be changed and his thoughts diverted ; if this can be accomplished, recovery will follow.'

So saying, he made Hua Tzu go naked till he begged to have his clothes again ; then he starved him till he begged for food ; then he shut him up in the dark till he begged for light. Thereupon the scholar turned joyfully to the patient's son.

' His disease is curable ! ' said he. ' But my prescription is a secret that has been handed down from generation to generation and may not be disclosed to others.'

So he turned them all out, and remained alone with Hua Tzu for seven days. No one knew what he did during that time but the long-standing malady was cured within the week.

When Hua Tzu recovered his memory he flew into a rage, turned his wife out of doors, beat his son, and drove away the scholar with a spear. A friend asked Hua Tzu why he behaved so strangely.

' When I had no memory,' Hua Tzu replied, ' I had no cares. I lived at ease, unconscious of anything in the wide world ; existence and non-existence were all one to me. But now, suddenly, I find myself remembering everything that has occurred for ten years past ; births and deaths, gains and losses, joys and sorrows, loves and hates, are mixed up in my memory in the most inextricable confusion, and the future bids fair to be as intolerable as the present. Would that I could recover my former happy state of oblivion. But that is impossible ; and there you have the reason why I drove the whole pack of them out of doors.'

BALFOUR

THE APES

A MAN who had a nagging wife decided to hang himself. He went into the forest and tied a rope round his neck. But at the last moment his courage failed and he went home again, only to hear from his wife that she had hoped that she had seen the last of him. He thereupon reiterated his intention of committing suicide, and returned to the forest. Being still unable to make up his mind to take the final step, he wandered about from one tree to another, finally sitting down exhausted in the attitude of a Buddha.

He soon fell asleep, and was presently found by an ape, who reported to his tribe that he had found their ancestor. A council was quickly called, and, whilst he still slept, the apes carried him off and made him their king. In their stronghold he found immense stores of treasure. He selected everything of value, and one day when his subjects were away, he escaped and made his way back to his home.

This time, thanks to the treasure he had brought back, his wife welcomed him warmly, nor could she resist the temptation to tell a neighbour that her husband had come home rich. Soon the neighbour's husband came over to inquire how the fortune had been made. Having learnt what he wished to know, he went off into the forest.

In the meantime, however, the apes had discovered the disappearance of their king and the loss of their treasure. As soon, therefore, as the second husband came amongst them, they surrounded him in crowds and literally tore him to pieces.

APPEARANCES

A CHILD hung a rosary round a cat's neck. The mice were delighted, supposing that their enemy, having become a Buddhist, would give up killing and forswear meat. They marked their new liberty by running about in the open in daylight. The cat, astonished at this bold change of front, but unable to resist profiting by it, killed several of their number. The remainder gathered at night and discussed the sad occurrence of the day. ' Ah,' said one, ' things were different in my young days. In these days those who make the loudest professions of religion are often the most violent and oppressive.'

THE ARREST

A COUNTRY constable, having arrested a Buddhist priest for a serious offence, fastened a chain to his waist and led him off to the nearest town to be tried. Half-way there he stopped for a drink, and before long was completely insensible. While he lay snoring the priest borrowed the key, unfastened the chain and put it on his escort. Then he took a small knife and shaved the top of the constable's head, and, after changing clothes with him, crept quietly away. Next morning when the constable woke, the priest was nowhere to be seen. But seeing the chain fastened to his own arm and finding himself with a tonsure when he scratched his head in bewilderment, the still dazed tippler muttered : ' Well, here's the priest all right, but where on earth can I be ? '

A THOUSAND DAYS AT HOME ARE LESS DIFFICULT THAN AN HOUR ABROAD

A TRAVELLER engaged a boat to take him down the river and arranged that the boatman's wife should cook for him. He measured out the rice for his first meal and saw the woman help herself to a bowlful and hide it away before putting the remainder on to boil. The traveller began to talk to himself aloud under the awning : ' Truly a thousand days abroad are to be preferred to one hour at home,' he exclaimed.

The boatman's wife lifted her head. ' Sir, you have the proverb wrong,' she corrected. ' It runs thus : " a thousand days at home are less difficult than an hour abroad." '

' Since you know the proverb so well,' retorted the traveller, ' perhaps you'll put that bowl of rice back and not add to the difficulties of my hours abroad by starving me.'

THE AUDIENCE

A SCHOLAR with his lute stopped in a busy market-place and began to play. A large crowd quickly gathered, but when they realized that the player was performing classical music which they could neither enjoy nor understand they soon melted away, leaving only one man, who stood by till the end of the piece. The scholar turned to his audience : ' Sir,' said he, ' I appreciate your attention, and I see that you appreciate good music.'

' Well,' returned the other, ' I don't understand that stuff any more than anybody else, and I should have been gone long since, but the table your lute is on is mine, and I can't go home without it.'

BAD GOVERNMENT

WHEN Confucius was travelling through a wild district he one day heard a woman wailing and sent one of his disciples to inquire the cause of her grief. She paused in her weeping to explain that her father-in-law, her husband and her son had in turn been killed by a tiger which haunted that place. 'Then why do you stay here?' asked the messenger in surprise. 'Because there is no bad government here,' replied the woman simply. 'Alas!' said Confucius, on hearing the explanation, 'bad government is more destructive than tigers.'

THE BARBER

A BARBER'S apprentice shaving the head of a young client clumsily cut his scalp. When he had done this several times he threw down the razor and refused to proceed. His master demanded the reason. 'He's too young, and his skin's tender,' said the assistant pettishly. 'Let him come back when he is older and his skin has had time to get tough.'

THE BEAR

AN emperor of the Han period went one day to the menagerie to see the tigers fight. Suddenly a bear got loose, and climbed over the railing. The attendants and courtiers all, with one exception, fled. One of the concubines rushed out and stood between the emperor and the bear until the attendants dispatched it with their cudgels.

'Why were you alone not terrified?' the emperor asked her when all was quiet again. 'I knew that he would be satisfied if he caught one person,' she replied, 'and I was afraid he might attack Your Majesty.' The emperor's respect and esteem for the lady was doubled.

THE deer fears the lynx ; the lynx fears the tiger ; the tiger fears the bear. The bear is covered with hair and stands upright like a man ; its strength is unsurpassed, and it is very dangerous.

There was once a hunter who, by blowing on a bamboo-pipe, could imitate all the noises made by wild beasts. One day, so the story goes, he took his bow and arrows and a fire-pot and went into the hills. He made deer noises to attract deer, and when one appeared he threw the fire at it and then shot it. Very soon a lynx smelt the deer and came seeking it. The terrified hunter made tiger noises and frightened the lynx away. But no sooner had it disappeared than a tiger bounded into sight. Still more afraid, the hunter made noises like a grizzly bear, and the tiger made off in turn. But a bear, attracted by the sound of the pipe, came ambling along to seek its fellow. Finding instead a man, it promptly seized him, tore him to pieces and ate him.

He who depends upon externals instead of perfecting essentials is undoubtedly in a fair way to be eaten by a bear.

LIU TSUNG-YUAN

BEAR AND FORBEAR

IN the course of a domestic quarrel a magistrate's wife snatched his official hat and trod on it. Her irate husband memorialized the Throne, outlining the circumstances and adding a request that His Imperial Majesty would Himself decide the appropriate punishment for this sacrilegious act.

A special edict from the Throne answered this appeal.

' Let Our minister show some forbearance,' it ran. ' We would have you know that Our Imperial Consort is not without the same sort of disquieting habits as your Lady, and no longer ago than yesterday, while having words with Us, she snatched from Our Head the cap of state, a far more expensive item than a mere official hat, and tore it to shreds.'

THE BEAUTIFUL VISITOR

ONE evening a young student named Wang was taking the air outside his gate, when he saw a woman approaching from the west. As she drew near he saw that she was a young girl of about eighteen, of singularly beautiful appearance. Next day he saw her again, and after that he watched for her and found that she passed every evening.

At length he ventured to speak. 'Where do you live, that you pass this way regularly every evening at this time?' he asked.

The girl laughed. 'I live near the South Hills,' she answered, 'but business obliges me to come every evening to the city.'

When they had chatted a while Wang invited her into the house, and she remained for the night, leaving at dawn. This happened on several occasions, until at last she came every night as a regular thing. Wang grew very fond of her, and suggested a visit to her family, but she put him off, saying that the house was too poor and mean to take guests to, and that there would be trouble if Wang went there, as she had a young cousin living with her who would be jealous. Wang believed all this, and was content to let things go on as they were. While they talked the girl sewed for him, and his attendants were astonished by her skill as a needlewoman.

After a year or so had passed very pleasantly in this manner, the girl came one night looking very unhappy.

'After all your love and tenderness, I must go away and leave you,' she told Wang. 'How shall I bear it?'

Very distressed, Wang asked for an explanation.

'Can we hope to avoid trouble?' the girl replied. 'Once I was the wife of a man who treated me badly. My parents in their kindness permitted me to return to the shelter of their roof, but soon afterwards I fell ill and died, and was buried near here. To-day I learn that I am to be taken to my old home, and I must go to-morrow. If you love me, do not be too angry.'

Wang asked what time she must leave, and learned that she could remain till the evening. Their parting was prolonged and sad ; they talked all night and could not sleep. When the time came for the girl to go she left him as a parting-gift a beautiful cup of gold and jade and a pair of jade rings, and received in return a chest full of beautiful clothes. Then clasping hands, they parted with tears.

At the time appointed for her removal Wang was at the South Hills. He saw the members of her family take out the body, which was just as he remembered it, with girlish beauty unchanged. Carried behind the coffin was the chest of clothes he had given her. But when they could not find the cup and rings that should have been in the grave the mourners knew that they were face to face with something supernatural. Wang therefore went forward and produced the missing articles and told his story, and amid the tears of everyone present, learned who his visitor had been.

' She is our little mistress who died at the age of ten,' they said.

When they had gone on their sad journey, Wang went home. For a few days he was so overcome that he was on the verge of a serious illness, but in time he recovered. Whenever he thought of his beautiful visitor, he would sit absorbed, forgetful alike of sleep and of food.

WANG YUAN-CHIH

BECAUSE

A YOUNG man having wasted his substance on riotous living, found himself a beggar singing in the streets and waiting about at doors for scraps of food. One day he happened to pass by the house of a courtesan whom he had often visited when he was rich. He could hear the sounds of entertainment within and his imagination pictured the once familiar scene. Then he heard the lady's voice raised in a tender song.

' Because of thee,' she sang, ' my beauty all has fled . . .'

Outside the gate the beggar raised his voice and finished the song in his own fashion, with all the bitterness of his heart and all the strength of his lungs.

' Because of thee,' he bawled, ' I've neither tea nor bread.'

THE BIRTHDAY-PRESENT

THE staff of a magistrate of some importance clubbed together to buy his Worship a birthday-present. After some consultation it was decided that, since he had been born in the year of the Rat, a golden rat would be a good mascot.

The magistrate was much gratified by the gift. After thanking the donors suitably, he added : ' I suppose you know it is my wife's birthday very shortly ? ' This hint could hardly be ignored. ' Indeed ! ' said the spokesman, ' how very fortunate that you told us. And is it permitted to inquire under which celestial sign your lady was born ? ' ' Oh, certainly,' returned the official affably, ' as a matter of fact she was born under the Ox.'

BLIND MAN'S LUCK

Two blind men were discussing their situation as they passed along a country road between fields in which were peasants toiling in the hot sun.

' We blind men,' said one, ' are the luckiest fellows on earth. Look how men who can see toil and moil. Think how hard these peasants we hear have to work. Who wouldn't be blind and live the life of a gentleman of leisure, going where we like and doing what we like ? '

This talk reached the ears of the workers nearest the road, as it was intended to do, and they quickly revenged themselves. Pretending the arrival of the local magistrate, some of them loudly hailed him with an imaginary complaint against the blind men ; another, assuming the voice of authority, cried : ' Seize them and beat them, here and now.' The peasants laid about the two blind men with a will, and then ordered them, in the language of the country-side, to ' roll along out of here.' The blind men needed no second order, but made off as speedily as they could, the peasants creeping along behind to hear what they would say now.

' We blind men,' said one to the other, ' are the luckiest fellows on earth. If we hadn't been blind we'd have been tortured as well as beaten.'

A BOASTFUL HUSBAND

A CERTAIN man who lived with his wife and concubine used regularly to come home and tell them how he had feasted and drunk with persons of wealth and distinction. In his absence one day the two women discussed the matter and agreed that seeing that no guests ever came to the house, it was strange that their husband should find so many hospitable hosts away from home.

' I shall follow him and see where he goes,' the wife declared, and accordingly, when her husband went out next day she followed him through the streets, keeping out of sight. All through the city they went, but nowhere did anyone stop him or speak to him, till at last they passed through the gate and out into the suburb, where people were offering sacrifices at the graves of their ancestors. Here the husband stopped at the first tomb he came to, and begged for the food and drink that was left over. Not having eaten enough there, he then went on to other parties, until he was satisfied.

His wife did not wait to see more. She hurried home and told the concubine what she had seen, saying : ' This is the man we have looked up to, and to whom we are tied for life ; and this is how he behaves.' And they reviled him and wept in the hall. Presently the husband, never dreaming that his secret was a secret no longer, returned home with his usual swaggering air, and his usual story, bearing himself before his wife and concubine in a very superior manner.

There are very few men whose method of seeking money and honours and promotion would not give their wives and concubines good reason to weep for them and be ashamed.

MENCIUS

A BOLD SPIRIT

A CHILD who was very brave and not at all afraid of ghosts was accidentally killed at the age of ten. At eighteen he was restored to life and told how he had worried the authorities in the Nether Regions till they had been glad to send him back to earth to get rid of him. At first, when he asked to be allowed to return to his family, the King of the Infernal Regions said that he would find his home destroyed if he insisted on going back, then he offered him a new birth in a good family of assured official position with adequate salary attached. Still the lad would not abate his cry to be sent home, and at length the King, weary of the noise, sent men to the Western Regions for the resurrection plant which grows there. The journey took several years, but the messengers returned at last and when the unwilling little ghost's bones were anointed with an extract made from the plant they immediately became covered with living flesh. Only the soles of his feet were somehow overlooked and did not revive, but remained with the bones showing.

When all was ready for his return, every member of his family dreamed that the boy was alive. The coffin was opened, and though at first the occupant seemed hardly to be breathing, he revived after a month of careful treatment and lived to a good old age.

*

The truly great man is the man who keeps his child-like heart.

Proverb

BOOTS

A MAN went out one day in odd boots. The sole of one was thick and the other thin, so that he found walking most uncomfortable. 'What's the matter with my legs to-day?' he said to himself; 'one is short and the other long.' Then he thought the awkwardness must be due to the unevenness of the road, but at last someone pointed out to him that his boots were not a pair. He then decided to remain where he was while his servant went home to fetch the other boots. After a long time the servant returned empty-handed, saying: 'It was no good bringing the others, Master; they have one sole thick and one sole thin too.'

THE BOOTS

Two brothers agreed to buy a pair of boots between them. The elder, by reason of his seniority, was to have the use of them by day and the younger by night.

The elder brother wore them so much and so often, what with going out to feasts and visiting friends and watching theatricals, that the younger found himself obliged to tramp the courtyard all night to get his fair share of the wear.

With this double wear the boots did not last long, and the elder brother suggested that they should share the cost of a new pair.

'No,' said the younger brother firmly, 'buy them yourself, then I shall be able to go to bed at night and sleep.'

BORROWING AN OX

ONE day a peasant sent a note to a rich neighbour asking for the loan of an ox. It chanced that the note was brought at a moment when the room was full of guests, and the rich man, who could not read but did not wish to display his ignorance to his visitors, made pretence of reading the message and then turned to the messenger. 'That's quite all right,' he said. 'You go on ahead, and tell your master that I will come presently.'

THE BRETHREN OF THE PEACH-ORCHARD

NEAR the close of the Han dynasty the widespread 'Yellow Turban' rebellion broke out. Notices were posted everywhere, calling for volunteers to serve against the rebels. One of these notices was put out in the Cho district, where it was seen by Liu Pei. This man was no mere bookish scholar, nor found he any pleasure in study. . . . He had always cherished a yearning for high emprise and had cultivated the friendship of men of mark. He was tall of stature. His ears were long, the lobes touching his shoulders, and his hands hung down below his knees. His eyes were very prominent, so that he could see backward past his ears. His complexion was clear as jade, and he had rich red lips . . . in short, he displayed every characteristic of the true hero.

The sight of the notice saddened him, and he sighed as he read it. Suddenly a rasping voice behind him cried : 'Noble Sir, why sigh if you do nothing to help your country ?' Turning quickly, he saw standing a man about his own height, with a bullet head like a leopard's, large eyes, a pointed chin and a bristling moustache. He spoke in a loud bass voice and looked as irresistible as a runaway horse. Liu Pei saw he was no ordinary man and asked who he was.

'Chang Fei is my name,' replied the stranger. 'I live near here, where I have a farm ; and I am a wine-seller and a butcher as well. Your sighs as you read the notice drew me towards you. I am not without means. Suppose you and I raised some men and tried what we could do to destroy these rebels and restore peace to the land.'

This was happy news for Liu Pei and the two betook themselves to the village inn to talk over the project. As they were drinking a huge, tall fellow appeared pushing a hand-cart along the road. At the threshold he halted and called for wine. 'And be quick,' he added, 'for I am in haste to get into the town and offer myself for the army.'

Liu Pei looked over the new-comer and noted his huge frame, his long beard, his dark brown face and deep red lips. He had eyes like a phoenix and fine bushy eyebrows like silkworms. Presently Liu crossed over and asked his name.

'I am Kuan Yü,' said he; 'I have been a fugitive on the river for some five years, because I slew a ruffian who, because he was powerful, was a bully. I have come to join the army here.'

Then Liu told him his own intentions and the three went away to Chang Fei's farm where they could talk over the grand project.

Said Fei: 'The peach-trees in the orchard behind the house are just in full flower. To-morrow we three will swear brotherhood before we enter upon our great task.'

All three being of one mind, next day they prepared the sacrifices, a black ox, a white horse, and wine for libation. Beneath the smoke of the incense burning on the altar they bowed their heads and recited this oath: " We three, Liu Pei, Kuan Yü and Chang Fei, though of different families, swear brotherhood and promise mutual help to one end. We will rescue each other in difficulty; we will aid each other in danger. We swear to serve the state and save the people. We ask not the same day of birth, but we seek to die together. May Heaven, the all-ruling, and Earth, the all-producing, read our hearts and if we turn aside from righteousness or forget kindliness may Heaven and man smite us.'

They rose from their knees and the two others bowed before Liu as their elder brother. This solemn ceremony performed, they slew other oxen and made a feast. Three hundred joined them, and they feasted and drank deep in the Peach Garden.

San Kuo Chih Yen I

THE BRIDE OF THE GOD

In the city of Yeh lived a witch who gave out that if a beautiful girl were not married to the river-god every year the city would be destroyed by flood. Any girl who was poor and pretty might be selected to be the bride of the god, and the city was in danger of being deserted altogether by parents with daughters, when a new magistrate arrived to take up his duties. As it was then the flood season the wedding of the river-god was the talk of the town, and the magistrate soon heard all about the ceremony of bathing and dressing the bride in silken garments and floating her down the river on a new bed with embroidered coverlets. He told his subordinates to give notice to the witch that he intended to be present at the ceremony.

The day arrived, and the magistrate took up his position near the red-curtained house occupied by the 'betrothed' girl. 'Bring out the bride,' he said to the witch, 'and let me approve your selection.' He looked the girl over and turned to the witch. 'She is not very beautiful, he said ; ' so do you go down and inform the river-god that I shall make it my business to choose a prettier bride for him and make the presentation shortly.'

He then ordered his soldiers to throw the witch into the river, and sat quietly waiting for five minutes.

' Why is she such a long time ? ' he asked at last. ' Let one of her disciples be sent after her.'

When three of the witch's disciples had followed their mistress and none returned, the magistrate declared that the river-god must have refused to listen to them because they were women, and he ordered the soldiers to throw one of his underlings into the water. By this time all the spectators, not knowing who might be the next to go, were seized with terror, and fell upon their knees begging that they might be spared.

' The god is keeping his guests a long time,' was all the magistrate replied. ' Let us go home.'

So they all went home, and from that time no one dared mention the subject of the marriage of the river-god again.

THE BURNING COAT

Yü T'an-tzu was sitting with a friend upon a couch beside which a brazier was burning. The friend was busily poring over a book, and did not notice that the skirt of his robe was lying in the fire.

The host, seeing what was happening, rose, and bowing politely with folded hands, addressed his friend as follows :

' There is, as it happens, an affair which I should very much like to lay before you for your consideration, but I have heard people say that your disposition is somewhat fiery, and I hesitate, therefore, to disturb you. Yet, if I do not do so I shall feel that I have failed in my duty as a friend. May I beg that you will be tolerant ? If I have your assurance that you will not be angry, I will then unfold the matter to you.'

' Tell me without hesitation what you have to say,' replied his friend.

The host, however, continued earnestly to beg his guest's indulgence in regard to the matter which he was about to divulge, but was at length prevailed upon to speak.

' Your robe has been on fire for some time,' he then said.

' The friend sprang to his feet and found that the skirt of his robe was indeed scorched beyond repair.

' Why did you not tell me at once,' he cried, reddening with anger, ' instead of shilly-shallying about all this time ? '

' No wonder people say you are hot tempered,' replied the host. ' I know now that they are quite right.'

*

He who knows he is a fool is not a big fool.

Proverb

195

THE BUTTERFLY

THE philosopher Chuang Tzu dreamed he was a butterfly, and when he woke up he said he did not know whether he was Chuang Tzu who had dreamed he was a butterfly, or a butterfly now dreaming that it was Chuang Tzu.

THE CARP

A FISHERMAN examining his traps saw a huge carp hiding close by. He tried to spear it, but it darted away. Presently he observed a young fish in the trap, and said to himself : ' This must be the off-spring of that big carp.' He hid in the rushes and waited, and after a time the big fish swam back to the trap and tried again and again to free its young.

As he watched, the fisherman recalled stories he had heard about the magic powers of carp, so he said to the fish : ' If you will give me a sign I will set your young one free.'

Immediately the big carp spouted a streak of yellow vapour twenty feet high, on top of which appeared the figure of a priest thirty or forty feet tall. As the fisherman gaped in astonishment at this vision, it dissolved slowly into thin air. He then hurriedly let the little fish go free, and the reunited parent and child darted away with every sign of joy. The fisherman determined to abandon an occupation which involved the taking of life, and became a Buddhist priest.

He himself often told this story, so it must be true.

YÜ T'I

A CHANCE ENCOUNTER

A CERTAIN official, having been appointed to a post in a neighbouring state, married a wife, and five days later, leaving her to minister to his parents in his absence, set out to take up his appointment.

At the end of five years, on his return home, as he drew near to his house he saw a woman picking mulberry-leaves, and being pleased with her looks, he descended from his carriage to converse with her ; but the lady went on picking leaves without stopping to look at him.

' You are working as if the year had not been plentiful,' the official remarked, trying to draw her into conversation, ' you pick your mulberry-leaves as if you would not deign to look at the lord of the land. I have gold which I would gladly give you, lady.'

' Away with you,' the woman cried. ' I want no man's gold.' The official went on his way, and when he reached home, gave the gold to his mother, who ordered his wife to be called. When she came in the official was mortified to find that she was the woman he had seen among the mulberries. She upbraided him, saying : ' You saw a pretty face and were willing to throw away your gold, the while entirely forgetting your mother ; this was very undutiful. If you do not honour your parents, you cannot be faithful to your prince ; not ordering your family properly, you will rule unjustly, and when filial duty and justice are both neglected, trouble is not far off. You may find another wife.' She then went out and threw herself into the river and was drowned.

WELLS-WILLIAMS

CHANGING THE FLOWER

IN the province of Shantung was the family residence of an official who for many years was a member of the Military Tribunal at Peking. It was his misfortune, however, at the age of sixty, to lose his lady, who left him no son, but only a daughter, named Ping-hsin, Icy Heart, a girl of remarkable beauty. Her eyebrows were like

197

the slender leaflet of the willow in spring, and her whole appearance was that of a delicate autumn flower. Brought up tenderly in the women's apartments, she surpassed in delicacy a silken tissue. However, when occasion called for it, she possessed talents and resolution beyond many of the other sex. Her father valued her as a gem, and being obliged to reside chiefly at the capital, left the management of the household in Shantung to her. It was in this manner that she reached the age of seventeen without any steps being taken towards her marriage.

Her father had unfortunately a very stupid and worthless younger brother, who had an exceedingly plain daughter, born in the same year as Ping-hsin. The younger brother longed to get into his own hands the management of his brother's estate, but this could not be while his niece remained single, and for this reason he engaged everyone who would to help him to persuade her to marry. Hearing that the son of a local official was in search of a wife he sent a go-between to propose his niece. The young man was not impressed, for being a dissolute person, he thought of nothing but the personal beauty of the woman he would marry, and was not to be caught by anyone whose attractions were not equal to his dreams. But being reassured by the lady's uncle, and allowed to take a stealthy peep into her room, he was soon all eagerness to become the husband of this uncommon beauty. When his emissaries went over to make proposals, however, the young lady rejected them altogether.

Much chagrined, the young man applied to the principal magistrate, endeavouring by rich presents to obtain his assistance. The magistrate called on Ping-hsin and endeavoured to influence her by argument, but finding it useless, thought proper to give up the scheme at once. But when he heard shortly afterwards that the young lady's father had been banished to the frontier for recommending a general who was unhappily defeated in an engagement with the enemy, he sent for Ping-hsin's uncle and advised him that it was his duty, in the absence of the girl's father, to see that the marriage was arranged.

Backed by this authority, Ping-hsin's uncle went straight to his niece, and pointed out that, since her father's consent could not be obtained, she must obey the wish of the magistrate.

' I have always looked upon my father's consent as indispensable,' said the girl, ' but if you wish to take the affair on youself, I will say no more, provided you do not consult *me* about it in any way.'

' Then make out in your own handwriting the paper with the eight characters showing the year, month, day, and hour of your birth,' demanded her uncle, delighted at the way things were turning out and determined to give her no opportunity to change her mind.

' It will be more proper for you to do that, if you are taking my father's place,' replied Ping-hsin, and wrote for him a rough draft of the eight birth-characters. Taking the place of her father involved his sending the nuptial presents, but Ping-hsin's uncle made light of selling a considerable part of the family wardrobe to provide the necessary money, and was amply rewarded when Ping-hsin herself begged him to receive into his house the much more valuable gifts sent by the prospective bridegroom in return, and to send thanks for them in his own name. ' For,' said Ping-hsin, when he protested, ' since my father is exiled, to use his name might be regarded as a mark of disrespect by the other family.'

During the ensuing month the preliminary feasts were held in the house of Ping-hsin's uncle, and great preparations went forward in the house of the bridegroom. At last the day came, and her uncle came hurrying over to tell his niece that it was time to prepare herself. She, however, affected ignorance, and asked what it was she was to prepare for.

' You seem disposed to joke,' exclaimed her uncle with some surprise. ' Your bridegroom is coming this very day to wed you —why affect ignorance ? '

' He is coming to wed *your daughter*,' replied his niece, ' what has it to do with me ? '

And so it proved. Ping-hsin had written her cousin's birth

characters in place of her own, and her uncle had sent and received the wedding-gifts, and there was nothing for the wretched man to do but to prepare his daughter secretly, with the help of Ping-hsin, for her marriage. Her hair was combed, her face smoothed, her teeth scrubbed, her eyebrows dressed, and she was duly perfumed with rare and precious unguents. She was also instructed to affect an access of modesty on being introduced to the inner apartments ; to insist on the lights being extinguished ; and, in order to prevent a premature exposure of her face, to retire to rest very early. Her maids were directed, when they offered the cups of alliance, to cause the bridegroom to get as tipsy as possible ; and if, after a view of her face next morning, he began to give vent to his anger and disappoint-ment, the new bride was instructed to pretend to search for some means of destroying herself. And so she was presently arrayed, and ready in all respects for the enterprise.

The bridegroom, on a fine horse, came in the evening to fetch home his bride. Her terrified father dried the sweat from his fore-head as he pushed his daughter into the state sedan and closed the door on her ; then the music striking up, she was carried off in nuptial procession.

The delighted young man escorted the bride to his own gate, where female attendants met and supported her into the hall. Her head being veiled, and her person adorned like some goddess, everyone took her for Ping-hsin and all were loud in their admiration. When the usual reverences had been performed, the bride and groom proceeded to the bridal chamber, but when she was invited to drink the pledge, the bride hid herself within the curtains, so the bridegroom went out again to the hall and soon became quite fuddled. On his return, tipsy as he was, he made his way to the bed and asked why she was not asleep. She, however, hid her face, and told the women to put out the lights, which, at a word from the bridegroom, they did, and took their departure.

The next morning, when both awakened, the bridegroom turned

his eyes towards his new wife, and to his utter dismay perceived, instead of the beauty like a fair flower after rain, or a willow seen through a mist, whom he had before beheld by stealth, a woman with a broad forehead, square face, and the most plain and ordinary features.

If the reader would know the husband's vexation on the occasion, and learn the further fruits of his folly, he must wait till the next chapter.

Hao Ch'iu Chuan

THE CHARM

A CERTAIN Taoist boasted that he could write charms so potent that they would prevent mosquitoes from stinging people. Among his audience was a man whose nights were so disturbed by mosquitoes that he willingly paid out good money for the antidote. He watched the Taoist write it, paid his money, took it home and stuck it up.

But the charm had no effect whatever on the mosquitoes, and next day he sought out the Taoist and complained.

' Where did you stick it ? ' the Taoist inquired.

' On the wall, of course,' replied the client.

' Ah, that's where you made a mistake,' said the Taoist, nodding his head, ' I should have told you. You must buy a mosquito-net, and tuck it well in all round you when you go to bed *with the charm inside*. If you use it properly it cannot fail.'

A CHINESE NEBUCHADNEZZAR

A CERTAIN unbeliever whom neither persuasion nor warning could turn from his wickedness was overtaken at the age of forty by a mysterious affliction. For ten years he remained bed-ridden, and then one day his son heard him calling for a bundle of hay. When this was brought he ordered it to be pushed round the edge of the door and told his son that on pain of death no one must enter the room. As the youth was withdrawing in obedience to his father's commands, he heard a loud sound of munching, and peeping through the door he saw to his horror that his father had been turned into an ox.

Wên Ch'ang Ti Chün Hui Hsiang Pao Hsün

THE CHOICE

THE King of Hades sent one of his demons to bring in a certain mortal for examination. In due time the demon returned alone. ' How is this ? ' cried the King, ' why have you come without the prisoner ? '

' Your Majesty,' replied the demon, ' the man is at present guarded by two such harridans, his wives, that I couldn't get near him. But if your Majesty will wait a little I am quite sure it will not be long before he comes here of his own accord.'

CIRCUMSTANCES ALTER CASES

CHUANG-TZŬ, having married a young and beautiful wife, retired to his native state to lead the life of a philosopher. He declined the offer of the sovereign of a neighbouring state, who had been led by the fame of his wisdom to seek his services as minister, with the following apologue :

' A heifer, prepared for sacrifice with high and luxurious feeding, marched in state, arrayed in all the ornaments with which victims are adorned. In the midst of her triumph she perceived some oxen at the plough, and her pride was redoubled. But when, on entering the temple, the victim saw the knife raised in readiness for her im-molation, she would gladly have exchanged lots with those whose condition had only just before been despised as inferior to her own.'

DAVIS

CONFUCIUS WORSTED IN DISCUSSION WITH A BOY

ONE day when Confucius was out riding in his carriage, he came across some boys playing in the road, and one boy standing alone, taking no part in the game. Confucius fell into conversation with him, and was astonished at his intelligence.

' Can you tell me,' Confucius asked after a pause, ' what fire has no smoke, what water no fish ; what hill has no stones, what tree no branches ; what man has no wife, what woman no husband ; what cow has no calf, what mare no colt ; what cock has no hen, what hen no cock ; what constitutes an excellent man and what an inferior man ; what is that which has not enough, and what has a surplus ; what city is without a market, and what people have no formal names ? '

The boy replied : ' A glow-worm's fire has no smoke, and well water no fish ; a mound of earth has no stones, and a rotten tree no branches ; genii have no wives, and fairies no husbands ; earthen cows have no calves, nor wooden mares any colts ; lonely cocks have no hens, and solitary hens no cocks ; he who is worthy is an excellent man, and a fool is an inferior man ; a winter's day is not long enough, and a summer's day is too long ; the imperial city has no market, and common people have no formal names.'

Confucius asked again : ' Do you know what are the connecting bonds between heaven and earth, and what is the beginning and ending of *Yin* and *Yang* : what is left, and what is right ; what is out, and what is in ; who is father and who is mother ; who is husband, and who is wife ? Do you know whence the clouds issue, and the dew arises ? And for how many tens of thousands of miles the sky and earth go parallel ? '

' Yes,' said the boy, ' nine multiplied by nine makes eighty-one, which is the controlling bond of heaven and earth ; eight multiplied by nine makes seventy-two, the beginning and end of the dual powers (*Yin* and *Yang*). Heaven is father, and earth is mother ; the sun is husband, and the moon wife ; east is left, and west is right ; without is out, and inside is in ; the clouds issue from the hills, and the dew rises from the ground. Sky and earth go parallel for ten thousand times ten thousand miles, and the four points of the compass have each their stations.'

' And which do you say is the closer relationship,' Confucius went on, ' father and mother, or husband and wife ? ' The boy responded : ' One's parents are close ; husband and wife are not so close.'

Confucius rejoined : ' While husband and wife are alive, they sleep under the same coverlet ; when they are dead they lie in the same grave ; how can you say they are not closely related ? '

The boy replied : ' A man without a wife is like a carriage without a wheel ; if there be no wheel, another one can be made, so it is easy to get a new one ; similarly if his wife die, a man seeks again, and can obtain a new one. . . . Three windows and six lattices do not give the light admitted by one door ; the whole host of stars, with all their sparkling brilliance, do not equal the splendour of the solitary moon. And so it is with the affection of a father and mother . . . it is unique, and alas if it be lost ! '

The boy then turned to the sage and said : ' I have answered your questions ; will the teacher now give me some instruction ? . . . Why is it that mallards and ducks are able to swim ; how is it that wild geese and cranes can sing ; and why are firs and pine-trees green through the winter ? '

Confucius replied : ' Mallards and ducks can swim because their feet are broad ; wild geese and cranes can sing because they have long necks ; firs and pines remain green through the winter because they have strong hearts.'

' Not so,' the youth returned, ' fishes and turtles can swim ; have they broad feet ? Frogs and toads can sing ; have they long necks ? The bamboo keeps fresh in winter ; is it on account of its strong heart ? '

Presently the boy went on ; ' How many stars are there altogether in the sky ? '

' How can we talk about the sky ? ' said Confucius. ' Ask me something about the earth.'

' Then how many houses are there on the earth ? ' the boy demanded.

The sage answered : ' Come now, speak about something that is before our eyes ; why must you ask about heaven and earth ? '

' Well,' said the lad, ' speak about what's before our eyes then—how many hairs are there in your eyebrows ? '

Confucius smiled and got into his carriage and rode away without replying.

CONFUCIUS, LAO TZU AND BUDDHA

ONE day Confucius, Lao Tzu and Buddha, the founders of the three sects of religion professed in China, were talking together in fairyland of the want of success which attended their doctrines in the world, and proposed a descent to see if there were any right-minded persons who might be commissioned to awaken the age. After travelling for some days, they came at length to a desert place where the smoke of human habitations was not visible. The three sages, being weary with their journey and their lack of success, looked about for some place where they might quench their thirst, when suddenly they espied a fountain, and an old man sitting by it on guard. They concluded that they had better ask him for a little drink, and consulted together upon whom the task should fall of soliciting the favour. 'Come,' said the other two to Buddha, 'you priests are in the habit of begging, you go forward and ask.' Buddha accordingly put the request. The old man asked : 'Who are you ?' 'I am Shikayamuni,' replied Buddha, 'who formerly appeared in the west.' 'Oh, you are the celebrated Buddha, then, of whom I have heard so much ; you have the reputation of being a good man, and I cannot refuse you a drink ; but you must first answer me a question, which, if you do, you may have as much water as you please ; but if not, you must go empty away.' 'What is it ?' said Buddha. 'Why,' said the old man, 'you Buddhists constantly affirm that men are equal, and admit neither of high nor low ; how is it then that in your monasteries you have abbots, priests and novices ?' Buddha could not answer, and was obliged to retire.

The sages then deputed Lao Tzu to ask for water, who, on coming up to the old man, was asked his name. 'I am Lao Tzu,' was the reply. 'Oh, the founder of the Tao sect,' said the old man. 'I have heard a good account of you ; but you must answer me a question or you will get no water.' 'Pray ask it,' Lao Tzu answered. 'You Taoists talk about the elixir of immortality ; have you such a thing ?' 'Yes,' said Lao Tzu, 'it is the partaking of this that has rendered me immortal.' 'Well then,' said the old man, 'why did you not give a little to your own father, and prevent his decease ?' Lao Tzu could not reply and was obliged to retire, saying to Confucius, 'Come, brother, you must try your skill, for I can make nothing of the old man.'

Confucius therefore advanced with the same request. 'And who are you ?' said the ancient. 'I am Confucius,' said he. 'Oh, the celebrated Confucius, the sage of China ; I have heard much of your discourses on filial piety, but how is it that you do not act up to them ? You say, When parents are alive do not wander far ; and if you do, have some settled place of abode ; why then have you strayed away to this uninhabited region ?' Confucius was unable to reply, and retired.

Upon this, the three worthies consulted together about the old man, and came to the conclusion that as he was so intelligent, they could not light upon a better person to revive their doctrines, and spread them through the world. They therefore made the suggestion. But the old man replied with a smile ; ' Gentlemen, you do not seem to know who or what I am ? It is the upper part of me only that is flesh and blood, the lower part is stone ; I can talk about virtue, but cannot follow it out.'

This, the sages found, was the character of all mankind, and in despair of reforming the world they returned to the aerial regions.

Chinese Miscellany

CONSIDERATION

A HUMANE general who lived in the tenth century A.D. was told that his house was falling down, and that it must be repaired at once. He replied, ' It is now the coldest time of the winter and the crannies of the tiles and bricks of the walls are filled with hibernating insects ; on no account must they be disturbed.'

CONSTANCY

' I SWEAR that when you die I will go with you to the grave,' cried the devoted wife to her husband on his death-bed.

' Nay, swear not that,' said the sick man tenderly.

' I swear that I will remain a widow to my dying day,' she protested, with tears.

' Swear not that either,' said he.

' Then I swear that I will not marry again till the sods are dry on your grave.'

Ten days later, a sage, chancing to pass that way, was astonished to see a woman in mourning garments vigorously fanning a newly-made grave.

THE COOK

ONCE, in the early years of the eighth century A.D., when the slaughter of animals had been forbidden by imperial order in hopes of ending a drought, a certain high official was alarmed to see meat on his table. He sent for the cook and reprimanded him for disobeying the imperial edict, and demanded an explanation.

' Sir,' said the cook simply, ' the animal was killed by a wolf.'

' Ah,' said his master, ' a perfectly satisfactory explanation ! ' And he ate his meat and enjoyed it.

Not long afterwards the cook served up some appetising fish, and was again summoned into the presence of his master.

' What does this mean ? ' the official cried angrily. ' Do you wish to get us both killed ? '

' No, Master,' said the cook, ' it is quite all right. This fish was bitten to death by a wolf.'

' Blockhead and fool ! ' exclaimed his master. ' Why can't you say by an otter ? '

' Yes, yes, Master, by an otter, ' the cook repeated, and left his master to enjoy the fish with an easy conscience.

The official found opportunity to recommend the cook for promotion.

T'ai P'ing Kuang Chi

THE COUNSELLOR

AN emperor newly enthroned was seeking counsellors and one of his ministers put forward the name of a man who was, he said, an admirable scholar and wise, but old.

' Send for him,' said the emperor, and when the aged man appeared he asked : ' How is it that one so wise has never held office ? '

' Sire,' replied the old scholar, ' your grandfather was interested in the civil administration and I in military affairs ; your father chose old men as his counsellors, and in his day I was young ; now you want young men, and I am old.'

THE COURIER

THERE was once a wizard with a special facility for driving out sickness by invocations and spells.

A certain inn-keeper had an epileptic son who was said to be incurable. Nevertheless, his father called in the wizard. When he arrived, the sick man pointed at him and cursed him loudly. 'The trouble has gone to his heart,' the wizard declared.

After he had set up an altar in the middle of the great hall, the wizard turned every one out, warning them not to peep. When night came he took the sick man and bound him with two thongs to the east wall. He then removed his heart and hung it under the eaves on the north side of the room. While he was reciting his invocations in the middle of the room a dog ate the heart, and when it was not to be found the wizard cut down the patient, left him on the floor, and rushed from the house.

The landlord, knowing no better, said: 'It is part of the operation, he will return,' and after a time the wizard did come back, carrying a heart in his hand. He went in and placed the heart in the sick man's breast, and by means of repeated invocations the patient was soon joined up again, and recovered his senses. But as he came round he kept crying out, 'Let the relay carry on! Let the relay carry on!'

No one in the house understood the meaning of this, but the facts were these: not far from the inn a courier bearing an official dispatch had died by the roadside just about the time the operation on the epileptic was taking place. Knowing that he was not far from the next post-house, and conscious of the importance and urgency of his message, the runner had died with the words, 'Let the relay carry on!' on his lips. And that was how it happened that the son of the inn-keeper regained consciousness completely restored to health and sanity crying: 'Let the relay carry on!'

Chi Shen Lu

COURTESY

A BURGLAR broke into a poor man's house one night in the hope of finding something worth stealing. When he entered the tenant was lying with his back to the wall, but on perceiving the thief he turned over with his eyes to the wall. The burglar was uneasy. ' He must know me,' he thought. ' He thinks I may be ashamed to be seen stealing and has looked the other way.' He was about to go without taking anything, when the man in bed sat up and said. ' Oh, please come in ! Don't let me disturb you. I'm so mortified that I haven't anything better for you to steal that I turned away to hide from you how much I felt the loss of face.'

CREMATION

A MAN who was going away said to his son : ' If anyone comes to see me when I am absent and asks for your " honoured sire " the correct reply is : " My papa has gone away. Please come in and take tea." '

Knowing his son's stupidity the father wrote this inquiry and the proper reply on a piece of paper and gave it to the boy, telling him to refresh his memory if a guest should arrive. For three days the lad kept the paper in his sleeve, but no one having called he burnt it that night when the lamp was lighted.

Next day a caller arrived and the boy went to the door to receive him. ' Your honoured sire ? ' inquired the visitor. The boy fumbled in his sleeve, then looked up at the guest. ' Gone ! ' he said sadly, referring to the paper. ' Gone ! ' cried the guest. ' Gone, and I did not even know he was ill ! How did it happen ? ' The boy's face brightened as he remembered what he had done with his scrap of paper : ' I burnt him last night,' he answered triumphantly.

*

The gods cannot help a man who loses opportunities.

Proverb

THE CROCODILE

THE present writer, when magistrate of a wild district in the south, finding it afflicted by the ravages of a crocodile, gave orders that the following notice, accompanied by a pig and a goat, should be cast into the river where it was :

' After the ancient kings had taken possession of the empire with net and spear, they drove out of the mountains and marshy places all reptiles and other evil creatures which were harmful to man, and banished them beyond the four seas.

' When the virtue of later rulers declined, the region to the south came under the sway of the barbarians, and here you, O crocodile, have hidden your eggs and brought up your young. But now, under the rule of the divine house of T'ang (A.D. 618–906) the whole universe is again united. Furthermore, this region once knew the footsteps of the Great Yü, the subduer of floods, and from it I must needs gather tribute to maintain the sacrifices to Heaven and Earth and the Imperial Ancestors. You and I, therefore, O crocodile, cannot both remain here. I hold the region and govern the inhabitants under imperial orders, while you disturb the river and devour people and animals on its banks in order to fatten yourself and breed children and grandchildren, and so you force me to contend with you for the mastery.

' What though I am puny and weak ? Shall I bow my head and submit my soul to a crocodile ? Rather will I die !

' But, acting under orders, I must first give you fair warning. If you are wise you will heed my words. A day's journey from here is the great ocean, in which there is room both for the mighty whale and for the tiny shrimp. Do you depart thither and there remain and live and feed. If you leave in the morning you will be there by nightfall.

' And now I charge you that in three days you begone, so that you may avoid the imperial mandate ; or if not in three days, then in five ; or if you cannot go in five days, then in seven. If by that time you have not gone I shall know that you will not obey . . . and I shall choose a skilful archer with a poisoned arrow and send him to exterminate you and all your breed. And then it will be too late for repentance.'

HAN YÜ

THE CROW

A VERY short-sighted man walking along a country road saw a crow perched on a large stone, and mistaking it for a person sitting by the roadside, he inquired the distance to the next town. Receiving no reply, he repeated his question, and at that moment the crow flew away. Annoyed by the continued silence he said : ' Very well, since you won't tell me how far it is to the town, I won't tell you that your hat has been blown off.'

DEAF AND DUMB

A DEAF man and a dumb man, each of whom wished to hide his defect, met one day. The deaf man, knowing the other to be dumb, asked him to sing. The dumb man, knowing that the other was deaf, went through all the motions of singing, opening and shutting his mouth and beating time with his finger, while the deaf man bent his head in the attitude of one listening intently and critically, and watched the dumb man's mouth. When the performance was finished the deaf man was loud in his congratulations. ' I have never had the pleasure of hearing you sing before, sir,' he said with perfect truth as well as courtesy, ' but now I can say that I have never heard anyone sing better.'

DEMON HUSBANDS

A CERTAIN sub-prefect lived near a river, beside which his two little daughters used to play at fishing. They never caught any fish, but one day they caught two curious creatures something like a hairy fish, and something like a turtle with gills. The family thought them so odd that they put them in a pond and kept them.

During the next year both the girls began to suffer from mental disturbances. Often at night they would be sewing, or dyeing, or rubbing ink by the light of the lamp. They were always busy doing something but no one could see for whom they worked. For six months these attacks continued and grew worse. Lamps were kept alight and paper-money was burnt regularly to appease the unknown demons. Then one night two tiny hands appeared beside the lamp, and loud voices begged for a copper.

The whole household began to heap reproaches on the now materialised demons.

' We are the husbands of the two daughters of the house,' the voices said, ' and you had better treat us with proper respect.'

After this they made themselves so much at home and were such a nuisance that a holy Buddhist priest with power over demons of every sort was called in to exorcise them. First he set out a fish-bowl, and made a rope circle all round it. Then, sword in hand, he summoned the demons to give themselves up. Next he had raw flesh and a large bowl of wine set outside the rope ring. At midnight something which resembled the nose of an ox became visible over the wine. The Buddhist leaped at it with a shout, and struck with all his strength. Dripping blood, the demon made off. Torches were lighted and they followed the blood-tracks to the corner of a neighbouring house, where they ended in an old black leather bag. A huge bonfire was made on the spot, and the bag burned. The smell spread through the whole district over a radius of three miles. As soon as the black bag was destroyed one of the sick girls recovered.

A day or two later, on a very wet, windy night, a wailing sound was heard outside the door, and the second daughter began one of her attacks. The Buddhist rose and took up a threatening attitude, reproaching her vehemently. The girl was so frightened that she fell to the ground, *kowtowing*. As she bent forward the priest noticed a black bag attached to her girdle. He ordered one of the maids to untie it, and inside he found a tiny key. He then searched the girl's possessions, and at last came upon a basket full of old black and yellow mourning clothes. But before he could think of a way of exorcising the second demon, his leave came to an end, and he was obliged to return to his monastery.

A year or two later, when the sub-prefect retired, he took his family to the capital and once more sought the Buddhist's help. His second daughter, who had never recovered from the attacks of madness, had since developed on her back a swelling the size of a melon. The priest removed the tumour and the girl eventually recovered.

NIU CHIAO

THE DISAPPOINTED TIGER

A PRIEST was returning from assisting at a funeral with his cymbals and his scripture-roll under his arm when he met a tiger. After his first gasp of terror he flung his cymbals at the beast one after the other. Finding that these had no effect he threw his scripture-roll at it in a panic. The tiger at once made off as fast as it could.

When it arrived at its den the tigress inquired what had so upset it. ' Why,' said the tiger, ' I met a likely-looking Buddhist priest just now, but he turned out to be a most unmannerly person, who threw both his noise-plates at me and then his subscription list. Mercifully I got away quickly ; in another moment he would have asked me for a donation.'

DISCIPLINE

THE first order issued by the victor was to spare the people. Instant death should be the punishment for murder or looting. The various officials of the city were retained in their offices and continued their functions.

One very wet day the conqueror, with a few horsemen as escort, was going round the walls and visiting the gates. One of the soldiers took from a passer-by his broad-brimmed hat, and put it on over his helmet to keep his armour dry. The general saw the action and the offender was seized. He was a fellow-villager of the general's, but that did not save him.

'You knew my order, why did you disobey it?' asked the general.

"I thought the rain would spoil my uniform, and I took the hat to protect it. I did not take it for my own advantage, but to protect official property. Spare me, O General, for the sake of our common dwelling-place.'

'I know you were protecting your armour, but still it was dis-obedience to the order against taking anything from the people,' was the reply.

The soldier was beheaded, and his head exposed as a warning. But when all was over the general had the body decently buried and wept at the grave for the loss of his friend.

San Kuo Chih Yen I

THE DIVINER

KUAN LU was a diviner. As a lad he loved to study the stars and would stay up all night to watch them. When he grew older he studied the *Book of Changes* and observed the winds.

The Prefect of An-p'ing heard of the diviner's fame and invited him to come on a visit. It happened that the wife of a neighbouring magistrate suffered from headaches and his son from pains in the heart. The diviner was asked to discover the cause. He cast lots and said that at the west corner of the main hall were buried two corpses, one of a man holding a spear and the other of a man who had a bow and arrows. The wall was built across them. The spearman's master had gashed his head and so his head pained. The archer's master had stabbed him in the heart and so his heart suffered anguish. They dug where he indicated, and found two coffins, one with a spear inside and the other with a strung bow and wooden arrows. All were much decayed. The remains were buried three miles outside the city and thereafter the woman and her son suffered no more.

Ibid.

DOCTOR BLACKBAG

THE surgeon who scraped the poison from the bone in the arm of the wounded general was once called in to attend the famous Ts'ao Ts'ao, who was suffering from an intolerable headache. The doctor felt his pulse and made a careful examination.

' Prince, your headache is due to a malignant humour within the brain-case. The humour is too thick to get out. Swallowing drugs will do no good. But I propose to administer a dose of hashish, then open the brain-case and remove the thickened humour. That will be a radical cure.'

' You mean you want to kill me,' cried Ts'ao Ts'ao angrily, and ordered his lictors to hale the doctor to prison, where he was tortured to find out who were his accomplices. His jailor was a certain Wu, who was kindly disposed to his prisoner, and saw that he was well fed. Thus the doctor conceived a liking for his jailor and said to him one day : ' I am doomed, I know. The pity is that my *Black Bag* treatise on medicine will be lost. You have been most kind to me and I should like to give you a letter to my wife, telling her to send it to you so that you may carry on my art.'

In due course the *Black Bag* arrived, and when the doctor had read it through, he presented it to Wu, who took it home and hid it away.

Not many days after the doctor died in prison. Wu bought a coffin and had him buried. This done, he quitted the prison and went home. But when he asked for the book he found that his wife had discovered it and was using it to light the fire. He snatched away what was left, but a whole volume was missing, and what was left amounted to only a few pages. He vented his anger in cursing his wife, and she retorted, saying : ' If you become a learned person you will only die in prison as the doctor did. What was the good of it to him ? '

It struck Wu that there was something in what she said and he stopped grumbling at her. But the upshot of all this was that the learning of the *Treatise of the Black Bag* was finally lost to the world, for what was left only contained a few recipes relating to domestic animals.

San Kuo Chih Yen I

DOING EVIL THAT GOOD MAY COME

THERE was once a man in Han-tan who presented a live pigeon to Chien-tzu at dawn one New Year's Day. Chien-tzu was delighted, and rewarded him liberally. A visitor asked him his reason for acting thus.

' Because,' said Chien-tzu, ' it gives me an opportunity of releasing a captive bird ; and to set living creatures free on New Year's morning is a special manifestation of mercy.'

' But if the people know that Your Excellency is so fond of setting birds at liberty,' returned the guest, ' they will vie with each other in catching them to give to you, and many birds will die. If your object is to save their lives, would it not be better to forbid the people to catch them at all ? To catch them first in order to let them go afterwards is surely to destroy the just proportions of good and evil.'

BALFOUR

THE DONKEY OF KUEICHOU

THERE were no donkeys in Kueichou so a certain busybody imported one by boat. When he got it there no one had any use for it and he let it go in the hills. A tiger, thinking from its size that it must be a supernatural creature, first watched it from a thicket, and then after a time ventured nearer, being careful, however, to keep out of sight.

One day the donkey brayed. The tiger fled in terror, thinking that it was about to be devoured. But after a while, looking at it frequently, the tiger came to the conclusion that the donkey was not, after all, a creature with unusual powers. It grew accustomed to its bray, and took to coming into the open and prowling about, though it still did not dare to attack. Nearer and nearer it came, growing more bold, until at last it plucked up courage and made a rush. The donkey was furious, and kicked out. ' If that's all it can do . . .' thought the tiger in glee, and leapt, with claws outstretched, at the donkey's throat.

Ah ! An awe-inspiring figure demands a nature to correspond, and a loud voice should be backed by appropriate strength. So long as the donkey had not shown what he could do the tiger, though fierce, hesitated and did not dare to attack. Alas ! How true this is to-day.

LIU TSUNG-YUAN

THE DOOR-GODS

A MAN went to buy pictures of the door-gods for the New Year, but brought home the wrong ones. However, he pasted them on the doors and said nothing. Presently his wife came out to have a look. 'What's this ? ' she exclaimed. ' This can't be right. Door-gods are always ferocious-looking beings, with swords and spears in their hands, and ugly enough to scare off evil spirits by their faces alone. What spirits will be scared by these mild-looking personages that you have pasted up ? ' ' Let be, wife,' answered the man ; ' in these days it is often the mildest-looking persons who turn out to be the most poisonous and the most dangerous.'

DRAGONS

THE surname Dragon-Keeper was conferred on a man who was greatly interested in dragons. He knew their tastes and habits and kept a pair in captivity.

Now dragons and men are very different creatures, but thinking he was allowing them to follow their natural instincts, Master Dragon-Keeper gave his pets a pond in the palace to bask in, though the hundred rivers and the four oceans are not large enough for them to sport in ; and he fed them with titbits, though the great whales in the vasty deep could not satisfy their appetite. Still, they grew very tame and were quite content to remain where they were.

One morning a wild dragon appeared, whom they eagerly hailed, saying, ' What are you doing ? To lie torpid between heaven and earth in the great ocean when it is cold and rise to the surface when it is warm is surely a dull existence ? You really should come here and live comfortably with us.'

The wild dragon tossed his head proudly and laughed. ' What,' he cried, ' all cramped up like you ? I am endowed by nature with a crest and horns and a scaly body ; I have power to lie hidden in the springs or fly through the sky ; mine is the spirit which blows the clouds along and rides upon the wind ; it is my business to crush the proud and to moisten the thirsty ; I see beyond the limitless ; I rest in the regions outside the bounds of space ; I go wherever I will, hampered by no boundaries and in whatever form I please. Is not this supreme felicity ? As for you, if you are satisfied in a puddle no bigger than a hoof-print, insensible as mud, and no better than earth-worms, led by your appetites, hoping for plenty to eat and drink, then, though your appearance is like mine, your pleasures are very different. He who fawns upon man, hoping to profit thereby, will be strangled and his flesh made into mincemeat ; it is only a matter of time. I pity you and would lend you a hand, and would you entice me also to enter the snare ? No, indeed, you will not escape.'

So saying, the wild dragon flew away, and before long the others actually were made into mincemeat for a rich man's table.

Lu Kuei-meng

DREAMING

A henpecked husband chuckled in his sleep and was roughly wakened by his wrathful wife and asked what had pleased him so. Not daring to conceal the truth the man said that he had dreamed he had a pretty concubine. The enraged wife made the unlucky dreamer kneel on the floor by the bed and looked round for something to beat him with.

' There's no truth in my dream,' protested the husband, ' why do you act as though there were ? '

' Any other dream you like,' his wife replied, ' but this kind of dream I will not allow. You are not to do it again, do you hear ? '

' I promise,' said her husband meekly.

' I don't believe you,' retorted the woman, ' how am I to know what you dream when you are asleep ? '

' I swear that from this time forth I will keep awake through all the three hundred and sixty nights in the year and never dare to go to sleep again,' was the reply.

THE DRUM AND THE OX

Two boastful travellers met and began to extol the merits of their respective provinces. ' In my unworthy region,' said one, ' we have a drum so large that the sound of it carries a hundred miles.'

' You astonish me,' replied the other, ' but in my disreputable part of the world we have an ox whose head is in one province on the north side of the river and his tail in another on the south side. Isn't that rather remarkable ? '

' I don't believe it,' said the man who had first boasted.

' No ? ' retorted the second. ' But if there weren't an ox as big as mine, where would you get a hide large enough to cover a drum as big as yours ? '

THE DRUNKARD

A CERTAIN youth of good family, who in his early years showed great promise of scholarship, gave way to drink and would often lie for days in a drunken stupor.

In due course he fell a victim to these excesses, and when he was dying the whole neighbourhood for miles around smelt so strongly of wine that for a long time it acted as a deterrent and a warning to all.

T'ai P'ing Kuang Chi

THE DUCK

THERE was once a villager who stole one of his neighbour's ducks and cooked it. That night his skin began to itch, and in the morning he found that he had a thick growth of duck's feathers, very painful when touched. He was much alarmed, knowing there was no remedy for such a complaint. The next night he dreamed that he was visited by a man who said : ' Your disease is a judgment from heaven ; you must persuade the man from whom you stole the duck to reprimand you and the feathers will fall off.'

Now his neighbour was a very broad-minded and refined person, who was never, in his whole life, known even to change countenance when anything was lost. The thief therefore approached the matter obliquely, saying : ' The fellow who stole your duck is very much afraid of a reprimand, but reprove him, and he will no doubt be more careful in future."

The neighbour laughed : ' Who has time or inclination to scold the wicked ? ' he asked, and refused to do it. The thief was thus obliged to confess, and the neighbour having obligingly reprimanded him the disorder was removed.

THE EARLY CREDITOR

A DEBTOR whose house was so full of duns waiting for their money that there were not enough chairs for them all, whispered to those who were standing : ' Come early to-morrow morning, gentlemen.'

Next morning the hopeful creditors put in an early appearance, thinking they were to be paid something on account at least. Presently the debtor came in : ' Ah, good-morning gentlemen,' he said, blandly, ' I am so pleased to see that you are here in time to get the seats this morning.'

THE ECHO

A CERTAIN scholar living at the capital was afflicted with an echo ; whatever he said was repeated in his throat.

His friends consulted a famous Doctor Chang who, after thinking the case over most carefully, proceeded to the house of the patient armed with a copy of the *Materia Medica*. The patient was ordered to read aloud from the beginning all the way through. The echoing voice accompanied the reading, but every now and then it was silent when the names of certain drugs were read out, and the doctor, sitting by and saying nothing, noted these down and from them made pills which effected an almost instantaneous cure.

CHANG TSU

THE EGG

A MAN who was so poor that he could not plan a day ahead, chanced one day to find an egg. He took it home in great glee and showed it to his wife.

'I have laid the foundation of our fortunes,' he cried, displaying his treasure, 'and in ten years we shall be rich beyond belief.'

He then began to calculate :

'Here is one egg. If we borrow a sitting hen from our neighbour we can hatch it out. When the chicken is grown it shall hatch out all the eggs which it lays, and in the course of a month we ought to have fifteen hens. Hens continuing to produce eggs, eggs hens, and hens eggs, by the end of two years we ought to have three hundred hens, which we may hope to sell for ten gold pieces. With the ten gold pieces we will buy five cows, which will produce more cows. In three years we shall own twenty-five cows, and in three more years these numbers will have increased to one hundred and fifty. These we shall sell for three hundred gold pieces. With this money I will start a money-lending business and after three years more we shall make a profit of five hundred gold pieces. Two-thirds of that we will spend on buying houses and fields, and with the remainder I will purchase a concubine, and so you and I will live happy ever after. Won't that be splendid ? '

No sooner did the wife hear the word concubine than she flared up and struck the egg from her husband's hand, crying :

'You shall not keep it ! It will bring trouble upon us.'

Livid with fury, her husband beat her soundly and then dragged her to court and accused her before the local magistrate.

'This wicked woman has ruined me. Please have her put to death.'

The magistrate inquired the extent of the damage the woman had done, and her husband related the whole story from the finding of the egg to the mention of buying a concubine.

' If such a fine establishment has been destroyed by this woman, she is very wicked and deserves to be killed,' said the magistrate. ' Take her away and boil her.'

' But nothing my husband has said has happened yet, so why should I be boiled ? ' protested the aggrieved wife.

' And your husband has not bought a concubine yet,' retorted the magistrate, ' so why should you be jealous ? '

' Quite true,' replied the wife gravely, ' but misfortune is best nipped in the bud.'

The magistrate laughed, and dismissed the case.

THE ELIXIR OF LIFE

ONCE upon a time it was rumoured that a person professed to have learned the secret of immortality. The King of Yen sent messengers to inquire about it, but they dawdled on the road, and before they had arrived at their destination the man was already dead. The king was very angry, and wished to slay the messengers, but his favourite minister expostulated.

' There is nothing which causes greater sorrow to men than death,' he argued, ' and there is nothing they value more highly than life. Now, the very man who said he possessed the secret of immortality is dead himself. How, then, could he have prevented Your Majesty from dying ? '

So the men's lives were spared.

BALFOUR

THE END OF AN INTRIGUE

Ts'ui Wu-tzu married the widowed sister of one of his ministers. Afterwards Duke Chuang took to frequenting Ts'ui's house and began an intrigue with his wife. He further insulted Ts'ui by giving one of his hats to someone else, and when the attendants protested that it was Ts'ui's hat he said : ' Even if it isn't Ts'ui, ought he to be hatless ? '

The duke at this time was on bad terms with one of the neighbouring states, whose ruler urged Ts'ui to murder the duke.

For some time he could find no excuse. At last however, by keeping about him a servant whom he had whipped, the duke played into Ts'ui's hands, giving him a spy at court.

During the summer the duke arranged an elaborate entertainment for a visiting envoy, from which Ts'ui excused himself, pleading illness. Next day the duke called in person, ostensibly to inquire for the invalid, and went straight into the house after his wife. Acting on their master's instructions, Ts'ui's servants shut the gate on the duke's followers, while Ts'ui hurried his wife through the inner apartments and out by a side door, and the duke waited in the hall patting a pillar and singing.

Presently, realizing his position, he attempted to escape, but Ts'ui's men-at-arms said : 'We have orders to capture an adulterer who is in the house,' and shot him down as he was trying to climb over the wall.

Tso Chuan

EVERLASTING FLOWERS

One fine evening in spring a student taking a country walk came upon a tree bearing the most exquisite blossoms he had ever seen. Their whiteness was almost unearthly, and they had a peculiar radiance which he was at a loss to explain or describe. Entranced with his find, he plucked a branch and took it home, and for twelve months the flowers remained as fresh in the vase as they had been on the tree. After that the student chanced one day to meet the daughter of a neighbour, and began an intrigue with her which had not lasted very long before her father caught him and accused him to the magistrate. He was found guilty and sentenced to a heavy punishment and the flowers immediately drooped and withered.

Wên Ch'ang Ti Chün Hui Hsiang Pao Hsün

EXAMINATION-FEVER

ON the day of the Literary Examination a young candidate was so nervous before setting out that his wife, to cheer him up, said jokingly : ' You make as much fuss over writing an essay as a woman over having a baby.' ' Having a baby is easy by comparison,' replied the young man gloomily. ' Really ? ' said his wife, genuinely surprised. ' How do you make that out ? ' ' Well,' answered the pessimistic candidate, ' the baby is all ready to be born.'

AN EXIGENT DEBTOR

A CERTAIN creditor, weary of dunning an obstinate fellow who owed him money and would not pay, sent two of his servants with orders to hide outside the offender's gate until he came out and then abduct him. ' For,' said he, ' since he will not pay I will keep him a prisoner until he does.'

Obeying their master's instructions, the servants waited till the debtor came out of his gate. Then knocking him down, they trussed him up, hoisted him on to their shoulders and went off. They had covered no more than half their road when the hot sun and the weight of the prisoner combined drove them to seek a place in which to rest for a few minutes. But their burden would not permit this.

' Hurry along ! ' he commanded. ' Don't stand still ! If you stop to rest some other creditor will come along and carry me off and you will lose me. What do you mean by not giving your whole attention to my affairs ? '

FAITHFUL TO HIS TRUST

A CERTAIN scholar who was himself very fond of wine found that his servant was stealing his supply. He decided to engage a teetotal servant and made inquiries among his friends. The first man recommended knew all the wines by name so he was not engaged ; the second could talk intelligently of quality, so he was dismissed ; the third said he had heard that there were such things as wines and spirits, so the scholar decided to give him a trial.

Next day the new servant was left in charge of the house. ' Be careful of the smoked ham hanging up, and of the fat chicken in the yard, and in particular be careful of the two bottles of white and red liquid,' said his master before he went out, ' for they contain poisons which burn the vitals.'

As soon as his master had gone the servant boiled the ham, and killed and roasted the chicken ; and when they were ready he ate them, drinking both bottles of wine to wash them down. By the time his master returned the man was lying on the floor helplessly drunk. Seeing the ham and the chicken gone and the bottles standing empty, the scholar kicked his new man wide awake and began angrily to question him. ' Oh, Sir,' whined the fellow, ' when you had gone I guarded everything carefully as you said, but suddenly a dog leapt over the wall and made off with the ham, while a cat came in and chased the chicken right out of the compound and I have seen nothing of either of them since. Then I was afraid that you would believe I had broken my trust, and I rushed in and drank both bottles of poison in order that I might die at once. After that I was so giddy and dazed that I could not tell whether I was alive or not, so I lay down on the floor there to wait for death.'

FATHER *v.* TIGER

HSIA YUNG was eminently filial, but lived in extreme poverty. One day having dreamed that his father was dangerously ill, he set out in haste to see him. As he was passing a forest by night, a tiger crossed his path.

'I am hurrying,' he exclaimed, without stopping a moment, 'to take care of my sick father. Let the tiger devour me if he will; I shall proceed without fear.'

The beast turned round, drooped its tail, and padded quietly away.

THE FAWN

A HUNTER caught a live fawn and carried it home. When he opened the door his dogs, tails up and hungry for blood, came running out and leaped at the deer. Out of pity for the little creature their master drove them off, and after that he made a practice of carrying it in his arms among the dogs every day until they grew accustomed to it, and by degrees he even taught them to play without harming it. After a time, the dogs were trained, and the deer, growing up amongst them, forgot it was a deer and felt they were its friends. It would push its way among them and lie down in the most friendly manner, and the dogs, fearing their master, behaved perfectly, even though they sometimes licked their lips.

About three years later the deer went out one day by itself, and, seeing some dogs in the road, ran up to play with them. The strange dogs, in fierce delight, tore it in pieces and lay about the road devouring it.

So the little fawn died, uncomprehending.

LIU TSUNG-YUAN

FIFTY-FIFTY

A BEGGAR met a rich man one day who offered him a thousand dollars if he would allow himself to be beaten to death. 'Sir,' said the beggar thoughtfully, 'I am not a grasping man; I should prefer to take half the beating and half the reward.'

THE FISHERMAN'S WIFE

IN Melon Village lived a fisherman whose wife became consumptive. The infection spread rapidly through the district, and several persons died.

Someone in the village then suggested that if the original victim of the disease were nailed in her coffin alive and cast into the river they would be rid of the trouble.

This was done, and the coffin, floating down to Golden Hill, was seen by a fisherman, who dragged it ashore to examine it. Finding in it a living woman, he carried her to his hut and nursed her back to life. Of necessity, he fed her on fish, principally on eels, and in course of time she recovered completely, married the fisherman, and lived a long time with no return of the disease.

HSÜ HSUAN

THE FLOOD

IN the remotest ages there was a flood in China which made the country almost uninhabitable. The emperor was so distressed by the sufferings of his people that he appointed Yü to find a means of controlling the waters. For thirteen years Yü laboured unceasingly, his hands growing more and more toilworn and his feet more calloused. Three times in the course of his travels he passed his own home without entering, and at last his devotion was rewarded. By making artificial canals he succeeded in draining the water off and leading it into the sea. After this the people were able to set up homes for themselves and live in peace, and this is why the proverb says : ' But for Yü we should all have been fishes.'

*

Let producers be many and consumers few ; let there be activity in production and economy in expenditure. Then wealth will always be ample.—CONFUCIUS.

Stories Short and Tall

THE FOUR DRAGONS

An artist of renown painted a picture of four dragons on a wall. When asked why he had left out their eyes he replied that if they had sight they would fly away. Being urged to finish his work he painted in the eyes and the dragons immediately broke down the wall and flew away.

THE FORTUNE-TELLER

A FORTUNE-TELLER sat by the cross-roads telling fortunes for passers-by. Presently his young son ran up to say that the house had been burned down and everything in it destroyed. The fortune-teller was very much put out by the news, and one of his clients standing in the group around his table turned to him and said jokingly : ' Sir, you sit here all day foretelling good and evil for others, but even when your house was burning you were totally unaware that the omens were bad for yourself. How are you going to explain this ? ' The fortune-teller could find nothing to say.

FOX OUTFOXED

One evening a man was returning home when he overtook a young man on the road. They saluted each other and entered into conversation, but there was something in the young man's appearance which excited the other's suspicions, and he resolved to be on his guard. They talked freely on various subjects, and the young man proved an agreeable companion ; finally, he begged his fellow-traveller to

give him a night's lodging as he was far from home. The request was readily granted. The young man then made several inquiries regarding his friend's home, asking particularly if he kept dogs. No, his friend kept no dogs ; so he was comforted.

' My greatest fear,' he said, ' is dogs ; what is yours ? '

' Oh ! ' said the other, ' my great terror is money ; the sight of it makes me shake and tremble.'

By this time they had reached the house. The owner carefully closed the front gate behind them and called to his dog, which in a moment came bounding towards him, but, on seeing the guest, rushed at him open-mouthed. Quick as lightning, however, that individual changed into a fox, bounded over the wall and was gone.

That night the man was aroused by a noise at the open window, and looking up saw the fox with a large bag of money in his hand, grinning at him maliciously. The man sprang up in seeming terror, and the fox pelted him with handful after handful of money, while he ran about the room crying piteously for mercy, to the fox's great delight. This continued night after night, until the fox grew weary and the man became rich.

Chinese Times

THE FRIENDS

Two very good friends named Kuan and Hua were digging in the garden when they turned up a piece of gold. Kuan glanced at it as if it had been a tile or a stone, and left it for Hua ; Hua picked it up and threw it away again.

On another occasion the two were sitting on the same mat studying when a procession passed the door. Kuan continued to read, but Hua got up and went out to see the sight. Kuan thereupon laid aside his book, rose and cut the mat in two and took his seat on one piece leaving the other for Hua, saying : ' One who leaves his studies to run after trivial matters is no friend of mine.'

T'ai P'ing Kuang Chi

Stories Short and Tall

FRIENDSHIP

A CERTAIN man had a friend lying sick in his house when news was brought of the approach of a large band of robbers. The whole neighbourhood fled, and the sick man said to his host : ' Do you go and leave me. Since I am so ill that I must die in any case, it does not matter whether I die of disease or at the hands of robbers.'

' A friend does not leave a friend in distress,' replied his host, and remained by the sick man's bed, tending him till the bandits arrived. He then begged that his life might be taken and the sick man left to die in peace. The robbers were astounded by this magnanimous conduct. Their leader cried : ' We who are sinners have indeed entered the country of the righteous,' and they withdrew without further molesting anyone.

Ibid.

A GENTLE OLD LADY

THERE was once a pious old woman whose rosary was never out of her fingers and who told her beads aloud constantly. One day she went out to the kitchen, saying, ' A-mi-t'o-Fo ; A-mi-t'o-Fo !' as usual. She broke off to call : ' Second son ! Second son ! Come here. Look at all these ants on the boiler. What a nuisance they are ! Light the fire underneath and burn them up, and get rid of them.' She then returned to her beads, leaving her son to destroy the ants while she went on invoking the Buddha. Presently another thought struck her. ' Second son ! Second son !' she cried again, ' don't use our wicker dust-pan to sweep the ants into ; you may burn it when you throw them on the fire. Go and borrow one from the people next door.'

*

Don't look at your reflection in water ; let other men be the mirror in which you see yourself.

Proverb

233

GRANDPA CAT

A CAT lay stretched out purring with closed eyes. Two mice, watching from afar, said in a whisper : ' Grandpa Cat has turned over a new leaf. How benign he looks saying his prayers to himself over there. Let's steal out and have a game.' No sooner had they left their hole than the cat pounced and one poor mouse was quickly eaten, head, bones and everything. The other fled back to the hole and said to its relations : ' I saw old Grandpa Cat saying his prayers with his eyes shut and I was sure he had undergone a change of heart. But instead he has become so fierce that, believe it or not, when he eats folk nowadays he doesn't even spit out the head or the bones.'

A GRATEFUL SPIRIT

DURING a skirmish between two armies the commander of the losing side was about to order a retreat when a god appeared among his men, strengthened their lines, and inspired them with such courage that defeat was speedily turned into victory.

When the fight was over the officer turned to his saviour and asked : ' Why should an honourable god have bothered to come to the rescue of an unworthy minor officer like myself ? May I inquire humbly who you are ? '

' I am the God of the Target,' was the reply.

' And in what way have I deserved your assistance and patronage ? ' the officer asked.

' Ah,' said the god, ' I owe you a lot. In all the years you have practised shooting, your arrow has never once hit me.'

*

A meagre soil produces late flowers ; worth in poverty develops slowly ; but let no man despise the snake which has no horns, for who can say that it will not become a dragon ?

Proverb

GRATITUDE

THE prince of Mu lost his war-horse, which was caught and eaten by three hundred peasants. The culprits were apprehended and tried, and were condemned to die. But the prince intervened, saying : ' After eating horse-flesh one should drink wine, otherwise one will certainly have indigestion. Give the poor fellows a drink and let them go.' Some time later, when the prince was at war with a neighbouring state, the three hundred begged leave to form a body-guard for him, and when he was hard pressed in battle they fought so fiercely that they saved the day and turned defeat into victory.

CHIH CHI

HALF-PRICE

AN official sent a note to a money-shop saying that he wished to buy two bars of silver. The merchant hastily packed them and went off to the official residence, where he was shown at once into the presence.

' Well,' said the magistrate, ' and what's the price of silver to-day ? '

' It should be so-and-so,' replied the merchant obsequiously, laying the bars on the table, ' but since it is for your Honour we will let you have it at half-price.'

' In that case,' the magistrate returned, picking up one of the bars and returning it, ' the best thing will be for me to give you back one of these.'

Taking the silver the merchant asked to be paid for the other bar.

' But I have just paid you,' said the official, looking surprised, ' what more do you want ? '

' When, your Honour ? ' asked the puzzled merchant.

' Stupid and ungrateful slave ! ' exclaimed the irate magistrate, ' you said you would take half-price, and I gave you one bar to pay you for the other at half-price. Do you insinuate that I have cheated you ! Begone before I have you flogged.'

HAPPINESS

CONFUCIUS one day met a man dressed in a deer-skin coat tied round the waist with a cord, who was playing on a lute and singing.

' Tell me why you are happy, Sir,' Confucius said to him.

' For many reasons,' the man replied. ' Heaven has created all things, and of them all man is the finest. It is my luck to be a man ... that is one cause for happiness. Further, take the difference between the sexes : men are honourable and women base. I happen to be a man . . . that is another cause for happiness. Then, too, some are born who never see the sun or moon ; others do not live through infancy. But I have already passed the age of ninety . . . that is a third cause for happiness. To be poor is the lot of the scholar ; death is the end of all. Shall I therefore be sad because I share the common lot ? '

Lieh Tzu

THE HEIR-APPARENT

IN the twenty-first year of the period ' Established Tranquillity ' (*i.e.* A.D. 216), a great memorial, signed by many officers, went up to the Emperor Hsien (last emperor of the Han dynasty), praying that Ts'ao Ts'ao be granted the title of prince for his manifest merits and signal services to the state. The memorial was approved and a draft edict prepared. Thrice Ts'ao Ts'ao, with seeming modesty, pretended to decline the honour, but thrice was his refusal rejected. Finally he made his obeisance and was enrolled as Prince of Wei, with the usual insignia and privileges, a headdress with twelve strings of beads and a chariot with gilt shafts, drawn by six steeds. But he arrogantly used an imperial chariot with bells, and had the roads cleared when he passed along.

Then he began to discuss the appointment of an heir-apparent. His real wife was without issue, but a concubine had borne him four sons. Wherefore he elevated her to the rank of consort in place of her senior. The third son was very clever and a ready master of composition, and Ts'ao Ts'ao wished him to be named the heir. Then the eldest son sought from a high officer of state a plan to secure his rights of primogeniture and was advised as to how he should act. Thereafter, whenever the father went out on a military expedition, the third son wrote fulsome panegyrics, but the eldest wept so copiously at bidding his father farewell that the courtiers were deeply affected, and remarked that though the one son was crafty and clever he was not so sincerely filial as the other. The eldest son also bought over his father's immediate attendants, who then sang the praises of his virtues so loud that Ts'ao Ts'ao before long declared his eldest son his heir.

San Kuo Chih Yen I

THE HINT

A THIRSTY guest was dining with a stingy host who had given strict orders to the servants that the wine-cups were not to be more than half-filled.

' Have you a saw in the house ? ' asked the guest.

' A saw ? What for ? ' demanded the host in surprise.

' Why,' said his friend, ' I thought I might saw off the top half of this wine-cup, which, being always empty, seems to me to be quite useless.'

HORSE-SENSE

PRINCE NING was passionately fond of horses. One day when he was talking with some visitors a groom arrived with two horses for sale. In size, colour, shape and appearance they were identical, but the price asked for one was just double that of the other.

The prince looked them over for a few minutes and then promised to give both horses to any guest who could solve the riddle of the difference in their value. They talked it over together but could come to no decision.

' Then,' said their host, ' since you cannot judge, we must try them out.'

Taking whip and reins he drove the two horses up and down in front of his guests, saying : ' Can you see the difference ? ' But each time, they all confessed that they hadn't an idea.

Pointing at last to the better horse, the prince said : ' This horse has been to and fro a hundred times and his hoofs have raised no dust, while this one,' turning to the second, ' has only been backwards and forwards a dozen times or so, but has raised clouds of dust with his hoofs. In this alone lies the superiority of the one over the other.'

HSIEH YUNG-JO

HOSPITALITY

ONE day a visitor called unexpectedly on a friend who had no tea in the house. A boy was sent to borrow some and meanwhile the boiler was lighted to heat the water. Time passed ; host and guest talked in the hall ; the host's wife added more and more water to the boiler ; but the messenger did not return with the tea. At last, after a long interval, the boiler was full to the brim of boiling water. The wife made signs from the door to her husband and led him outside. ' It is plain,' she whispered, ' that the guest will not get his tea, but there is plenty of hot water, so you had better invite him to take a bath instead.'

HOT AND COLD
The Legend of the ' Half-and-half' Spring

LEGEND says that the Weaving-Maiden (the star Vega, daughter of the sun-god) brought the Herd-Boy (Aquila) to visit this spot. The Herd-Boy was thirsty, and she took water from the spring and gave it to him. He complained that it was cold, so the Maiden put a spell upon the water and made it warm. The Herd-Boy then said it was hot, so she pulled out her precious six-flowered hairpin, spoke an incantation and drew the hair-pin across the water. One half at once became cold and the other hot, and she gave him both mixed together.

CHANG PI

THE HUSBANDS' CLUB

IT happened one day that ten men met and made the startling discovery that they were all afraid of their wives. With this bond between them they naturally repaired to the nearest temple and there swore eternal brotherhood, and further agreed that whenever domestic affairs permitted, they would meet at the temple to enjoy a feast and a little peace and quiet in each other's company.

On the first of these pleasant occasions, while the meal was in progress, it happened that the ten wives forgathered by accident at the temple, each having come in search of her husband.

As soon as the women's voices were heard nine of the brethren fled, and having taken up their positions in secluded corners, well out of sight, watched with admiration the silent, statuesque dignity of the tenth man while the wives berated him.

When at last the ladies had left, the nine came out of their hiding-places and with one accord proclaimed their brave brother as head and honourable leader of their band. But the tenth brother still answered not a word . . . on first hearing his wife's voice in the courtyard he had died of fright.

239

IN THE RIGHT

A CORRUPT magistrate took a bribe from the plaintiff in a case which came before his Court. Later he accepted twice the amount from the defendant. When the time came to give judgment, no higher offer having come from the first man, the case went in favour of his opponent. ' But, your Honour,' the plaintiff protested, ' you yourself said I had right on my side.' ' True,' replied the magistrate curtly, ' but the defendant had twice as much on his.'

THE INVITATION

A CERTAIN man who had plenty of money but no education was advised to engage a tutor for his son so that the boy might have the advantages which his father had missed. The tutor arrived and after the first day's lesson the lad came to his father and said : ' Father, why should you waste money on a teacher ? I have now learned all the rudiments of writing and counting and the rest is simple. He has to-day explained that one horizontal stroke stands for *one*, and two strokes mean *two* ; in fact, this reading and writing business is now quite clear to me.' The father was delighted at his son's intelligence and rapid progress, and dismissed the tutor.

A day or two later the boy was told to write an invitation to his father's old friend, Mr. Million, asking him to dine. At noon the father went to the study to see why the note was not forthcoming. ' Father,' protested the boy, looking up tired and dishevelled from his task, ' could you not have invited some other friend to dine ? Here have I been working since dawn and up till now I have written only five hundred strokes. I can't think how long it is going to take to write a million.'

*

The King of Hades is easily seen, but it is hard to avoid small devils.

Proverb

Stories Short and Tall

IS THE EARTH SQUARE ?

SOMEONE asked one of Confucius' most famous disciples if it was true that the sky was round and the earth square. ' If it were true,' he replied, ' the four corners would stick out ; and since this is not so, it follows that the earth is round. Even the ancients knew that.'

THE JUDGMENT-SEAT

A MINOR military official named Sun was killed in an accident, but after a time he revived and was able to recall what had happened to him in the interval. He said he had been taken to a place which looked like a royal palace, strongly guarded. His conductor, now a satelite of the King of the Infernal Regions, had been a Buddhist priest on earth, but had consistently broken his vows and had no compensating merit to save him.

' You have been brought here so that I may enjoin you to earn merit through copying the *Fa hua Sutra*,' he told Sun. ' You are not to be examined this time.'

Presently he led Sun before the dreaded King of Hades himself, who told Sun that as he had no sins to answer for he was free to return to earth.

Sun also described the arrival in the palace of a barbarian-looking king with a guard of several hundred soldiers, whom the King of the Infernal Regions had received with great respect and conducted to the upper end of the great hall. Hardly had the honoured guest seated himself than a great gust of wind brought a new arrival to judgment. The newcomer, it appeared, had always carried about with him a copy of the *Diamond Sutra*, but he was also very fond of meat, and he stood awaiting sentence, with a pile of several thousands of rolls of the sutra on his left hand, while on his right was a huge mound of flesh. The judge declared the latter to be the larger heap and the man was therefore condemned. But suddenly, from the pile of sutras, a spark flew across to the mound of flesh and very soon it was completely consumed. The prisoner was therefore allowed to go free, and left the judgment-hall ' walking on air.'

TUAN CH'ENG-SHIH

JUSTICE

AI Tzŭ supervised the education of his grandson, aged ten, and punished every tendency to laziness by a whipping. The boy's father, fearing that his child would not survive such severity, begged the old man, with tears in his eyes, to treat the boy more leniently.

' Are you dissatisfied with my methods ? ' demanded the philosopher, angrily.

His son was silent, and although the punishments became even more severe, he was restrained by filial piety from further criticism.

One winter morning, waking to find a heavy fall of snow on the ground, the little boy ran out to play in it. As a punishment for this neglect of his studies, his grandfather ordered him to kneel in the snow naked.

Made desperate by the sight of his child's suffering, the father threw off his clothes and knelt beside his son in the snow. Presently the grandfather appeared.

' You are not being punished,' he said to his son, ' so why are you kneeling there ? '

The boy's father looked up.

' If you freeze my son,' he said, ' I'll freeze yours.'

KICK ME, DOCTOR !

A FUEL-CARRIER ambling along the road carelessly bumped his load against a doctor whom he knew by sight. The doctor raised his fist and struck him, but the fuel-carrier fell on his knees crying : ' Kick me, Doctor, please ; kick me.'

Having vented his annoyance the doctor went on his way while the puzzled bystanders asked the reason of the coolie's strange request

Ah,' said he sagely, ' a few kicks won't hurt, but preserve me from the hands of a doctor with a reputation like his.'

THE LEAF MAKER

THERE was once a man of Sung who made some leaves of jade for the king. He carved the stems and veins, and reproduced even the down and gloss, so that the result had all the appearance of a luxuriant cluster of bright leaves and could not be distinguished from real ones. The man received a regular salary from the state, and took three years to finish the work.

' Well !' exclaimed a philosopher when he heard of it, ' if when God created the world He had taken three years to make one bunch of leaves, there would be very few trees in the world to-day !'

BALFOUR

A LEGEND OF HSIU-HSING

MANY generations ago, the Prefect of Hsiu-hsing dreamed a dream in which he saw myriads of devils who declared they were going to overthrow the ruling dynasty. The Prefect expressed disbelief and desired some distinguishing mark by which to recognize the devils in any altered form which they might assume in carrying out their threats. To this they agreed, and allowed him to mark each of them with a red spot on the forehead.

He awoke much troubled, not knowing whether the devils were

243

a reality or an idle vision. He went out to consult wise men, but what was his surprise, on returning to his Yamen, to find it strewed with small round stones, on every one of which was a red spot.

'These,' thought he, 'are surely the devils I marked last night, and what a good opportunity is this to get them in my power.'

Accordingly he caused all the stones to be collected in earthenware jars and locked up in a strong room in his Yamen. Before they were finally secured they entered into a parley with the Prefect, who finally persuaded them to agree to submit to incarceration till a certain tree in the Yamen should come into blossom, when they were to be released.

The wily Prefect knew that this particular tree never did blossom in the latitude of Hsiu-hsing, and he congratulated himself on having saved the Government from these powerful enemies. It was understood, however, that to render their imprisonment valid the door was to be sealed with the Prefect's seal, which was to be renewed by each successive holder of that office.

Prefect after prefect occupied the Yamen, and each faithfully resealed the door of the devils' prison, until at length the story began to be forgotten, and one unlucky prefect neglecting to perform this duty, the door was thoughtlessly opened and a jar of devils broken. At the moment this occurred it happened that an official retinue was in the Yamen, and the followers had hung their red-tasselled caps on the tree, the blossoming of which was to have been a signal for the release of the prisoners. Perceiving that their release was the result of an accident, mistaking the red tassels for flowers and assuming that the tree had thus blossomed every year during their long confinement the devils were much incensed at this breach of faith, and in retaliation they caused the city to be submerged below the waters of the river, where it remained until they were recaptured and the door resealed. Taught by woeful experience, each succeeding prefect was from that time careful to reseal the door on assuming office, and thus the devils were long restrained from doing mischief.

Time passed on, and faith in the necessity of sealing the door was shaken, and in 1854 a prefect named Ma assumed office, utterly despising the story of the devils. Not only did he omit to seal the door, but he caused the red spotted stones to be taken from the strong room and thrown away. In that very year the red-turbaned rebels —the devils with red marks on their foreheads, now appearing in human form—captured the city !

THE LEECH

THE King of Ch'u found a leech in his salad, and swallowed it. He became so ill that he could take no food of any kind, and being questioned, at length confessed what he had done. ' But why did you not leave the leech ?' he was asked. ' If I had not swallowed it,' the king replied, ' the cook would have been put to death for carelessness.' ' In that case,' said his questioner, ' you will not die. One cannot die as the result of a good deed.' And before long the king vomited the leech and recovered.

LET WELL ALONE

ONE day a man of Sung was looking at his springing corn, and feeling distressed because it was not longer, he pulled it up. He then went home, complaining that he was tired, and said : ' I have been working hard, helping the corn to grow long.' His son ran out to the field, and found the corn lying withered on the ground.

MENCIUS

*

Don't enter a widow's house alone.
Victory is the result of strategy, not of bravery.

Proverbs

THE LIARS

A MAN who could never resist the temptation to boast told some country cousins that he possessed an ox thirty feet long that could travel three hundred and thirty-three miles in a day ; a cock that announced not only the dawn but every watch with the correct number of crows ; and a dog that could read. ' Such possessions as these must not be hidden from sight,' said his hearers ; ' we shall call to-morrow and see them for ourselves.'

The man went home and told his wife of his predicament. ' What shall I do ? ' he asked. ' How can I avoid losing face ? '

' Don't worry,' his wife replied, ' leave it to me and keep out of sight when they come.'

Next day the visitors came at the appointed hour. ' Is Mr. So-and-so at home ? ' they asked his wife, who received them. ' No, he went off on his ox this morning to Yunnan, but he'll be back in a couple of days.' ' Really ! ' said the visitors. ' We should have liked to see the ox, but you have a cock which announces the watches of the day and night . . . can we see that ? ' At that moment, which as it happened was noon, a cock in the farm-yard crowed. ' That,' said the wife, ' is he. He not only announces the watches as you hear, but he always crows when strangers come.'

' Wonderful,' exclaimed the country cousins, ' and what about the dog that can read ? May we have a look at that ? '

' Well,' said the wife, ' I won't deceive you. This family is so poor that we have had to find the dog a situation as a tutor.'

THE LIKENESS

' SIR,' said an artist to a sitter whose portrait he had just completed, ' would you mind if we took this picture out and asked a few people in the street what they think of it ? '

' Not at all,' said the sitter, so they went out carrying the portrait with them, and the subject of it stopped the first person he saw and asked him to be good enough to say whether he thought the portrait a good likeness. After a careful examination of the picture and the owner, the man unhesitatingly replied : ' The hat's a good likeness.'

A second person whom they stopped to interrogate studied the portrait and the original and said : ' Aren't the clothes like ? '

When they accosted a third man, the artist did not wait for his client to speak, but said quickly : ' The hat and clothes have already been commented on ; no need to tell us what you think of them. What about the face ? Is that a good likeness ? '

The third critic finished his examination and then appeared to think hard. Finally he replied : ' The whiskers seem to me to be remarkably like.'

THE LISTENER

THERE was once a monk who began to preach to a woman he met in the road. The woman knelt and listened with streaming eyes, so that the monk's zeal increased and he talked on till midnight. The woman still wept, and at last the monk inquired what it was in his discourse that so affected her. ' Oh,' cried the woman, ' our donkey died last night ; is it not terrible ? '

THE LOST CORD

ONE day a man came upon a friend wearing the great wooden collar of the criminal and asked the cause of his misfortune. ' Oh,' replied the offender airily, ' I was just walking along the road when I saw a bit of straw rope lying on the ground and thinking it was of no use to anyone, I picked it up and took it away, and then they arrested me.'

' But that's monstrous ! ' his friend exclaimed, ' to punish a man for picking up a piece of rope.'

' I ought perhaps to add that there was something attached to one end of the rope,' said the man in the collar.

'What thing?' asked his friend, still indignant at this manifest injustice.

'Oh, just a small, small ploughing-ox,' was the reply.

THE LOST PEARL

THE mother of the Emperor Yuan of the Liang dynasty lost a pearl. Yuan, who was a very little boy at the time swallowed it and said that one of the attendants must have stolen it. He then swallowed the eye of a broiled fish to avert trouble. This made him sick, however, and in consequence the pearl was restored to its owner. But Yuan was blind in one eye all his life.

YÜ T'I

A MAGICIAN TESTS HIS WIFE

ONE day a philosopher out for a walk saw a woman fanning the newly-made grave of her husband, to whom she had made a promise that she would not marry again before his grave was dry. On returning home the philosopher related the incident to his young wife, adding that he had no doubt that she would do the same or worse. His wife expressed her indignation at such conduct and declared that she would remain a faithful widow, according to the rules of propriety, to the end of her days.

Now the philosopher, being possessed of magical powers, was in a position to put the matter to the test. Almost immediately he pretended to have a fit and die. In accordance with the rites he was placed in a coffin and the lid fastened down. His widow, dressed in mourning garments, was burning incense when a good-looking young man came and knelt beside her. At first she was indignant, but it was not long before the stranger's ardent attentions caused the widow to exchange her mourning garb for wedding attire, and before the old husband had been carried away for burial she had married the new.

While the marriage feast was still in progress the bridegroom suddenly manifested signs of the illness which had carried off her former husband, and fell to the ground in a fit, crying out that the only remedy was the brain of a living man or one recently dead. The wife rushed to the coffin and broke it open. Immediately the young man disappeared, and sitting up in the coffin was the elderly philosopher. Seeing his wife in wedding garments, he cried out upon her faithlessness : ' And you have been drinking too,' he added angrily.

' Ah,' replied the wife, without a moment's hesitation, ' I had a feeling that you were not really dead, so I dressed like this to welcome you back, and took a glass of wine as a disinfectant against any germs which might be disturbed in the opening of the coffin.'

Moral : Be not over hasty in your judgments, nor too ready with your promises.

A MAN IN THE MOON

In the olden times an aged man, while trudging along a country road, was accosted by a fairy, who, perceiving him to be a worthy fellow, desired to translate him to the heavenly land.

' Take,' he said, ' these two pills ; keep them until midday on the fifteenth of the eighth month when, if you look towards the southern heavens, you will see a door appear. As soon as the door opens swallow the two pills, and you will be changed into a genie.'

The old man in simple faith pocketed the pills and returned to his home, where—alas !—he was not long able to keep the secret from his wife.

When the appointed day arrived, the husband having left the house, the wife bethought herself of the pills and determined to try their virtue. Looking towards the southern heavens, she saw the door. As it slowly opened she swallowed one of the pills, considerately leaving the second for her husband. Forthwith a stool descended to the earth and no sooner had she seated herself than she was wafted away into space.

Shortly afterwards the husband returned, and was much distressed to find himself minus a wife and a pill too. But he did the best he could in the circumstances. The heavens indeed did not open for him, and no door appeared. But the hour had arrived, and no sooner had he hastily swallowed the remaining pill than another stool descended from the sky, on which he was carried away after his wife. But ere he reached the door of heaven the bolt had been shot, and he was left like a peri weeping at the confines of paradise. Touched by his distress, the guardian angel turned him into a genie and gave him the ' Palace of Chilly Vastness ' in the moon for a residence, where he still lives in dreary solitude.

Meanwhile his wife had entered the heavenly portal and been changed into a female genie. Once a year, on the anniversary of their separation, she opens the door of heaven and gladdens the heart of her wronged and suffering husband with a sight of his spouse. It is to join and support him in his transitory bliss, and to drink to his health, that mortals carouse at the mid-autumn festival.

Chinese Times

A MAN IN THE WELL

A CERTAIN Master Ting had no well in his garden and one of his men was always out, drawing water from a well some distance away. When he dug a well of his own and the man could remain at home to work, Master Ting remarked : ' By digging a well I found a man.' Soon the story spread that Master Ting had found a man when he was digging a well in the garden. When it came to the ears of the king he sent for Master Ting, who was obliged to explain that he had meant that he had found the services of a man, and not that he had found one in the well.

MAN INTO TIGER

TOWARDS the end of the ninth century of the Christian era a young official named Chang begged leave of absence from his post. To all inquiries as to where he was going he would only say that he had an old mother, as well as a wife and child, and that he wanted to see them.

Leave was granted and Chang went away. That night loud lamentations were heard, and in the morning it was learned that Chang had gone home, said farewell to his family, and departed into the hills to become a tiger.

A few nights later the sound of wailing was heard again. This time it appeared that Chang, being homesick, had returned during the night. The upper half of him had already been transformed into a tiger but he was still able to talk.

YÜ T'I

THE MEETING

TWO persons belonging to the same clan met in the street. One was quick-tempered, the other slow-witted. The latter, a rather obsequious man, bowed to the ground saying : ' My dear Sir, what must you think of me ? You brought me gifts at New Year ; you sent me greetings at the fifth month festival ; you gave me moon-cakes at the mid-autumn feast in the eighth month, and all this time I have not . . .'

Lifting his head, he saw that the other had gone, and was by this time out of sight. ' When did my friend leave ? ' he asked, turning to the little crowd that had been waiting to enjoy his embarrassment.

' Oh,' replied a wag, ' he left as soon as he had brought you his gifts at the New Year.'

*

The idol-maker doesn't worship Buddha.

Proverb

THE MONKEYS

THE keeper of a monkey-house one day told his charges that he proposed to give each of them three nuts every morning and four every evening. The monkeys were very annoyed at this arrangement, which did not suit them at all. 'Very well,' said the keeper, 'I will change my plans to suit your wishes, and will give you four in the morning and three in the evening.' The monkeys were very content.

CHUANG TZU

MOSQUITOES

THE country mosquitoes invited their town relatives to a banquet. The provisions were ample, but thick-skinned, and the town mosquitoes left the feast hungry and bad-tempered. Knowing, however, that they must return the invitation, they discussed the form of the banquet to which they would invite their country cousins. So many people were using mosquito-curtains, they pointed out, that if the always-hungry country mosquitoes got enough to eat, their hosts would have to go without. 'Invite them to the temples,' some one said, and this suggestion was carried unanimously. So when the country mosquitoes came to town they were offered painted clay gods to satisfy themselves on, and one and all agreed, after the politest of farewells, that for the future they would neither invite, nor accept invitations from their relatives in town.

雀鹿

蜂猴

253

THE MOUNTAIN

MR. STUPID was ninety years of age, and he began to find the mountain just outside his gate a little inconvenient when he went in and out. So one day he gathered his sons and grandsons and led them with spades and baskets to dig up the mountain and remove it out of the way. His neighbours laughed at him and pointed out the folly of his attempt. ' Indeed, you are stupid ! ' they exclaimed. ' You have only a few more years to live, and you are wasting the little strength you have and shortening the time that remains by trying to remove a mountain to which all your efforts will make scarcely a hair's-breadth of difference.'

' Not at all,' the old man replied, ' when I am dead I shall be followed by my sons, and they by my grandsons and their sons and so on without end, and, since the mountain will not continue to increase correspondingly in height, what fear is there that it will not in the end be removed ? '

THE MUSSEL AND THE HERON

A MUSSEL was lying on the river bank sunning itself when a heron came by and pecked at it. The mussel closed its shell, nipping the bird's beak, whereupon the bird said : ' If you don't let me go to-day or to-morrow there will be a dead mussel.' The fish replied : ' If I don't open to-day or to-morrow, there will be a dead heron.' Just then a fisherman came along and seized them both.

THE MYSTERY OF THE LICE

ONE night a man lying in bed heard several human voices coming from under the clothes, reciting in unison, in thin, tiny voices, a poem which he knew. Hurriedly throwing back the covers he found nothing except a dozen or so lice about as big as beans. When they were destroyed the voices ceased.

LIU HSUN

NON-COMMITTAL

' BE non-committal in your speech,' said a father to his son. ' Never sound too cock-sure.'

' What does non-committal mean ? ' the boy asked.

' I will explain,' his father said. ' Suppose someone in the street wants to borrow something, you should never say how much you have of it, nor should you say definitely how little ; rather say that maybe you have some at home and maybe you haven't. That is what I mean by non-committal speech. Don't forget what I have told you.'

The next day a friend of the family called and asked the boy if his father was at home. Mindful of yesterday's lesson, the boy replied : ' My father ? Well, I wouldn't like to say definitely how much or how little, but maybe we have some of him at home and maybe we haven't.'

' NOTHING—BUT DOTH CHANGE '

IN A.D. 266 the mother of a well-known official in Tan-yang, being eighty years of age, was given a bath and as a result she became a turtle. Her sons kept the gates shut and guarded her carefully ; they made a little house for her and a pond. She entered the water and swam about in it, but after two days she stretched her neck and

255

looked around, then seeing the gates ajar, slipped out and went off to a distant pool and never came back again.

HSIEH YUNG-JO

ORDINARY MOON

THERE was once a man who flattered everyone else and always described his own possessions as ' ordinary.' One day he invited a few guests to wine, and they sat drinking with him till the moon rose. The evening was lovely and one of the party remarked : ' I did not think there would be such a beautiful moon to-night.' The host bowed low and rubbed his hands together. ' You are too kind ; you are too kind !' he exclaimed. ' I am sorry this poor establishment is unable to provide anything more than an ordinary household moon.'

OUR MUTUAL ADVANTAGE

THE tailor's son was watching his father cut out a coat for a customer. First this way and then that the scissors hesitated over the cloth but still the first snip was not made. ' What's the matter, Father,' the boy asked, ' why don't you cut it ?' ' Ah, my boy,' said his father sadly, ' it is by no means as easy as that. You see, if I cut this cloth to the customer's advantage I shan't get any of it, and if I cut it to my advantage he won't get his coat.'

PAINLESS EXTRACTION

A MAN named Li had an abscess on his left eyelid the size of a duck's egg, which entirely prevented the eye from opening. One day a doctor came along and began to talk to him. They sat talking and drinking till Li was so drunk that he lost consciousness. The doctor then lanced the abscess, and out of the hole came an oriole, which flew away singing.

T'ai P'ing Kuang Chi

THE PARAMOUR

SHORTLY before her death a certain royal widow gave orders to bury her lover with her. The lover hastened to send a servant to his mistress with this message : 'The dead either have or have not knowledge. If they have not, what is the use of taking me with you ? If they have, your dead husband is probably so incensed already by your behaviour that it would be madness for you to appear before him in the company of your lover.' The queen decided to be buried alone.

THE 'PATENT' MEDICINE

IN the West Market in Ch'ang-an there used to sit a man who sold a patent medicine containing several drugs of his own compounding. He never troubled to feel a pulse, or even to inquire into the nature of the disease to be treated. He merely sold his draught, and people suffering from every kind of disease drank it and were cured.

One day a servant of an official named T'ien saw for himself how remarkable were the effects of this medicine, and on arriving home he reported to his master, who had been seriously ill for some time, what he had seen.

'Send a man on horseback to buy some at once,' ordered the sick man. Accordingly, a rider set off post-haste, bought the draught, and rode quickly back again. Not far from home, however, his horse stumbled and the precious mixture was spilt. Not daring to return without it, and having no money to buy more, the wretched man refilled the bottle from the nearest runnel in the dyers' quarter of the city and carried it home.

No sooner had the sick man taken the dose than he recovered completely. Then, knowing only that he was better, but not the origin of the medicine that had cured him, he not only went in person to thank the medicine-seller, but presented him with a banner as a testimonial of his skill.

T'ai P'ing Kuang Chi

PATRIOTISM

PU SHIH was a sheep-breeder of the Han period, who owned more than a thousand sheep. Once, when China was about to send an army against the marauding tribes on her western borders, Pu presented a memorial to the Throne offering half his possessions as a contribution towards the expenses of the expedition. The Emperor sent a messenger to ask if Pu was looking for a post in the government. This Pu denied. 'Then,' said the envoy, 'have you a complaint against someone which you wish to open a way to lay before the Emperor ? ' ' I have no quarrel with anyone,' Pu replied, ' so why should I want to lodge a complaint ? ' ' Well,' cried the messenger, ' what *do* you want ? ' ' The Son of Heaven is about to punish the enemies of the state,' answered Pu simply, ' and it is the opinion of this stupid person that the able-bodied ought to join the army and the rich to give of their substance. If this were done the barbarians would quickly be exterminated.'

SSU-MA CH'IEN

THE PEAR-TREE

A COUNTRYMAN was offering a barrow of pears for sale in the market one day when a Taoist priest begged one. The request was refused, and when the priest became importunate the owner of the pears cursed him roundly.

' You have several hundreds there,' the priest protested, ' and I only want one ; why should you be so angry about it ? ' The bystanders also urged the salesman to pick out a poor specimen and give it to the priest, but the obstinate fellow still persisted in his refusal.

Finally the people who had gathered to hear the argument contributed enough cash to buy a pear, and settle the affair. The priest thanked them, and speaking to the crowd, said : ' I don't want to be greedy ; I hope you, my kind friends, will condescend to share this pear with me.'

' Why don't you eat it yourself and be done with it ? ' some one asked.

' All I want is the seeds to plant,' the priest returned, and quickly eating the pear, he saved the seeds in the palm of his hand and, picking up a spade, dug a hole and dropped them in one by one· He then covered them with earth and begged a little water from a near-by stall to water them. The eyes of the crowd were fixed on the spot where the seeds lay hidden. In a few moments a crooked sprout poked its way through the soil, and, gradually increasing in size, soon became a tree, with branches and leaves. Before long flowers bloomed, and these were quickly followed by quantities of large and fragrant pears which almost hid the branches. These the priest plucked as fast as they appeared, handing them to the delighted bystanders, who were soon all eating pears. Before long the last one was eaten, and then the priest chopped down the tree with an axe and walked away with it.

The countryman meanwhile had been too interested in the priest's magic to think of his own affairs, but turning to go back to his barrow, he saw that it was empty, and knew that the pears on the tree had been his pears, and on examining the barrow he knew that the tree had been one of its handles, which had been chopped off with an axe. Hurrying after the priest, he found the handle thrown down by a corner of the wall, but of the priest there was no sign.

*

Those who steal property are executed ; those who steal kingdoms become princes.

Proverb

THE PEKING MOON

A YOUNG man from the provinces who had lived for some years in Peking returned home full of the superiority of everything in the capital. One night he was out walking with his father when they met a friend who remarked that the moon was beautiful. ' Ah,' said the young man, before his father could answer, ' you should see the moon we have in Peking ; that's something like a moon ! '

His father was so put out by this rudeness that he boxed his son's ears soundly. The youth burst into tears, but through his sobs he was heard to say : ' You think that a box on the ears, but that's nothing to the sort of box on the ears one would get in Peking.'

THE PICNIC

DURING the T'ang period (A.D. 618–906) the third son of a court official was betrothed to the younger daughter of a President of the Board of Rites. The wedding-day was fixed, but the sudden transfer of the girl's father to a new post caused the marriage to be postponed until the spring of the following year.

A day before the young man was due to arrive at the new home to claim his bride, her father sent the entire family on a picnic, and after a happy day they were returning in the evening through the woods, when a tiger sprang out and carried off the little bride-to-be. The horror-stricken party rushed home and told their tale. All night the house was filled with wailing and men were sent to seek the bones of the victim and bring them back for burial.

That same night the bridegroom, when still about ten miles from his destination, left his boat, and, attended by half a dozen companions, walked along the river-bank, the boat travelling slowly close in to the shore. They had not gone far when they came upon a wooden hut and went inside to examine it. Suddenly they were startled by the sound of a creature coming out of the woods, and kept perfectly still. Through the chinks in the wall they saw a tiger enter the moonlit clearing round the hut carrying something in its mouth. They made such a clatter, beating upon the wooden walls of the hut and shouting at the tops of their voices, that the beast dropped its burden and made off.

When they found that the tiger's prey was a girl, the young men were amazed, and carrying her quickly to the boat, they gave her into the care of the waiting-women who were to attend upon the bride on the return journey. She soon recovered consciousness and began to cry, but she would not, or could not, tell them who she was, though her appearance proclaimed her to be of gentle parentage and no village-maid.

While they were discussing her, voices were heard from the bank, and presently someone entered in a hurry and told the story of the search for the remains of the victim of yesterday's tragedy. Leaving the girl in charge of the women, the young men hurried off to carry the news of her rescue to her family. Presently they all reached the house safely and the wedding took place as arranged.

Ever since this incident occurred people in that locality have from time to time set up tablets to commemorate this 'Tiger-go-between.' Some of these may still be seen at the present day.

HSIEH YUNG-JO

THE PRICE OF A LIFE

A MAN fell into the river and was in danger of drowning. His son on the bank cried out to the passers-by to rescue him, promising a handsome reward. But the father, coming to the surface in time to hear this, protested. 'Make it thirty cents and no more, my boy. If they won't come and save me for thirty cents, let them stay away.'

*

Those who think must govern those who labour ; those who labour must provide necessaries for those who think.

Proverb

A PROBLEM OF AGE

MR. CHANG had a daughter aged one ; Mr. Li had a son aged two. It occurred to the latter that it might be a good thing to arrange a marriage between these two children, so he sent a go-between to Mr. Chang to make the proposal.

Mr. Chang, however, disapproved strongly, and said so. 'My daughter is one, while his son is two,' said he indignantly, 'so that by the time she is ten he will be twenty. I wouldn't dream of letting her marry such an elderly husband !'

'Oh, my dear,' protested his wife, who was present at this interview, ' you are wrong in your calculations. Next year our daughter will be two too, and what could be more suitable than a match between two persons of the same age ?'

THE RABBIT

WHILST a farmer was ploughing one day he saw a rabbit in headlong flight dash against a tree-trunk with such force that it killed itself instantly. He picked it up, very pleased at having a meal provided so easily, and from then onwards he gave up farming and watched every day beside the tree trunk for rabbits to kill themselves for his profit. But no other rabbit obliged, and his farm fell into ruin.

RATS

MR. MA was a magician. One day he met another man also called Ma, who, presuming on their having the same family name, begged to be taught some tricks, or at least to be given a demonstration of magic. The magician obliged. He produced untold sums of money from his clothes, and threw into a well coins which at his command flew out of the well one at a time and were handled by the onlookers.

Hearing that the city was over-run by rats, the magician wrote a charm and ordered it to be pasted on the south wall. Then gongs were beaten in long rolls of sound and the rats came out in hosts and squatted in front of the wall. The magician called out one of the largest size and said : ' What do you mean, you vermin, by boring holes in the walls and making your nests in people's houses and annoying Mr. Ma here, day and night ? If you don't want to be exterminated altogether, you will be well advised to take your entire tribe with you and clear out from this place.'

The large rat turned to the hosts around, who bumped their heads on the ground as if recognizing their guilt. Then, arranging themselves in troops, so many that none could count them, they went out by the gate and from that time forth not a single rat was ever seen again in the city.

CHIANG FANG

*

Mr. So-and-So was very superstitious. Being born in the year of the rat, he was fond of these creatures, and would not keep a cat or a dog nor allow his servants to destroy them. In his kitchen and his barns the rats did as they liked and no one interfered with them.

The rats naturally advised their friends, who all came to live with Mr. So-and-so, where the food was plentiful and there was no danger. Before long there wasn't a sound article in his house nor a whole garment in his clothes-chests, and rats swarmed all over the food.

By day strings of them ran about with the family, and at night the noise of gnawing and scratching kept everyone awake.

Some years later Mr. So-and-so went to live in another district and a new tenant took possession of the house. The rats continued to behave as before.

'There are no limits to the depredations of these filthy vermin!' said the new tenant. He acquired five or six cats, blocked all the doors, flooded the rat-holes, and hired rat-catchers. The army of rats that were caught and killed and thrown out was so great that it was months before the smell of them quite disappeared.

Well, well! Those rats thought they could continue for ever gorging themselves without interference.

LIU TSUNG-YUAN

RECOGNITION

YANG PU, younger brother of the philosopher Yang Chu, one day went out wearing a white robe, but being wet through by heavy rain, he changed and went home wearing black. His dog, not recognizing his master, barked at him. Pu was annoyed and would have beaten the animal, but Yang Chu remonstrated. 'You would do just the same,' he said. 'If your dog went out white and came home black would you recognize him?'

Lieh Tzu

REFORMATION

THERE was once a man who used every day to steal his neighbours' strayed fowls. When he was told that this was not the act of a gentleman, he answered: 'Very well, for the rest of this year I will reduce my appropriations to one fowl a day, and next year I will give up the practice altogether.'

MENCIUS

RELATIONSHIP

A MAN was standing outside his gate, holding his son in his arms. 'Good gracious,' exclaimed a passer-by, to annoy the father, 'isn't that child like me?' 'That's so,' replied the father quickly, 'one can see that you and the child are sons of the same mother, but isn't it a dreadful thought that he may grow up to look like you?'

THE REPAIR

A MAN fell from his horse and broke his leg. The doctor ordered a draught of powdered copper in wine, after which the patient recovered completely and lived to a good age.

Ten years after his death it chanced that he was for some reason being reburied, and when the skeleton was in process of removal it was discovered that the shinbone was bound round with a piece of copper where it had been broken.

CHANG TSU

RESCUE THOSE WHO ARE IN DANGER

A CERTAIN merchant had reached middle age without the good fortune of possessing children. To add to his chagrin, a skilful physiognomist said to him:

'Before you are many months older you will meet with a dangerous accident.'

The merchant, knowing this practitioner's extraordinary skill in his art, packed up all his goods and proceeded in haste towards his home.

In the course of his journey by water he saw a woman throw herself into the river with her child. He immediately called some fishermen, and promised them twenty ounces of silver if they would save them from drowning. The men thereupon drew them both out of the water. Having paid the promised sum, the merchant turned to the woman and asked why she had thrown herself into the river.

' My husband,' she replied, ' is a day-labourer. We had fattened a pig, which he carried to sale yesterday, but returned home without perceiving that he had been paid in bad money. His anger was turned against himself, and he scolded and beat me. We have now nothing left to buy food.'

When he heard her story, the merchant gave her twice the value of the pig, and sent her home.

The woman, on her return, related her adventure to her husband, who would hardly believe her. However, they went together to see the merchant and thank him, arriving at his lodging after he had retired to rest. Having knocked at the door, the woman cried out, telling him who they were, and the merchant left his apartment to see them. No sooner had he quitted his room than the wall and roof fell in, crushing the bed on which he had been lying. He went forthwith to see the man of destinies.

' I perceive that you have just escaped an imminent danger,' exclaimed that worthy as soon as he saw him, ' but more—you have entitled yourself to unlooked-for good fortune, and will have no further occasion to bewail your want of offspring.'

Ere long the merchant achieved an heir, who afterwards attained to high distinction and office.

DAVIS

RETRIBUTION

A COMMONER named Huang fell off his horse and broke his leg, and knowing that the tortoise was supposed to be an efficacious mender of broken bones, he looked round for one, smashed it with a stone and bound it on his leg. The leg soon healed, but the tortoise had not been killed, and while it was healing Huang's flesh it also healed its own with his so that they grew as one. Huang went to cut the loathsome thing from his leg, but it was like cutting his own flesh so he had to put up with it. Thereafter he could see things through the tortoise's eyes in his leg just as well as through his own eyes. Such was the retribution which overtook him for his cruelty to a living creature.

YÜ T'I

★

The Marquis of Chin saw in a dream a ferocious demon with long untidy hair reaching to the ground, which accused him of killing and ill-treating its descendants. When the marquis awoke he called a witch and related his dream. ' You will not live to eat of the new wheat-crop,' was her interpretation.

In the sixth month the Marquis expressed a wish to eat of the new wheat and the superintendent of his fields brought some. While it was being cooked the witch was also sent for and executed, but before it was ready for the table, the marquis went outside, and being taken ill, fell into the privy and died there. An attendant who had dreamed the previous night that he was carrying his lord up to heaven on his shoulders bore the marquis's body back to the palace, and was afterwards buried alive in his tomb.

Tso Chuan

THE RETURN OF THE SPIRIT

A CERTAIN Mr. Li who had lived for many years in complete harmony with his wife, died suddenly. The widow was inconsolable and spent all her time beside the bier, refusing to allow the coffin to be nailed down.

There was a general belief in that region that on the seventh night after death a messenger from the world of shades brought the spirit back to its body. No one had ever dared to be present on such an occasion, but Madame Li placed her children in safety in an adjoining room, and at the appointed time took up a position close to her husband's body. At midnight an icy wind heralded the arrival of a spectre, and a ferocious demon, leading the spirit of her husband by a rope, made its appearance. Now, knowing that spirits, good and bad, are always hungry, Madame Li had spread an appetising meal by the side of the coffin, and as soon as the demon saw the food it dropped the rope, and throwing down its pitchfork, gave all its attention to satisfying its hunger, while Madame Li threw a coverlet round the spirit of her husband and clasped his body, all icy as it was, in her arms.

Her cries, when the monster had finished its meal and turned to look for its prisoner, brought her children and servants to her help. Between them they drove off the demon and after a time succeeded in reviving the corpse.

REVENGE

The Duke of Ch'i employed as his chariot-driver a man whose father's corpse he had mutilated, and as his second attendant in the chariot, one whose wife he had taken. One day, during a halt, the two attendants were bathing in a river, when the driver annoyed his fellow servant by hitting him with a stick.

' You let your wife be taken from you without showing annoyance,' protested the driver, ' but as soon as you are touched yourself you say you are hurt ; how can that be ? '

' What about one who shows no anger when the feet of his father's corpse are cut off ? ' retorted the other.

Thereupon they killed the duke and hid his body among the bamboos on the river-bank. Then, returning to the city, they drank a cup of wine, and went away.

Tso Chuan

THE REWARD

A MAN who had the misfortune to own a house which stood between a blacksmith's shop on one side and a coppersmith's on the other let it be known that he would pay a considerable sum to either or both if they would change their address. A few days later both turned up and claimed the reward. When their delighted neighbour had paid the promised sums he inquired : ' And where, may I ask, are you moving to ? ' ' Oh,' said the two smiths in unison, ' he's moving into my house and I'm moving into his house.'

RICH AND POOR

A RICH man was boasting of his wealth to a poor man. ' I am a millionaire,' he said ; ' did you know ? '

' And so am I,' declared the poor man, ' so there's nothing remarkable in that.'

' Where are your millions ? ' asked the rich man sceptically.

' You've got a million and won't spend it,' replied the other ; ' I could spend a million and haven't got it ; so you are no better off than I am, and I am as much a millionaire as you are.'

RICH MAN, POOR MAN

' I HAVE a thousand pieces of gold,' said a rich man to a poor man, ' and you ought therefore to treat me with respect.'

' Why ? ' demanded the poor man bluntly, ' what has it to do with me ? '

' Suppose I gave you half my gold, would you treat me with respect ? ' the rich man went on.

Why ? ' asked the poor man again, ' if we had half each we should be equals and there would be no occasion to treat you other than as an equal.'

' Well then, suppose I gave it all to you, would you treat me with respect ? '

' Certainly not,' returned the other, ' for in that case it would be you who ought to treat me with respect.'

RIDING A TIGER

A MAN who had climbed a tree to escape from a tiger trembled so much that he fell out of it on to the tiger's back. The beast rose and made off, the poor man sitting as if stunned, not knowing whether to let go or hang on.

People seeing him pass exclaimed : ' Such courage ! Doesn't he look like an Immortal, riding a tiger with so much dignity ? '

Hearing these comments the terrified rider shouted : ' You may think I *look* dignified, but you don't know what I feel like, nor how I am suffering through not being able to decide whether to get off or not.'

ROCKING THE BOAT

THE Marquis of Ch'i and one of his ladies were sailing in a boat on the lake in his park, when she rocked the boat. The marquis turned pale with fright and told her to stop, but she would not, so she was sent home in disgrace, though not regularly divorced, and her family married her to someone else.

Tso Chuan

SALTED EGGS

A COUNTRYMAN arriving in Peking was invited to dinner by a friend and was given salted duck-eggs.

' How strange ! ' he cried, at the first bite. ' Why are these eggs salt ? '

' Oh,' said his host, ' have you never heard of Peking salted ducks ? As the ducks are salt, of course their eggs are salt too.'

THE SCHOOL-TEACHER

A CERTAIN man who could find no other means of making a livelihood set up a school. His attainments were extremely limited and he often found it impossible to answer the questions put to him by his scholars. On the first of these occasions he pleaded the soporific after-effects of intoxication and postponed answering the question until next day. At night he asked his wife about it and next morning appeared in the school-room all primed with the answer and expounded it to his students. 'And now do you understand, dullards?' he concluded. 'Yes, I understand that,' replied the bright boy of the class, 'and now, Sir, will you please tell us the meaning of the sentence which follows?'

This was too much for the teacher. His eyes glazed and he swayed slightly. 'Be quiet,' he said, 'don't bother me. That wine has gone to my head again.'

SECRECY

A WIFE went to the edge of the village fields and called her husband in to dinner. 'One moment,' he shouted, 'I'll just hide my hoe and come.' When he came in his wife warned him that it was unwise to shout about hiding things and that someone might steal the hoe. After dinner he went out again to work but was soon back. Creeping softly to his wife's side, he whispered in her ear : You know that hoe I hid? Well, you were quite right ; somebody has stolen it.'

SHEEP MOUNTAIN

In the midst of the sea is an island called Sheep Mountain. On it is a temple, the presiding spirit of which is reputed to be the Emperor Yang of the Sui Dynasty. The Mountain consists of several peaks, among which lie three lakes known as the Three Maidens. Here water-chestnuts and caltrops grow luxuriantly and wild-duck and water-fowl are plentiful. There is a god standing at the entrance to the temple. If anyone's kitchen is overrun with mice or flies and he reports it to this spirit, the matter will be attended to promptly.

YÜ T'I

SINGLE COMBAT

The rolling of drums at dawn next day announced the arrival of Ma. He wore a lion helmet and his belt was clasped with the shaggy head of a wild beast. His breastplate was silver and his robe of white. He emerged from the shadow of his great standard and stood below, challenging Chang Fei, who at length rode out with half a company to meet him. About a bow-shot distant from the enemy Chang halted his men. When all had taken their places he set his spear and rode out.

'Do you know who I am?' he shouted. 'I am Chang Fei of Yen.'

'My family having been noble for many generations,' Ma shouted back, 'I am not likely to know any rustic dolts.'

This reply upset Chang Fei, and in a moment the two were rushing towards one another, with poised spears. After a hundred bouts neither appeared to have any advantage, and a gong was sounded as a signal to cease the fight. It was then growing late and Chang's brother said to him: 'You had better retire for to-day; he is a terrible opponent. Try him again to-morrow.'

But Chang's spirit was roused. 'No,' he shouted, 'I will die and not come back.'

' But it is late ; you cannot go on fighting,' protested his brother.

' Let them bring torches and we will have a night battle,' said Chang, his excitement rising higher. And hastily changing horses with his brother he rode forth.

Both sides cheered. They lit torches till it seemed as light as day, and the two great captains went to the front to fight.

After the twentieth bout Ma thought to try a ruse. By a false flight he would inveigle Chang into pursuit. He picked up a copper hammer secretly, and kept a careful watch for the most favourable moment to strike. But his enemy's flight only put Chang on his guard, and when the moment came for the blow with the hammer, he dodged and the weapon flew harmlessly past his ear. Then Chang turned his horse and Ma began to pursue. Chang then pulled up, took his bow, fitted an arrow to the string and let fly. But Ma also dodged and the arrow flew by. Then each returned to his own side.

Then Chang's brother and leader came out to the front of his battle-line and called out : ' Note well, O Ma, that I, who have never treated men other than with kindness, justice and truth, swear that I will not take advantage of your period of repose to pursue or attack. Wherefore you may rest awhile in peace.'

Both armies then withdrew for the night.

San Kuo Chih Yen I

A SINGING DOG

A CERTAIN man possessed a dog which was bewitched. It squatted in the hall, beat time on the floor with its foot, and sang a song in most lugubrious tones. Then one morning its owner could not find his cap, and at last he discovered the dog sitting on the kitchen stove with the cap on its head. In that month great trouble overtook the dog's owner.

LU HSUN

THE SLEEPER

A NUMBER of students who lived together found one of their fellows fast asleep, and wishing to play a practical joke on him, they set out candles at the head and foot of his bed as if he were a corpse, and retired to wait the result. Presently the youth woke, and seeing the candles, said to himself : ' I am dead,' and lay down and really died. After a while the other boys returned, and finding their companion dead, removed the candles hastily, and in their terror agreed to say nothing of what had occurred.

What had happened was that the youth's soul having left his body while he was in a heavy sleep, and finding the candles round the bed when it returned, would not re-enter the body, but abandoned it for ever.

Chiang Hsing Tsa Lu

THE SNAKE

A MAN who was given to exaggeration, having seen a snake for he first time, described it to a friend as being at least a hundred feet wide and a thousand feet long. When the friend refused to believe him, he gradually reduced his estimate of its length until he came down to a hundred feet. Then, pulling himself up, he said : ' No, no, I'm wrong ; it couldn't have been so short, because then it would have been square.'

SNEEZING

A TEACHER at home for the holidays heard his wife sneeze. ' Somebody talking about me behind my back,' she remarked.

' I often sneeze when I'm away,' said her husband.

' That's because I'm thinking about you,' his wife replied sweetly.

When the teacher went back to his post down the river a few days later, he had not been long on the boat when one of the boatmen sneezed because the wind tickled his nose.

' This is too much ! ' exclaimed the teacher. ' It's not more than an hour since I said goodbye to my wife, and already she's thinking about a sailor.'

A SOPORIFIC

A FOSTER-MOTHER whose foster-child cried continually and would not sleep thought of a remedy. ' Father ! Father ! Bring me a book,' she called to her husband.

' What do you want a book for ? ' he shouted in reply, trying to make himself heard above the baby's howls.

' I want to see,' his wife answered in the same tone, ' if opening it and holding it up will have the same effect on the child as it always has on you.'

A SPEAKING LIKENESS

A YOUNG portrait-painter who could not find sitters complained to a friend. ' Hang portraits of yourself and your wife outside the gate as an advertisement,' counselled the friend.

Some days later this was done and it chanced that the first caller was the artist's father-in-law. ' Who is the girl in the picture outside your gate ? ' the visitor inquired when greetings were over. ' Why, Sir, that's your own daughter,' the young man cried. ' Then tell me,' said her father angrily, ' why you have dared to hang her portrait outside the gate side by side with that of a complete stranger.'

THE SPOTTED DOG

SOME monks who kept a spotted dog were building a commemorative pagoda. The dog used to follow the workmen about and carry bricks for the building. They came upon a stone statue of the Buddha in the foundations of an old monastery on the site. The right ear of the statue was missing when they found it, and the dog at once leapt down into the foundations and scratched till it found the missing ear. When the pagoda was finished the dog died.

YÜ T'I

THE STUDENT

A STUDENT took lodgings in a Buddhist monastery. On the day after his arrival he went out in the morning for a stroll and on returning in the afternoon he called the book-boy to bring his books. The boy brought an anthology. 'Too low,' said the student. *The History of the Han Dynasty* was next produced and laid on top of the other. 'Too low,' was his only comment. The *Historical Records* were then brought and added to the pile at his side, but still the student repeated: 'Too low!' Now a monk whose room was next door overhead the conversation between the student and his attendant, and each time he heard the student say: 'Too low,' when the lad announced the name of the book he had brought he was more astonished. At last his curiosity overcame him. He appeared at his neighbour's door. 'Sir,' said he, 'each of the books offered to you is regarded as containing material for a lifetime's study, why do you call them low ?'

'Oh,' said the student, 'I don't want them to read. I want to go to sleep and require a pile high enough to make me a pillow.'

A STUPID DOCTOR

A STUPID doctor married and had two children, a boy and a girl. His diagnoses were often at fault and his treatment of his patients fatal. He was threatened with legal proceedings by the parents of a little boy who had died under his care, and to avoid the consequences he gave them his son in place of their own. Before long he lost his little daughter in the same manner, and shortly afterwards, while he and his wife were still very depressed by the loss of their children, they were wakened one night by someone calling for the doctor. 'Who is it ?' the doctor cried apprehensively. 'Who is ill ?' 'It's my wife,' answered a voice from outside the door. 'Come quickly, she's dying.' 'There,' exclaimed the doctor to his wife in the voice of one whose worst fears are realized, 'I knew it! Someone must have seen you, my dear.'

SUBSTANCE AND SHADOW

YUAN CHING-MU once fainted with hunger on the road. A bandit named Hu-fu Ch'iu, seeing him in this condition, brought out a bowl of soup and fed him, and when the traveller had swallowed a few mouthfuls he recovered sufficiently to open his eyes.

'Who are you?' he asked, gazing at his deliverer.

'I am Hu-fu Ch'iu,' replied the bandit.

'What!' exclaimed Mr. Yuan. 'But you're a robber, aren't you? How is it you have given me food? My honour forbids me to accept your hospitality.'

Whereupon he knelt with his two hands upon the ground and retched. He was unable, however, to vomit what he had eaten, but coughed and choked so violently that he fell down flat and expired.

It is true that Hu-fu Ch'iu was a bandit, but his food had been honestly come by; so that to refuse to eat food because it is given by a robber, who only *may* have stolen it, is to lose both the substance and the shadow.

BALFOUR

THE SURGEON

A SOLDIER with an arrow in his leg sent for a famous surgeon to extract it. ' A simple matter,' said the great man nodding his head. Taking a knife from his bag, he cut off the shaft of the arrow level with the skin, replaced the knife and asked for his fee.

' But you have left the head of the arrow in the flesh,' cried the wounded man.

' A surgeon's functions are limited to externals,' replied the doctor severely, ' and as far as externals go there is no more to be done. The rest is internal, and belongs to the province of the physician, with which I may not interfere.'

SURGERY

3rd Century A.D.

SEEING that their leader would not retire, and the wound showed no sign of healing, the captains inquired far and near for a good surgeon to attend their general.

One day a person arrived in a small ship. He wore a square-cut cap and a loose robe, and in his hand he carried a small black bag. He said he had heard of the wound sustained by the famous hero and had come to heal it.

The general was engaged in a game of chess, for although his arm was very painful he kept up appearances so as not to discourage the men. The physician was introduced, and after the tea of ceremony, was shown the injured arm.

' I know how to cure this,' said the visitor, ' but I think you will be afraid of the remedy.'

' Death, after all, is but a return home,' answered the general, ' what do you propose to do ? '

' This,' replied the doctor, ' is what I shall do. In a private room I shall erect a post with a ring attached. I shall ask you to put your arm through the ring and I shall bind it firmly to the post. Then I

278

shall cover your head so that you cannot see, and with a scalpel cut down to the bone and scrape away the poison which has penetrated it.'

' It sounds simple enough,' smiled the general, ' but why the ring and the post ? '

Refreshments were then served and after a few cups of wine the warrior extended his arm for the operation, which the surgeon performed as he had explained. He found the bone very much discoloured, but he scraped it clean. ' *Hsi, hsi,*' went the knife over the surface, and all turned pale. But the general went on with his game, only drinking a cup of wine now and again, and his face betrayed no sign of pain. When the wound had been dressed and sewn up with a thread, the patient stood up smiling and said : ' The arm is now as good as ever it was ; there is no pain. Indeed, Master Leech, you are a marvel.'

San Kuo Chih Yen I

TAKING THE PLEDGE

LIU LING used to drive about in a deer-cart, carrying a bottle of wine. ' Bury me where I fall,' he would say to his attendants. To save him from his folly, his wife hid the wine and destroyed the bottles. ' This is no way to keep fit,' she admonished him, ' you must give it up.' ' You are quite right,' Liu answered, ' and I will make a vow before the gods to do so. But there must be wine and food for the offering and the libation.'

No sooner were these prepared than Liu, kneeling down, spoke thus : ' All my life, I, Liu Ling, have been a noted drinker. At a sitting I have consumed as much as a gallon, and less scarcely makes me drunk. The sage was right who said : " A man should not listen to the words of his wife." '

Thereupon he rose, poured the libation wine into a cup, and set himself down with the meat for the offering, and ate and drank till he was again completely overcome.

Chin Shu

THE TALKING DUCK

THE fame of Lu Kuei-meng's talents filled the whole empire, but he was a man of undignified character. He lived near the bank of a river, and one day a metropolitan official, passing that way, shot a mandarin duck on the bank. The owner reported the matter to Lu, who took a small boat and followed the official down river, taking with him a report on the affair which he himself had written. This he presented to the official, saying : 'So-and-so trained that duck so that it could talk, and meant to present it to the emperor. Why did you kill it ?'

When the official read the report he was greatly agitated and handed over a large sum of money in compensation. As he was leaving he asked : 'What could the duck really say ?'

Lu answered : 'After quite a number of years of teaching it had learned to call itself by saying, "Quack, quack."'

YÜ T'I

TALL STORIES

A SHANTUNG man had heard so much about the size and height of the bridge at Suchou that he determined, despite the distance, to go and see it for himself. When half-way there he met a man from Suchou on his way to Shantung to see the enormously long carrots which were said to be grown in that region. When the Shantung man said where he was going, the other replied : 'Why not save yourself the fatigue of the journey ? I can tell you all about the Suchou bridge. On the third of June last year a man fell off it, and on the third of June this year he had not yet hit the water. That will give you an idea of the height of it.'

'I am very much obliged to you for the information,' answered the Shantung man, 'and the least I can do in return is to save you going all the way to Shantung to see our carrots. I can promise you that if you go home and wait till this time next year you will find that their roots have reached Suchou.'

THE TEST

A MINOR military officer arrested a man for being out after dark without a lantern. ' I am a student, and I have been with a friend writing essays,' the man declared.

' Writing essays, is it ? ' said the officer gruffly, ' we'll soon see about that.'

' Well,' said the culprit, ' if you don't believe me, test me. Give me a title and I'll make you an essay.'

The officer thought a long time, but not an idea for an essay-title could he suggest. ' Get out,' he said at last, ' and think yourself lucky that there aren't any essay-subjects about to-night.'

THE THIRSTY DOG

A STONE-DEAF man was calling on a friend. When he knocked at the door the owner's dog stood in the street barking incessantly, but to the visitor inaudibly. At that moment rain began to fall heavily, and his friend opened the door. ' Your dog is suffering from thirst,' remarked the guest. ' Why don't you look after him better ? He has been standing outside the gate with his mouth open waiting for a drop of rain to quench his thirst.'

THE THREE SAGES

A CERTAIN student was conceited beyond measure. One day he said to some friends : ' Have you ever realized how rarely a sage appears ? First, there was P'an Ku, who created the world and all that's in it.' He crooked his first finger, to indicate that P'an Ku might be counted as the earliest sage. ' Then,' he went on, ' there was Confucius. In view of his contribution to literature and to ethics and government we may accept him as the world's second sage.' A second finger was bent to show his acceptance of Confucius. ' Except for these two,' he continued, ' there is no one for whom to crook a finger.' He sat for a while wrapped in thought. Then he nodded his head, and said : ' Don't you agree that sages are difficult to come by ? ' ' Of course,' he added, crooking a third finger, ' if you take me into account there are three.'

TURN AND TURN ABOUT

Two brothers who shared the produce of the same fields and were always quarrelling about the division of the harvest finally agreed to a suggestion made by the elder that they should take in turn the top of the crop one year and the bottom the next.

In the first year they sowed corn, and the elder brother took the grain and left the other to make what he could of the stalks, promising that the next year he should have all the tops. When spring came, the younger brother said : ' It is time to sow our corn, brother.'

Oh, no,' replied his elder brother, ' not corn ; we're planting roots this year.'

TIT FOR TAT

WHEN the Duke of Chin set out with an army against a neighbouring state, his son stood by, laughing heartily.

' Why do you laugh ? ' asked the Duke.

' I was laughing at something which happened to a neighbour.' The prince replied. ' He was taking his wife home to see her family, when a woman picking mulberry-leaves beside the road took his fancy, and he stopped to talk to her. Happening to look up, he discovered that his own wife was also being ogled by an admirer.'

The point of the story was not lost upon the Duke, who forthwith led his army home again, to find an invading force already across his frontier.

Lieh Tzu

THE TORTOISE

THE philosopher Chuang Tzu was fishing on the bank of a river when a messenger appeared with an invitation from the King of Ch'u offering him the post of prime minister. Without taking his eyes from the river, the philosopher replied : ' They say that the King has in his treasury the shell of a supernatural tortoise ; if the tortoise had been allowed to choose, would it have preferred to adorn a king's treasury or to continue to wag its tail in the mud of its native marsh ? ' ' It would have preferred to remain wagging its tail in the mud,' said the messenger. ' And I, too,' answered Chuang Tzu, ' prefer to live obscure but free. To be in office often costs a man his life and always costs his peace of mind. Go back to the King and say that I will continue to wag my tail in the mud.'

CHUANG TZU

★

It is unlucky to gamble after taking a bath.

Proverb

A TWITCHING FINGER

Two officials named Kung and Chia were chatting one day when the former's finger began to twitch. He held it up to Chia, saying : ' Whenever this happens I am offered some rare delicacy to eat.'

Next day the officials had an audience with the local duke, and as they entered the palace they chanced to see his cook cutting up a large turtle. Seeing them laughing over the incident, the duke inquired the reason for their amusement. But when the turtle was cooked, though Kung was bidden to remain, he was not offered any. He was so annoyed that he dipped his fingers into the dish, helped himself, and then left the palace. This made the duke so angry that he wanted to kill Kung, but Kung prevailed upon Chia to help him, and together they murdered the duke.

Tso Chuan

THE TWO GEESE AND THE TORTOISE

On the edge of a pond lived two geese who had made friends with a tortoise. When the heat of summer caused the pond to begin to dry up the geese took counsel together.

' Now that the pond is drying up our friend must be suffering,' they said, and spoke to the tortoise about it.

' When the pond is dry you will have no means of subsistence,' they told him. ' Take hold of this stick with your mouth and we will carry you to a place where water is plentiful.'

They set out at once, flying high over towns and villages with the tortoise between them. Their flight was observed by two little boys.

' Look at the two geese carrying a tortoise,' they cried in delight.

The tortoise, hearing the exclamation, was furious.

' What is that to you ? ' he opened his mouth to retort, but losing his hold on the stick, he fell to the earth and expired.

VENGEANCE

ONE morning a little boy of eleven named Ma, looking out of his bedroom window on the first floor just before dawn, saw the old gardener next door watering his pots of chrysanthemums on a raised terrace at the rear of his house. As he watched, another man, carrying two buckets on a pole, climbed the ladder and joined the gardener, offering to help him. The offer was refused, but the stranger persisted and would not be hurried off. Finally the gardener grew angry and gave him a push so that he missed his footing and fell down the ladder with the buckets on top of him. The horrified gardener hurried down, and the little boy watching knew from his face that

the man was dead. He saw him drag the corpse through the gate at the bottom of the garden and leave it, with the buckets, by the river-side ; and then, thinking that it was better to know nothing of such an affair, the boy hurried back into bed and went to sleep. He was wakened by an outcry, and before long the magistrate arrived upon the scene. No one confessing to a knowledge of the man or of how he came by his death, and no relatives appearing, the inquiry was soon closed with a verdict of accidental death.

About ten years later, young Ma, now a candidate for the examination for the first degree, was working at his books at dawn one morning, when, chancing to look out of his window, he saw coming slowly along the road the same man with the buckets who had died by falling from the terrace next door.

' It is his ghost returning to avenge itself on the gardener,' he thought. But the ghost passed the gardener's house and went on past Ma's front gate to a house on the other side owned by a wealthy family named Li. Thinking that he had better warn the neighbours, who had always been his good friends, Ma hurried downstairs, and was about to knock at their gate when one of the servants rushed out, almost knocking him down.

' Where are you going ? ' Ma inquired.

' To find the midwife,' replied the man.

' Did you see a man carrying two buckets come into your court-yard a few minutes ago ? ' Ma went on.

' The gate was shut, so no one could have gone in,' answered the man, turning as he heard his name called from the house.

' There is no need to fetch the midwife,' a woman-servant was saying, ' the mistress has just given birth to a fine boy.'

Then Ma realized that the ghost of the dead man had come to be reborn, and had taken up its abode in the newly-born child of the Li family, and he decided again that it would be better to say nothing, so, after offering congratulations, he returned home.

The baby grew into a fine, good-looking lad with a strong distaste for books and a great love of birds. One morning when he was ten, he was seen by Ma opening the door of his dovecot, while on the terrace of the house on the other side the old gardener was watering his chrysanthemums. Ma watched the doves circle round several times and then settle on the balustrade of the terrace, quite close to the gardener. He heard the boy call, and when the birds failed to return, he saw him pick up a small stone and fling it with all his strength in the direction of the terrace. But instead of hitting the birds, the stone struck the gardener on the temple just as he was beginning to descend the ladder and, losing his balance, he fell to the ground and was killed outright.

The small boy then went quietly indoors, and Ma, knowing that the ghost had now had its revenge and would cause no further trouble, decided for the third time in his life to know nothing and to say nothing.

VICARIOUS SACRIFICE

On the death of a certain philosopher his wife and secretary decided that since someone would have to be interred with him, the most suitable person would be his brother who was expected in time for the funeral.

' Your dead brother requires a companion on his journey to the underworld,' they therefore informed him on his arrival, ' and we must ask you to accompany him into the grave.'

' To sacrifice the living with the dead,' replied the brother, ' is contrary to the rites. But if you are sure that my brother should be attended, no one could be more suitable than his wife and secretary. If you think he can do without attendants I have nothing to say ; if not, then I fear you will both have to undertake the duty.'

From that time the custom fell into disuse.

THE VINE-TRELLIS

The magistrate's clerk came into court with his face all scratched.

' What has happened to your face ? ' his superior inquired.

' Why, Sir,' replied the clerk, ' I was enjoying the breeze last night beside the vine in my courtyard when a gust of wind blew the trellis down and it scratched me.'

The magistrate was sceptical. ' Those scratches look like the marks of finger-nails to me,' he returned. ' I should say without doubt you have been quarrelling with your wife and she has left her marks on you. Bring her along to me and I will arrange to relieve your feelings by ordering her a beating.'

At that moment angry sounds from the back of the court-room announced the arrival of the magistrate's lady. ' What's that about a beating ? Who's to be beaten ? ' she demanded as she came into view.

The magistrate rose. ' The court is adjourned,' he said hurriedly. ' Get out, all of you. Unless I am much mistaken my vine-trellis is going to fall too in a minute.'

THE VISIT

To the west of the Long White Mountains was the grave of a woman. One night a traveller riding that way alone suddenly came upon red walls and painted doors, within which halls and pavilions were grouped in splendid array. As he gazed with astonishment a servant came out and said : ' My mistress would be very pleased to see you, Sir.'

Dismounting in silence, the traveller entered the courtyard, where another servant waited to conduct him to the mistress of the house. When they reached the inner apartment the guest was given a seat on a couch, while his hostess stood near the door and exchanged remarks about the weather. In spite of a feeling that she was not human, the visitor was not conscious of fear or agitation. To decide the matter he presently asked a question about an event which had occurred three centuries earlier. The lady replied that she had been born about that time and gave him particulars of that and other matters. When the visitor rose to leave, the lady said : ' In ten years we shall meet again.' Looking bach from a little distance the traveller saw nothing but an old tomb, so thinking the whole affair, and particularly the lady's parting words, inauspicious, he sought purification from a Buddhist priest.

Ten years later he was telling his adventure to a friend when he remembered that the ten years were at an end. Greatly disturbed in mind, he went into the garden to seek distraction. He picked an apricot, and suddenly cried : ' The lady's message has come ; I must go at once ! ' Before he could bite the apricot he died.

CH'ANG I

A WASTED WISH

A CAT chased a rat into a jar, where it lay trembling while the cat crouched in wait. Suddenly the cat sneezed. ' Good luck and God bless you ! ' said the rat from inside. ' That won't wash ! ' replied the cat. ' Good wishes or no good wishes, I mean to eat you.'

WEDDING RICE

Now the origin of wedding rice was in this wise.

In the days of the Shang dynasty, some fifteen hundred years before Christ, there lived in the province of Shansi a famous sorcerer called Chao. One day a Mr. P'ang came to consult the oracle, and Chao, having divined by means of the tortoise diagrams, informed him that he had but six days to live.

In such a strait, it is not to be wondered at that P'ang should repair to another source to make sure that there was no mistake. To the fair Peachblossom, a young lady who had acquired some reputation as a sorceress, he unfolded the story of his woe. Her divination yielded the same result as Chao's ; in six days P'ang would·die, unless, by the exercise of her magical powers, she could avert the catastrophe. Her efforts were successful, and on the seventh day great was Chao's astonishment, and still greater his mortification and rage, when he met P'ang taking his evening stroll and learned that there lived a greater magician than he. The story would soon get about, and, unless he could put an end to his fair rival's existence, his reputation would be ruined.

He therefore sent a go-between to Peachblossom's parents who, believing the story that he had a son who was seeking a wife, were induced to engage Peachblossom to him in marriage. The marriage cards were duly interchanged, but the crafty Chao chose as the most unlucky he could select for the wedding, the day when the 'Golden Pheasant' was in the ascendant, knowing that as the bride entered the red chair the spirit-bird would destroy her with his powerful beak. But the wise Peachblossom knew all these things, and feared not.

'I will go,' she said, 'and I will fight and defeat him.'

When the wedding morning came, she gave directions to have rice thrown out at the door, which the spirit-bird seeing made haste to devour. While his attention was thus occupied, Peachblossom stepped into the bridal chair and passed on her way unharmed.

And now the ingenuous reader knows why he throws rice after the bride.

WHAT'S IN A NAME ?

A CERTAIN man owned a remarkably fine and intelligent cat which he called Tiger.

He was describing its beauties to some friends one day, when one of them objected to its name.

'A tiger,' he said, 'is fierce, I know, but a dragon is more wonderful ; change its name to Dragon.'

'The dragon may indeed be more remarkable than the tiger,' said another. 'But to mount to heaven, the dragon must ride upon the clouds, and thus clouds are more wonderful than dragons. Therefore, I think you should call your cat Cloud.'

'Clouds may cover the sky,' another broke in, 'but a gust of wind will scatter them. Clouds cannot oppose wind, and I would suggest Wind as a more suitable name.'

' However fiercely the wind may blow,' chimed in someone else, ' you can break it with a wall. So I think the cat should be called Wall.'

' Not at all,' said the last of the group, ' for a wall may be gnawed by a rat, which will make a hole right through it. I say let the cat be called Rat.'

' Well, well,' said the owner, ' since cats catch rats, I may as well call it plain Cat.'

THE WINE-CUP

A MAN who liked his wine in large quantities was invited by a mean man to a banquet. Observing at his entry that the wine-cups set out were of the smallest size obtainable the thirsty man burst into well-simulated tears.

' Whatever is the matter ? ' cried his host, in distress.

' Oh,' wailed the guest, ' I am reminded by the sight of these cups of the day my father died. There was nothing whatever the matter with him, but that day he too was invited by a friend to drink wine, and the cups they drank out of were exactly like these. In a moment of inadvertence my father swallowed both the wine and the cup, and choked to death. Ever since that day I have been unable to look at cups of this size without weeping.'

A WONDERFUL ESCAPE

THE (non-Chinese) people of the region south of the Yang-tzu river are extremely callous, and look upon children as marketable commodities. From the age of eight they may be sold by their parents or elder brothers ; in other cases children are stolen from their homes and sold as slaves. The Chinese magistrates, who themselves make a profit out of these transactions, take no action in the matter, and in consequence the population of the region steadily decreases, for very few escape being sold into slavery. This makes the escape of an eleven-year-old boy named Ch'u Chi all the more remarkable.

Chi was a herd-boy. One day while he was minding his ox he was seized by two bandits, gagged, and carried away some distance to be sold. Now Chi was a particularly sturdy boy, but he wept with pretended terror and the bandits thought him an easy prey. They set him down and began to drink. Soon they were intoxicated and one went off to arrange for the sale, while the other lay down on the ground to rest, placing his sword beside him. Chi waited till the bandit was asleep, and then cut his bonds by rubbing the ropes with all his strength up and down the sword. He then slew his sleeping captor and fled. He had not gone far before he met the second bandit returning. He was soon caught and questioned, and the bandit was about to kill him when Chi said : ' Who would not rather be slave to one gentleman than two ? That one was unkind to me. If you could bring yourself to spare me all would be well.'

The bandit reflected. ' After all,' he thought to himself, ' is it not better to sell this slave than to kill him ? And is it not better for me to sell him and take all the profit myself than to have had to share with the man he has killed ? Seeing that he has killed him, so much the better for me.' So he hid the corpse of his dead companion and went off with the boy to a house where he was once more firmly bound, and they lay down to sleep.

In the middle of the night Chi rolled over till he was able to reach the brazier, over which, in spite of the pain of burnt hands, he held his bonds till they parted. Then, as before, he killed his sleeping guard and made such an outcry that the whole neighbourhood was roused. He told his story, demanding that report be made to the magistrate. In due course the case was brought to the notice of the governor of the province, who was so struck by the courage and resource of Chi that he offered him a position in his household, and when this was declined, he loaded the boy with presents of clothes and sent an escort to see him safely back to his village, where those who made a trade of abduction did not dare to pass his door, ' For,' said they, ' if a child of that age can unaided slay two grown men, it is better to keep at a safe distance.'

*

PROVERBS

A desirable neighbourhood is one where good manners are the rule ; only a fool will choose to live anywhere else.

Ill-grown trees do not fear the axe, nor diseased pigs the sacrificial knife.

When the melon is ripe it falls of itself.

Without wind the grass does not move.

If the tree is large the shade is large.

There is no fence that the wind cannot penetrate.

The grub in the cabbage dies in the cabbage.

One tree doesn't make a forest.

The trees won't sway if the wind doesn't blow.

The bird chooses the tree, not the tree the bird.

A wise man adapts himself to circumstances, as water shapes itself to the vessel that contains it.

The greedy man becomes a merchant, the lazy man a priest.

FLOWERS AND GARDENS

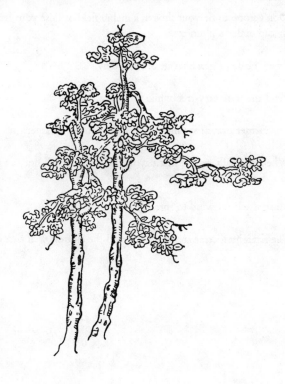

PROVERBS

Don't stoop to tie your shoe in a melon field or raise your hand to your cap under a plum tree.

*

Every blade of grass has its drop of dew.

*

Bend the mulberry-tree while it is still small.

*

The farmer prays for rain, the traveller for fair weather.

*

When rain falls on the first day of the moon it will not last more than a day.

*

Musk needs no wind to spread it.

*

The straightest trees are first felled and the clearest well first dried up.

IKEBANA

THE ART OF FLOWER-ARRANGEMENT

W<small>HEN</small> flowers are scarce one can derive much pleasure from experimenting in the Japanese cult of flower-arrangement. Although this art is believed to have been learned in China and carried to Japan by students of Chinese culture, it has not survived in the country of its supposed origin. In China pot-plants are generally preferred for decorative purposes, and the Chinese market-gardener is a past-master in the art of growing these. But cut flowers in a vase are apt, in China, to look very much as they do in many French homes, like a Victorian posy.

In Japan, however, the arranging of flowers has developed into a cult, and many schools of thought exist, in each of which certain definite principles of arrangement are followed. The word ' flower ' is used in a broad sense, to cover not only flowering plants, but also blossoming, and even flowerless, trees and shrubs. The fundamental principle underlying all the schools seems to be the same : whether the material for an arrangement consists of several flowers, a single branch of a flowering shrub, or a handful of grasses, it should be so disposed in the container that it symbolizes Heaven, Earth and Man.

The Dragon Book

In the case of a plant or miniature tree, the main stem represents Heaven, a short branch growing (or bent) outwards and upwards on one side of the main stem signifies Man, while a third still lower and shorter branch on the opposite side denotes Earth. The same effect may be achieved by using a small branch of a tree or shrub, or again with flowers, leaves or grasses. The drawing in Fig. 1 shows the Heaven, Earth and Man arrangement in its elementary form.

Unusual flowers and shrubs, and winter branches with or without berries, which do not look well in our ordinary wide-mouthed vases, can be made to yield artistic and decorative effects in narrow-necked vessels by a free use of scissors to remove superfluous twigs or by bending the stems into the curves required by the Heaven, Earth and Man arrangement; and many modifications of the fundamental principle will be suggested by the materials and by the background against which the arrangement is to be shown. Even a trained Japanese lady could not have excelled the effect, in its particular surroundings, of an arrangement seen in a London suburban house, consisting of a leafless branch of wild-rose, rich in scarlet berries, set in a rough grey-blue Chinese ginger-jar.

Modern pottery vases are often well-adapted to Japanese flower-arrangement, or *ikebana*. It is possible too, to buy quite reasonably at the big stores the square, oblong, and oddly-shaped shallow Japanese dishes in subdued brown, green, or grey pottery which so delight the eye and which are used for those arrangements in which it is intended to suggest a tiny garden with water-plants growing in a stream.

Fig. 1

One of these dishes, or a substitute in earthenware from the kitchen, a few upright vases of modern pottery, and a lead-based flower-holder with easily-bent wires curled into rings at the top, are all the equipment needed to make experiments in *ikebana*. Pebbles and stones to hide the holder in the water-garden arrangements may be collected on walks or from the beach during holidays. A handful of tiny white pebbles will hide the holder of a group of grasses, or a rough stone some four inches square may be set against the stalks of an ' island ' of iris.

The suggestions for modified *ikebana* given below include only two of its simplest forms—the ' water-garden ' style, in flat, shallow containers, with (*a*) formal groups of suitable flowers, or (*b*) vertical or horizontal branches, as illustrated by Fig. II, and the ' vertical ' style, which requires a slender or a deep vase for upright arrangements of the kind suggested by Fig. I.

Fig. II

MATERIALS FOR JAPANESE FLOWER ARRANGEMENTS

THE discovery of a plant or a branch suitable for an *ikebana* arrangement makes a pleasant object for a country walk. It adds to the enjoyment of the garden or the park to try to discover, without picking, growths which conform to, or are modifications of, the fundamental principle. Such arrangements need not be always upright : a branch of cherry-blossom or azalea hanging horizontally may be just as good an example as one whose direction is vertical. Nor need there be an air of scantiness about a group. Bushy flowers may be used, though it is generally better to keep to normal arrangements for English flowers such as roses, delphiniums, and others which can be easily and beautifully grouped in ways to which we are accustomed, experimenting with unusual materials and those which are difficult to dispose well.

All sorts of unexpected discoveries will be made. Wild parsley often grows into excellent examples of the Heaven, Earth and Man arrangement ; a yew-tree in fruit may yield either a Male-style branch, in which the Man-twig curves upwards and outwards on the right of the main stem with the Earth-twig on the left, or a Female branch in which the secondary and tertiary twigs grow the other way. Held fast in the end of a spring clothes-peg dropped upright into a pottery vase of suitable size, this will strike an unusual note if carefully placed, and if you are not too superstitious to use it. The yew is reputed to be the longest-lived of all trees, and might well share the popularity of the pine-tree as a symbol of long life.

The Orchis family is one which lends itself both to a naturalistic style of *ikebana* and to variations of more severe or ' classical ' styles. Whether arranged in a holder hidden among stones at one end of a long black or grey dish, and balanced by a small stone at the other end in the former style, or, in the latter, set at an angle in an upright holder with the leaves bent suitably, a fly-orchis or early purple orchis with spotted leaves can be very decorative. A feature of wild-flower arrangements which commends itself is that only a single branch or a very few flowers are required, nor is it ever necessary to pull up plants by the roots.

Though in the East flower-arrangement is essentially a feminine art, it is believed to have been first practised in Japan by priests in their temples, and the clean, strong lines and absence of ' fussiness ' of many *ikebana* compositions suggest the hand of man.

SUGGESTIONS FOR MODIFIED JAPANESE FLOWER ARRANGEMENTS

I. ' WATER-GARDEN ' STYLE

A ' WATER-GARDEN ' arrangement, as has already been said, may be either a group composition, or a line composition as illustrated by Fig. II, the same receptacle being used for both. A large, shallow dish about two inches deep and preferably oval or oblong, and one or more glass or wire flower-holders are all the essentials.

Fill the bowl with water, and set the holder at one end. Avoid a group in the middle of this type of receptacle, as the desired aesthetic balance is best achieved by setting a larger group at one end and a smaller one at a distance from it.

A number of suggestions are given below for this arrangement, which can be varied, within limits, to suit individual taste, but which should always conform to the principle that every group is a complete unit, a triangle the extreme points of which are indicated by the ends of the primary, secondary and tertiary branches.

The Dragon Book

(a). *Group Compositions in Shallow Containers*

1. King-cups or marsh-marigolds and common rushes, with lily-pads or other leaves to disguise the holders. A rust-coloured stone at a distance from the main group to give balance. A black or greenish dish is effective for this arrangement.

2. Grasses, flowering or otherwise, with some of the leaves bent sharply downwards. Two groups, in the smaller of which no flowering stalks are used. Relative height of the two elements must be considered and the 'triangle principle' kept in mind.

The Japanese use a flower-holder which looks like a flat wooden pin-cushion with the points of the pins all turned upwards, on which they impale stems individually in an arrangement of this kind. There used to be a pricker used by pastrycooks in making holes in shortbread which would serve admirably.

3. Narcissi or daffodils, the holders masked by stones. A larger group arranged realistically at one end and at the opposite corner of the dish a single flower, with its leaves curving sharply over and beyond the edge of the dish, which is effective in modern white pottery.

4. Orchis, as described above.

5. Arum lilies. Three of these cut to correspond in height with the three-fold Heaven, Earth and Man lengths, and arranged with a sparing accompaniment of leaves, standing erect in a round, black bowl several inches deep and about twelve inches in diameter. Such a composition as this should not be much higher than the width of the container or it will look 'leggy.' Stones hide the holder.

6. Iris, the flowers used sparingly, with a preponderance of leaves, and, if more than one colour is introduced, dark flowers below lighter

ones. A single flower can be effective, particularly if ' balanced ' by a water-lily bud, or even a lily-pad. An oval white or grey pottery dish is preferable to a green one for this.

7. Water-lily, with a bud as balancing feature, and rushes arranged stiffly to give height. The choice of colour for the receptacle depends on the colour of the flower.

(b). *Line Compositions in Shallow Containers*

Ikebana depending on linear arrangement need not necessarily be limited to three stems or branches. Secondary and tertiary branches are often multiplied, and even the primary element is sometimes a group of three. Care should be taken to keep the numbers odd, however. Nine is a favourite number, three for each of the main branches. In these experiments it is not necessary to adhere to fixed rules regarding the number of twigs, etc., but it must always be remembered that we are working to an imaginary triangle which should enclose the whole composition.

Apart from the vertical arrangements such as have been suggested above under ' Group Compositions,' many beautiful effects can be obtained by using the same dishes and holders for flowering sprays and branches of shrubs and trees. Small pine, willow, or maple branches, twigs of larch with flowers and a cone or two, catkins, and flowering shrubs will all yield material for these groups.

1. Small branches of azalea of golden or apricot shade cut from the taller varieties, arranged in a shallow black pottery dish with smooth white pebbles heaped over the holder.

2. A single branch of rhododendron about eighteen inches or two feet high, with or without flowers. Trim and bend so that the three elements are clearly marked, the primary line rising in a bow-like curve, the secondary bending upward and outward to one side, and the tertiary jutting out horizontally or drooping downwards a little to the other. In this case there should be no superfluous twigs, as the foliage is plentiful. A suitable receptacle is a vessel with a shallow

edge and a deep hole in the centre in which the holder can be firmly wedged to prevent it being overturned by the weight of the branch. Such vases are often seen in coloured glass, and sometimes in art pottery. The colour of the vessel must depend on the shade of the flowers.

3. Japonica. A difficult but intriguing subject, which, though apt to look straggly may, by judicious persuasion, be disposed in striking lines along the length of a greyish oval or rectangular dish. Three stems may be needed in order to produce the basic triangular effect.

4. Syringa in flower is beautiful and easy to arrange. It is often possible to find a single branch with curving medial stem, and two or four other stems growing out from it in the desired directions. Set in a vessel such as that described for rhododendron, it forms a delightful flower-study.

5. It is unnecessary to do more than mention flowering shrubs as a class. They are well adapted to arrangements similar to the one suggested for azaleas.

II. VERTICAL GROUPS IN SLENDER VASES

A number of flowers and shrubs already mentioned as suitable for other styles of composition lend themselves also to this arrangement. Irises, lilies and some of the shrubs may be utilized for both.

Among wild flowers the taller and stronger varieties such as sea-lavender, foxgloves, mallows and many others may be used either alone or with flowers of a shorter variety to add breadth to the composition or for colour contrast.

1. A spray or two of sea-holly may be effectively arranged in a pewter pot with a wide base and a narrower neck, though some difficulty may be experienced in finding specimens which branch at the correct angles. This problem can be solved by wedging twigs into the mouth of the pot criss-cross fashion, or by the use of a flower-displayer of pliable copper wire twisted into rings.

2. The natural curves of wall-flower stems as well as the lovely colours of the flowers make them a good subject for this type of arrangement. A pottery vase suggestive of a boat, or a glass one of basket shape, or a rose-bowl in which a wire holder may be hidden, form admirable containers for them, and three groups of flowers carefully graded in height make an interesting modification of the primary arrangement. Care should be taken not to make this group too ' bunchy.'

3. Pussy-willows and yellow jonquils. Two or three twigs of pussy-willow for the primary line, four or five for the secondary and a group of three yellow jonquils with leaf spikes dropping gracefully for the earth-line make an effective variation of the spring theme. A narrow-necked vase of greyish-green sets off the silver of the pussy-willows.

4. Single twigs or sprays of flowering shrubs such as almond or apricot, even if carefully curved to the desired form, make a narrow and over-classical group by themselves. Width may be given by making the earth-line of pheasant-eye narcissi and leaves, as in 3.

5. The kind of barberry often seen in suburban gardens—*Berberis aquifolium*, I think—yields some interesting results if the branches are carefully trimmed into shape. The vivid colouring of its tiny flowers and glossy leaves make it an excellent subject for experiment. A straight slender vase in heavy ware of a warm brown colour is an appropriate receptacle.

*

Experiments such as are suggested, though only touching the fringe of the complex art of flower-arrangement as practised in Japan, nevertheless provide new and interesting studies in home decoration, *ikebana* being well adapted, because of the simplicity of its lines and its atmosphere of restraint, to modern interiors.

A few general rules with regard to experiments in *ikebana* may be helpful.

1. Even numbers of flowers or twigs are regarded as unlucky, and should be avoided.

2. Avoid anything approaching symmetry.

3. Bend carefully with the fingers or trim with the scissors in order to achieve the shape desired.

4. Before you begin to design a composition make up your mind what you wish it to look like when finished.

5. Metal vessels—copper, brass, bronze, or the new coloured aluminium—do excellently to hold branches, but unless they are of appropriate shape they are better left empty.

6. Pegs, both the old-fashioned and spring varieties, assist enormously in holding branches in position. With a small saw they can be shortened if necessary to allow them to be wedged into the neck of a vase, one or more twigs being held firmly in the peg.

ON THE CARE OF FLOWERS

THE problem of keeping flowers fresh is one which exercises the minds of many housewives. The battle is half won if the blooms are picked either in the early morning or in the evening, when the sun is not on them. All cut flowers, whether picked from the garden or bought, should be placed in a large vessel of cold water in a darkened room and allowed to stand for an hour or two before being arranged in vases. A sheet of paper wrapped lightly round them and pinned serves to exclude light but not air, and gives support to any weak ones which show signs of drooping.

Certain varieties of flowers may be revived, or have their life lengthened by giving them special treatment before they are set aside in the dark.

1. Branches of blossoming trees and shrubs.

Woody stems should be broken, not cut. Split or crush the ends of the stems and dip in boiling water for a few minutes, then stand in cold water for two hours. This treatment will be found satisfactory for apple, cherry, peach, almond and plum-blossom.

2. Singeing the ends of their stems is good for dahlias, chrysanthemums and roses. Be careful to hold the flowers at right angles to the flame so that the heat does not reach the blossoms. The stem of a drooping flower should be recut under water before singeing.

3. Tulips, forget-me-nots, primroses, iris and lily-of-the-valley should all be dipped for a minute or two in boiling water before being set aside to stand in cold water for one or two hours. Roses and chrysanthemums may be treated in this way instead of being singed.

4. Some flowers like freesia, gladioli, hyacinths, larkspurs and sweet-peas respond to treatment if allowed to stand in a limited quantity of water containing a few drops of methylated spirit. One to two hours is generally long enough for this treatment.

CHINESE GARDENS

CHINESE Gardeners use many sorts of scenes, which they employ as circumstances vary ; all which they range in three separate classes ; and distinguish them by the appellations of the pleasing, the terrible, and the surprising.

The first of these are composed of the gayest and most perfect productions of the vegetable world ; intermixed with rivers, lakes, cascades, fountains, and water-works of all sorts : being combined and disposed in all the picturesque forms that art or nature can suggest. Buildings, sculptures and paintings are added, to give splendour and variety ; and the rarest productions of the animal creation are collected, to enliven them. . . .

Their scenes of terror are composed of gloomy woods, deep valleys inaccessible to the sun, impending barren rocks, dark caverns, and impetuous cataracts rushing down the mountains from all parts. The trees are . . . forced out of their natural directions and seemingly torn to pieces by the violence of tempests ; some are thrown down, and intercept the course of the torrents ; the buildings are in ruins . . . and in the most dismal recesses of the woods . . . are temples dedicated to the king of vengeance, deep caverns in the rocks, and descents to gloomy subterraneous habitations, overgrown with brushwood and brambles. . . .

Their surprising, or supernatural scenes, are of the romantic kind, and abound in the marvellous ; being calculated to excite in the mind of the spectator quick successions of opposite and violent sensations. Sometimes the passenger is hurried by steep, descending paths to subterraneous vaults, divided into stately apartments, where lamps, which yield a faint and glimmering light, discover the pale images of ancient kings and heroes, reclining on beds of state . . . flutes, and soft harmonious organs, impelled by subterraneous waters, interrupt, at stated intervals, the silence of the place, and fill the air with solemn sacred music.

CHAMBERS

Flowers and Gardens

FLOWERS

THE Chinese Gardeners do not scatter their flowers indiscriminately about their borders . . . but dispose them with great circumspection ; and, if I may be allowed the expression, paint their way very artfully along the skirts of the plantations or other places, where flowers are to be introduced. They reject all that are of a straggling growth ; of harsh colour and poor foliage ; choosing only such as are of some duration, grow either large or in clusters, are of beautiful forms, well-leaved, and of tints that harmonize with the greens that surround them. They avoid all sudden transitions, both with regard to dimension and colour ; rising gradually from the smallest flowers to holly-oaks, peonies, sun-flowers, carnation-poppies, and others of the boldest growth ; and varying their tints by easy gradations, from white, straw-colour, purple and incarnate, to the deepest blues, and most brilliant crimsons and scarlets. They frequently blend several roots together, whose leaves and flowers unite, and compose one rich harmonious mass ; such as the white and purple candituff, larkspurs, and mallows of various colours, double poppies, loopins, primroses, pinks and carnations ; with many more of which the forms and colours accord with each other ; and the same method they use with flowering shrubs ; blending white, red and variegated roses together, purple and white lilacks ; yellow and white jessamine ; altheas of various sorts ; and as many others as they can with any propriety unite. . . . By these mixtures they encrease considerably the variety and beauty of their compositions.

In their large plantations, the flowers generally grow in the natural ground : but in flower-gardens, and all other parts that are highly kept, they are in pots, buried in the ground ; which, as fast as the bloom goes off, are removed, and others are brought to supply their places ; so that there is a constant succession, for almost every month in the year ; and the flowers are never seen, but in the height of their beauty.

Ibid.

A PEKING GARDEN

AROUND the villa . . . was an inclosure of at least twelve acres. It contained a garden laid out in serpentine walks, a rivulet winding round an island, a grove of various trees interspersed with patches of grass ground, and diversified with artificial inequalities, and rocks rudely heaped upon each other. The buildings in this place consisted of several separate pavilions, erected round small courts. The apartments were handsome, and not ill contrived. Several of them were adorned with landscapes, painted in water-colours. The objects appeared to be correctly drawn ; nor were the rules of perspective unattended to ; but what instantly showed them to be the works of Chinese artists, was the total neglect of light and shade. A lake was represented, with trees and houses near it, almost on every side ; but a Chinese would consider it a blemish, to render the shadow of any of these objects perceptible on the water.

CHAMBERS

THE PLEASURE GROUNDS AT JEHOL

ONLY a part of the great pleasure-grounds of the palace at Jehol are open to men, the remainder being reserved for the use of the female part of the Imperial family. . . . They rode through a verdant valley, in which several trees, particularly willows of an uncommonly large girth, were interspersed, and between which the grass was suffered to attain its most luxuriant height, with little interruption from cattle or the mower. Arriving at the shores of an extensive lake of an irregular form, they sailed upon it till the yachts, in which they had embarked, were interrupted by a bridge thrown over the lake in the narrowest part ; and beyond which it seemed to lose itself in distance and obscurity. The surface of the water was partly covered with the *lien-wha* (lotus) which adorned the lake with its spreading leaves and fragrant flowers.

. . . The grounds included the utmost inequality of surface ; some bearing the hardy oaks of northern hills, and others the tender plants of southern vallies. Where a wide plain happened to occur, massy rocks were heaped together to diversify the scene and the whole seemed calculated to exhibit the pleasing variety and striking contrast of the ruggedness of wild, and the softness of cultivated, nature.

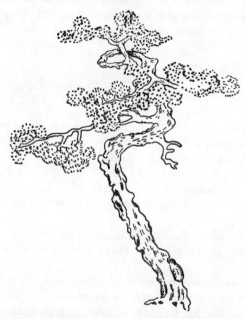

The gardens were enlivened by the movements, as well as sounds, of different kinds of herbiverous animals, both quadrupeds and birds; but no menagerie of wild beasts was perceived. Some monstrous varieties of gold and silver fishes were seen playing in ponds of pellucid water, upon a bottom studded with pebbles of agate, jasper and other precious stones.

Throughout these grounds they met no gravel walks; no trees planted in belts nor collected in clumps. Everything seemed to be avoided which betrayed a regularity of design. Nothing was observed to be directed, unless for very short distances, by straight ines, or to turn at right angles. Natural objects seemed scattered round by accident, in such a manner as to render their position pleasing ; while many of the works of human labour, though answering every purpose of convenience, were made to appear the produce of rustic hands, without the assistance of a tool.

STAUNTON

*

PROVERBS

Prisons are shut, day and night, and yet they are always full ; temples are open day and night, and they are always empty.

Would you understand the character of the prince, examine his ministers ; would you know the disposition of any man, look at his companions ; would you know that of a father, look at his son.

Though a tree be a thousand feet high, its leaves must fall and return to its root.

If you are afraid of leaving tracks, do not walk in snow.

Borrowed money makes time short ; working for others makes it long.

Great wealth comes by destiny ; moderate wealth by industry.

If there is a cart in front there is a rut behind.

When the boat is in the middle of the river it is too late to mend the leak.

If two men keep a horse it gets thin ; if two families own a boat it leaks.

When the river is crossed the boat-pole is finished with.

With money you can get the devil to turn the mill.

When you enter a house find out what words are tabooed there.

One day's frost won't give you three feet of ice.

The best swimmer may be drowned or the best rider thrown.

Flowers and Gardens

Weave your grass-coat before the rain comes and dig your well before you are thirsty.

' I have heard ' is not as good as ' I have seen.'

Do not ascend the hills and catch birds in a net ; do not go down to the river and poison the fish ; do not kill the ox that ploughs ; do not throw away paper with writing on it.

A cloudy day . . . leisure to beat the children.

Good men don't become soldiers ; good iron isn't made into nails.

It's no good stopping your ears when you steal a bell.

Don't look at a thief while he is eating, look at him while he is undergoing punishment.

When the fire breaks out the thieves steal forth.

Even the best needles are not sharp at both ends.

He who wants his pig to grow must be diligent in washing the trough ; he who wants his child to grow must be diligent in shaving its head.

The pestle produces white rice ; the rod makes good children.

He who dons a rush coat to go and put out a fire will only bring trouble on himself.

When you throw stones at the rat beware of hitting the vase.

The wise forget old injuries.

The first come is prince, the last is minister.

Walls have ears, and there is sure to be someone outside the window.

Rather patch clothes as a poor man's wife than be a rich man's concubine.

MEDICAL LORE

PROVERBS

If the slave-girl is very cheap she probably has the leprosy.

*

Old age and a withered flower no medicine can remedy.

*

When disease enters the marrow no drug can avail.

*

Illness enters by the mouth and great evils come out of it.

*

The tongue, which is yielding, endures ; the teeth, which are stubborn, decay.

*

The blind have the best ears and the deaf the sharpest eyes.

*

An ignorant doctor is no better than a murderer.

MEDICAL SKILL

Dᴏᴄᴛᴏʀ Hsü was a physician of almost supernatural skill. ' Why don't you write a book ? ' he was asked, ' so that your knowledge may be passed on for the benefit of posterity ? '

' Medical skill is a matter of intelligence,' the doctor replied, ' and depends partly on a man's power of concentrated thought, and partly on his skill in feeling the pulse. The pulse, as the ancients knew, may be of many different types difficult to distinguish, and each indicates a different disease. Facility in these two matters cannot be taught. When the nature of the pulse is skilfully distinguished, then the disease can be diagnosed, and treatment can be given with the proper drug, on which alone recovery depends.'

' The way in which medical men go on in these days,' continued the doctor after a pause, ' failing to diagnose correctly by the pulse, and treating a disease with a whole collection of ameliorating drugs instead of the one appropriate one, is just like a hunter who, having not the slightest idea where the hare is, wastes endless men and horses over a large area, in the vague hope that one or other of them may meet it and be lucky enough to catch it.'

T'ai P'ing Kuang Chi

*

At the first glass the man drinks the wine ; at the second glass the wine drinks the wine ; at the third glass the wine drinks the man.

The mouth is the door of misfortune.

Proverbs

317

ANTIDOTES

THE *Book of Medicine* says : 'A tiger shot by a poisoned arrow eats mud ; a wild boar rootles about for harebell or kikio-root ; a pheasant wounded by a hawk seeks the leaves of the *ti-huang* plant. Chang Ao tried giving powdered *yü*-stone to rats, and found that they became unconscious of the presence of man, yet they could be completely restored in a few minutes by a drink of medicine compounded from jelly-fish.

Birds, beasts and even insects know the antidotes for things which are poisonous to them ; how much more should man ? A silkworm sting may be cured by an application of powdered snake ; the bite of a horse by rubbing it with the ashes of a burnt whip-holder. . . . In short, to be effective, an antidote must correspond to that which has caused the injury.

T'ai P'ing Kuang Chi

AN ANTIDOTE FOR POISONS IN GENERAL

IF a person believed to have taken poison is feeling acute discomfort, try the following experiment : Fill the patient's mouth with yellow beans. If there is no offensive smell he is really poisoned, and should immediately be given an emetic consisting of a pint of water in which hemp has been boiled. This will induce vomiting and promote recovery.

BITTER-ROOT POISONING

TAKE two or three eggs from the nest of a brooding hen. Mix with sesamum oil. Force the patient to swallow the mixture, or alternatively, give a drink of onion-juice.

*

An inconstant man will never make a wizard or a doctor.

Proverb

BLISTERS

To cure a blister caused by walking, cover the part with a paste made from flour and water and leave on all night.

CHICKEN WITH FOXGLOVE

A GOOD cure for pains in the back is chicken with foxglove.

Half a pound of foxgloves, five ounces of sugar, and one black chicken are the ingredients required. Pluck the chicken and draw it in the usual way ; cut up the foxgloves and stuff the bird with them and the sugar. Stew in a bronze vessel and eat with rice. Neither salt nor vinegar should accompany this dish, and only the flesh should be eaten.

Yin Shan Cheng Yao

CHINESE DENTISTRY

TOOTH extraction as described by the Chinese themselves is somewhat as follows :

' A medicine is made from horses' perspiration and is rubbed on the gum over the tooth. The patient is then asked to cough and the tooth tumbles out.'

Several other recipes are known for making medicines to extract teeth without pain and they all end by promising that the tooth will come out after a cough or sneeze. The simplest, and what is said to be the most efficacious medicine is made as follows :

A certain kind of fish is killed and its abdomen filled with white arsenic ; it is then hung up for some days till a white mould appears on the surface. Some of this mould is put on a piece of cotton and pressed into the cavity of the tooth, or some of it may be rubbed on the gum.

A CURE FOR TOOTHACHE

TAKE one black plum, 7 ounces of raw sweet liquorice-root, and 5 small pieces of ice. Pound and form into pills. Hold one in the mouth until it dissolves then spit it out. Repeat till cured.

DOG-BITE

IF a person is bitten by a mad dog apply a plaster made of flour and human excrement, and cover with a piece of the white bark of the locust tree. Cauterize with moxa in the fourteen appropriate places. When the heat penetrates the patient will sweat and will soon recover.

DREAMS

BAD dreams may be prevented by placing large lumps of cinnabar on the head when going to bed.

DROWNING

A PERSON rescued from drowning should be laid across the back of a buffalo or a person bent double, and gently moved about, his mouth being kept open with a chop-stick to allow the water to run out.

Administer raw ginger, and apply a pad of hot salt wrapped in a cloth. Cover the patient warmly and leave him to sleep quietly.

DRUNKENNESS

IF a drunk person falls into a coma so deep that he appears to be dying draw water from the well and wet his head thoroughly. Old cloths wrung out in very cold water should be laid over the diaphragm and re-wetted from time to time until the patient regains consciousness.

*

The best cure for drunkenness is to look at a drunken man.

ELIXIR OF LIFE

THE elixir of life can be prepared by mixing peach-tree gum with cinnabar and the powdered ash of mulberry wood.

DENNYS

EPIDEMICS

IF a really serious epidemic is prevalent, it is a good thing to throw a handful of black beans into the water-jar every morning. A large handful should also be thrown into the well at the fifth watch. If this is done unseen, no one who uses the well will be infected by the disease.

If it is necessary to visit an infected house the nostrils should first be stopped with a paste of aromatic oil and flowers of sulphur. On leaving, sneeze it out and drink a bowl of sulphur-wine.

FITS

To cure a person lying in a fit take a large head of garlic and a quantity of warm yellow dust from the road. Pound and mix together till soft, add fresh well-water, and strain. The sufferer must be induced to swallow the draught, his teeth being forced open if necessary.

FREEZING

IF a person is found freezing to death, or has fallen into icy water, he may be saved so long as there seems to be any warmth in his chest.

Quickly remove his wet clothes and wrap him in under-garments taken straight from the body of a healthy person among the by-standers. On no account must the patient be placed near a fire, but it is a good thing to lay on the pit of his stomach a cloth containing hot ashes, which should be changed as often as necessary. As soon as he opens his eyes he should be forced to swallow warmed wine with ginger in it.

Medical Lore

EXORCISING FRIGHT

When a child has been badly frightened a bowl of rice covered with a cloth is rubbed over its face and head, while the mother cries : ' If the left ear have fright, at the left ear go out ; if the right ear have fright, at the right ear go out ; and enter the bowl of rice.'

Morrison

FAITH-HEALING

A certain doctor who was deservedly famous for curing nervous complaints invariably prescribed the same method—sleeping on a dead man's pillow. The pillows, which were of wood, were taken from decaying coffins in broken-down tombs, and the faith of the patients in the efficacy of this remedy was such that they never failed to recover.

T'ai P'ing Kuang Chi

HEALTH

In the house of the body the heart is the husband and the lungs the wife ; if there is not harmony between husband and wife the whole house is soon in disorder.

HOW TO KEEP YOUNG

On the seventh day of the seventh month pick seven ounces of lotus flowers ; on the eighth day of the eighth month gather eight ounces of lotus-root ; on the ninth day of the ninth month collect nine ounces of lotus-seeds. Dry in the shade and eat the mixture and you will never grow old.

Yin Shan Cheng Yao

*

It is not the wine that makes a man drunk but the man himself.

Proverb

INSECTS IN THE EAR

IF an insect gets into the ear do not disturb it. If it is in the left ear, press the right hand tightly over the right ear and hold the nose firmly with the other hand. Keeping the mouth closed, force the breath in the direction of the left ear, when the insect will come out of itself.

KEEPING FIT

A FAMOUS Chinese doctor of olden days was once asked the best way of keeping fit and preserving health. Here is his recipe :

Man requires exercise to aid the process of digestion and cause the blood to circulate freely. If he took enough exercise, sickness would be unknown. The pivot of a door never becomes rotten and running water is never foul for the simple reason that they are always moving. If I were sick I should cure myself by leaping and dancing about like the birds and beasts.

THE MAGIC PILLOW

TAKE a piece of cedar wood cut on the fifth day of the fifth month or the seventh day of the seventh month and hollow it out to make a pillow. The log should be one foot two inches long and four inches high, and its capacity should be one and one-fifth pecks. Keep a piece of the inside wood two inches thick to make a stopper for the open end, and bore in it one hundred and forty-seven holes the size of a grain of rice, arranging them in three rows of forty-nine holes each. Then insert into the pillow one ounce of each of the twenty-four beneficial and eight poisonous drugs. Among the former are :

cassia, peony, ginseng, dry ginger, magnolia, broomrape, angelica, plumeless thistle, kikio root, Chinese pepper, Job's tears, Japanese pepper, and japonica ;

while the eight poisonous drugs include :

aconite root, aconite seeds, *penellia tuberifera*, slough grass, and cockscomb.

When the pillow is full, close the stopper and cover with a pillow-case. After using the pillow for a hundred days the face will become glossy and smooth ; in a year all the ills of the body will be cured and it will become fragrant ; in four years colour will be restored to the hair, the teeth will be renewed, and sight and hearing will become perfect again.

Yin Shan Cheng Yao

MANIPULATIVE SURGERY

IF a man's ribs were displaced by any accident, the sufferer was made to rest his feet upon two piles of thin bricks. He then laid hold of two loops suspended from a cross-bar resting upon two crutches about the height of goal-posts. The surgeon stood behind, and by means of a belt, shifted the patient backwards and forwards as he thought fit, while an attendant withdrew the bricks from under his feet alternately. He was desired to breathe before each successive descent of the foot, and, in this way, to give the muscles concerned in respiration a chance of lending their assistance in the good work. When the operator was satisfied, he put a sort of corset of bamboo strips on the chest and bound it round eight times. The patient was then laid upon his back, forbidden the use of a pillow, or to turn to the right or the left.

LAY

MEDICINE

WHEN a ruler is ill and has to drink medicine, the minister first tastes it. The same is the rule for a son and an ailing parent. The physic of a doctor in whose family medicine has not been practised for at least three generations should not be taken.

Li Chi

PILLS TO PREVENT HUNGER

TAKE three pints of sesame, three lbs. of red dates and three pints of glutinous rice. Dry over a fire and grind to powder, then form into pellets the size of bullets. Dose : one pill in a little water.

In times of famine or on long journeys these pills will be found invaluable.

PRE-NATAL INFLUENCES

THE sages of old laid down certain rules relating to pre-natal influences. Expectant mothers were forbidden to lie on the side, to lean when sitting or to lounge when standing. They might not eat any food that was strongly flavoured, nor any that was not properly cut up, nor sit on a mat that was crooked. They were required to look at beautiful things, such as jewels and pictures of lucky birds and animals, to listen to wise discourse and beautiful music. But above all they had to exercise care in their choice of food. They did not eat rabbit and hare for fear of giving birth to a child with a hare lip ; eggs and dried fish they refused lest it should suffer from boils ; mulberries and duck-eggs they avoided, in case of an unpropitious presentation at birth ; they denied themselves wine lest the child should grow up dissolute and shameless ; game and bean-sauce they did not eat because these cause spots on the face ; they believed that donkey-meat would cause the birth to be delayed ; and turtle was forbidden lest the child should be short in the neck.

Yin Shan Cheng Yao

A ROYAL REMEDY

AN elephant has just died at the Palace. Consequently the Luan-i wei Office has officially requested the Kuang-lu ssŭ Office to dispatch a trustworthy officer to skin the elephant and take out his bones. The said skin and bones will then be placed in the Wu-pei yuan Office for His Majesty's consumption when he feels indisposed.

From a Memorial to the Throne submitted in 1885

RULES OF HEALTH

1. KEEP out of draughts when you are sweating after eating hot food. Fits, headache, affections of the eyes and sleepiness are all caused by neglect of this rule.

2. Don't eat much at night.

3. Rinse the mouth with warm water after eating. This prevents toothache and bad breath.

4. If you go out at night, don't sing or shout.

5. After a day's fast on the anniversary of the death of the emperor or of a parent or friend, don't gorge yourself in the evening.

6. After a month's abstinence during mourning for the death of a parent, don't go and get blind drunk on the last day of the moon.

7. During the year of mourning for parents don't travel to a distance.

8. A thousand doses of medicine are not equal to a good night's rest.

9. On the anniversary of your birthday and that of your parents don't eat the flesh of the animal associated with that day.

10. Sit upright ; this will make your heart upright.

11. Stand straight ; this will make your body straight.

12. Don't stand long ; standing is bad for the bones.

13. Don't sit long ; sitting is bad for the blood.

14. Don't walk far ; walking is bad for the sinews.

15. Don't lie long ; lying is bad for the breath.

16. Don't keep the eyes fixed long upon one object ; staring is bad for the mind.

17. Don't wash your head after a full meal ; this is apt to bring on fits.

18. Keep out of draughts when you have had a bath ; the pores are open and malign winds penetrate easily.

19. Don't climb, run, ride or drive till you are out of breath and exhausted, or your soul may fly away and disperse.

20. Be careful not to act disorderly either at home or abroad during a high wind, heavy rain, or when it is very cold or very hot.

21. Don't blow out a lamp ; blowing is injurious to health.

22. Don't try to distinguish objects at a distance ; this weakens the sight.

23. Don't sleep with a lighted candle by you or you cannot hope to guard your soul.

24. Don't sleep in the daytime ; it injures the constitution.

25. Don't rush unceremoniously into every shrine and temple you see.

26. When there is a storm with thunder and lightning you should shut the door and sit in a formal manner, burning incense in case gods are passing by.

27. Don't be violent when you are angry as this causes boils.

28. It is better to spit near to you than far away, but it is better not to spit.

29. Don't lie on, or wear, tiger and leopard skins ; they are bad for the eyes.

30. Avoid lust as you would arrows ; avoid wantonness as you would an enemy.

31. Don't drink tea on an empty stomach, and don't eat cereals in the evening. The ancients had a saying : ' Travellers should not remain hungry in the morning nor over-eat at night.' Not only travellers, but everyone, should take a meal early in the day.

32. The ancients used to say : ' Flour-paste should be cooked to rags, meat till tender. Drink moderately ; sleep alone.'

33. The ancients got up and went to bed early all their lives for the sake of their health. Nowadays people do nothing to prolong life till they are old, when it is too late.

34. When you go to bed rub your hands till they are warm and then rub your eyes, and you will never have eye troubles.

35. On retiring rub the hands till warm and then rub the face, and you will never have boils or spots.

36. To strengthen the eyes wash them in hot water first thing every morning.

37. It is better to clean the teeth at night than in the morning.

38. If you comb your hair one hundred times on going to bed you will never have headaches.

39. To prevent chilblains bathe the feet every night before going to bed.

40. Don't wash your face in cold water during hot weather as it is bad for the eyes.

41. Don't bathe on the first day of autumn as this makes the skin coarse and causes it to peel.

Yin Shan Cheng Yao

SHOCK

THE best way to revive a person who is suffering from severe shock is to force him to swallow a draught of strong wine.

THE SPIRIT LEAVING THE BODY DURING SLEEP

WHEN a person is asleep his spiritual soul removes to his liver, the seat of his animal soul. If the liver happens to be weakened by noxious influences, the visiting soul does not return to its proper place. In such cases the following remedy is efficacious :

> Ginseng, 1 mace
> Dragon-brain (*i.e.* camphor), 2 mace
> Red China-root, 1 mace.

Boil together and strain ; add fine cinnabar, 1 mace. Give one dose nightly in warm water at bedtime. The soul will return and the patient recover after three doses.

SUNSTROKE

IF the attack is severe, and there is much dizziness, the following remedy is unfailing and rapid : Dig a hole about three feet deep and pour in freshly-drawn well-water. Stir well and give the patient several cups of the mixture to drink.

TO CURE

(1) a sick child :

Take five hundred paper cash, one paper horse, eggs, water, and rice, and offer them, facing the south-west. You will thus expel the devils and the child will recover.

(2) a cold in the head :

Drink an infusion of peppermint leaves before going to bed.

(3) headache :

Apply small discs of fresh radish peel to the temples.

(4) depression :

Take the snuff of three lamp-wicks, twelve bamboo leaves washed in water, and one gold hairpin. Boil in river water and take three doses.

(5) irritability, when the mind is like tangled hemp :

Comb the hair and wash the feet. Boil some last season's allspice flowers in dew and take three doses.

(6) to banish sickness :

Wrap a few small coins in red paper and throw the packet into the road. Whoever picks it up will carry away the sickness and the patient will be cured. Mottoes may be written on the paper, as for example, ' I sell out my interest in a bad cold.'

(7) a slight ' touch of the sun ' :

Pinch the skin between the eyes and on the breast with a couple of copper coins, until a livid red line or patch is raised upon the surface.

(8) smallpox, measles and scarlet fever :
Take white and red coral, rubies, pearls, emeralds, musk, and crush into powder ; roll into pills with gum and rose-water, and coat with gold-leaf.

BALFOUR

TO PREVENT SUNBURN

IF you eat the seeds of the *Schizandra chinensis* for sixteen years your face will look like jade and you will be able to walk through fire without being burned and water without becoming wet.

Yin Shan Cheng Yao

TO REVIVE A PERSON WHO HAS DIED SUDDENLY

LIGHT a charcoal brazier and sprinkle on it strong vinegar. Hold close to the dead man's nose. He will revive as soon as the smell reaches him.

Garlic or onion juice injected into the nose is also excellent for the purpose.

TO WEAN A CHILD

TAKE three gardenia-nuts and dry them over the fire. Add small quantities of yellow ochre, cinnabar and calomel. Grind to powder and mix to a smooth paste with sesamum oil. When the child is sleeping heavily rub his eyebrows with the paste and he will waken with a distaste for milk. If not successful the first time, repeat, and the result will be certain.

WHEN THE HOUR STRIKES

A GOOD doctor may apply his knife and his medicine with success so long as the patient is not doomed to die and provided his disease is not incurable. But if a man has come to the end of his allotted span of life and is suffering from a fatal disease, not even the most famous physician can help him. It all depends on fate and on time.

WANG CH'UNG

WORMS IN TEETH

BORE a small hole in a gall-nut. Insert some salt and fill up the hole with powdered lime. Rub the tooth with this several times and no further trouble will be experienced.

*

PROVERBS

To lie like a matchmaker.

He who can swallow an insult is a true man.

Generals and statesmen do not grow from seed ; the young must make an effort.

If you do your duty to your parents at home, there is no need to burn incense abroad.

A man's words are like a soldier's arrow ; a woman's words are like a broken fan.

The boat must go to the landing-place ; the landing-place won't go to the boat.

He who does not know there are ghosts does not fear the dark.

One hand can't screen the heavens.

One bamboo pole can scare a whole boat-load of people.

You can't press oil out of old chaff.

An unruly wife and an obstinate son cannot be governed.

The best swimmers are oftenest drowned and the best riders have the worst falls.

A leaky house on a rainy night—one misfortune on top of another.

Wife, children, fortune and profession—all are predestined.

Listen to your wife, don't believe her.

A woman's mind is of quicksilver, her heart of wax.

THE EPICURE

PROVERBS

He who carefully orders his eating and drinking assures for himself good health and long life.

*

One never digests well what one does not digest easily.

*

Peculiar dishes result in extraordinary diseases.

*

The more dishes appear on the table the more drugs will be needed in the medicine.

*

We keep count of the number of those assassinated, poisoned and killed in battle, but not of those who die through their own intemperance and gluttony.

*

' The fewer the dishes on my table,' said a thoughtful emperor, ' the fewer the ailments I suffer from ; the less I indulge my appetite, the less I am conscious of the weight of my years.'

*

Wine and good dinners make a multitude of friends ; but in time of adversity none remains.

THE FEAST

THE feast spread out, the splendour round
Allowed the eye no rest ;
The wealth of China, of all Ind,
Appeared to greet each guest.

All tongues are still ; no converse free
The solemn silence broke ;
Because, alas ! the foreign guest
No word of Chinese spoke.

.   .   .   .   .

But presently he brightened up,
And thought himself in luck
When close before him, what he saw
Looked something like a duck.

Yet cautious still, to make quite sure
His brain he set to rack ;
At length he turned to one behind,
And, pointing, said : ' Quack, quack ? '

The Chinese gravely shook his head,
Next made a reverend bow ;
And then expressed what dish it was
By uttering, ' Bow-wow-wow.'

By an Old Resident in Canton

FOOD

SOME animals are good for food ; others are not. But avoid even those which are normally edible if there be anything unnatural in their appearance. Do not eat horse's feet ; they have eyes in them at night. A black chicken or sheep with a white head, or a sheep with only a single horn, or a horned horse, should never be used for food. The same rule applies to meat which falls on the ground and does not leave a wet patch, or which is found to be warm after having been left over-night.

Yin Shan Cheng Yao

*

Apart from foods which are poisonous in themselves, there are many which should not be eaten together as they do not harmonize and are apt to cause great discomfort and inconvenience. Horse-flesh, for example, should not be accompanied by ginger ; neither should hare. Pork and beef, or pork and sheep-liver are equally unsuited to be eaten together.

Ibid.

COMPOSITE COOKERY

RECENTLY I dined at a Chinese restaurant in London in which, with the exception of three Indians, all the diners were Europeans. This suggests that Chinese food is becoming increasingly favoured. But there are many people who have no opportunity of visiting a Chinese restaurant who would welcome an occasional change of cookery provided that it did not involve the addition to the store-cupboard of quantities of dried and tinned Oriental foodstuffs. For the woman who yearns to cook ' proper ' Chinese food at home, there are cookery-books in plenty, and materials for preparing them at the

Chinese emporia. It is for the cook who would like to experiment in Chinese methods of preparing appetizing dishes that the following menus and recipes are intended. Nothing that is not likely to be found in the ordinary English kitchen is needed. Many have been tried out in a kitchenette too small to contain two well-grown persons, and therefore not large enough to allow of any lavishness in the matter of equipment.

No sharks' fins or birds' nests, no carp or lily-petals, will make these recipes tantalizing impossibilities; but chicken stewed with almonds, and new ways with fish and omelettes, easily and reasonably quickly prepared offer a new reply to the question: ' What shall we eat ? '

I am aware that these views will sound unorthodox. I know very well that Chinese cooking depends on the combining of a number of subtle flavours. I shall be told that only by using Chinese oils and sauces can the refinements of the Chinese cuisine be discovered. It is also true that in the preparation of certain Chinese dishes charcoal is preferred to gas or electricity, but this need not prevent us from experimenting with the means at our disposal. Half the interest of experimenting in cookery lies in adapting it to our own needs and tastes, and we need not be deprived of an adventure into the realms of Chinese cookery because a certain number of substitutes must be found. In every case the recipe is purely Chinese, and where a substitute is used the fact is stated.

English cooks will be surprised at the small quantities of many of the dishes prepared by the Chinese. This is easy to understand when one realizes that the basis of the meal is generally rice, and that the meat and vegetable dishes are only accompaniments, intended to give interest and flavour to the staple food. Furthermore, a number of these small dishes of various kinds of meat, fish, and vegetables, or combinations of some or all of these, are set on the table at the same time and the diners help themselves at will, but always in small quantities.

The Chinese do not eat a great deal of beef or mutton, and to speak the truth, their method of cooking is apt to make red meats tough and flavourless. Chicken, duck and pork are made more delicate and palatable on the other hand, and lend themselves to these simple recipes.

Chinese food may be classified under a number of headings, and one or more dishes from any or all of these groups may be chosen as an accompaniment to rice. The groups represented by the recipes given here are :

> Chicken
> Duck
> Shell-fish
> Fish
> Meat
> Eggs
> Vegetables

The selection and number of dishes given in each group depends on the ease with which they can be prepared, and the availability of materials.

THE EDITOR

CHICKEN WITH ALMONDS OR WALNUTS

AN unusual and particularly delicious combination of chicken with almonds or walnuts deserves a place of honour on the table. The method of preparation does not differ very much, but both recipes are given.

1. *Chicken with Almonds*

> 6 small white mushrooms, diced
> 1 onion chopped very small
> ¼lb. blanched almonds, split
> 6 oz. diced cooked chicken

Fry the almonds in 1 oz. of hot lard for a few minutes. Remove and cook the onions in the same pan for 4 minutes. Add the mushrooms and cook 3 minutes longer.

Pour over ½ teacupful of stock ; add a lump of sugar, and pepper and salt to taste, and stir for a minute. Then add the diced chicken and thicken (*see* THICKENING). Stir in a tablespoonful of sherry and add the almonds.

If desired, ½ teacupful of diced celery may be added, though the flavour of the almonds is then less marked. Chinese cooks might add the same quantity of bamboo-shoots chopped into cubes.

Either of these additions should be cooked with the mushrooms and onions.

This quantity is enough for two people if it is the only dish.

2. *Chicken with Walnuts*

    1 cup of diced cooked chicken
    1 cup of shelled walnuts fried brown in deep fat
    6 small white mushrooms, diced
    ½ teacupful of diced celery

The walnuts should be fried in boiling lard deep enough to cover them. Use a frying-basket, and shake them gently till they are a pale brown, then remove and dry on kitchen-paper.

Heat 1 oz. of lard in a pan and add the celery. Cook without browning for 3 minutes ; add the diced mushrooms and cook all for a further 5 minutes. Sprinkle over a teaspoonful of salt and the same of sugar. Throw in the diced chicken, stir well, and thicken (*see* THICKENING). Add the walnuts, heat through, and serve.

CHICKEN AND CHESTNUTS

    A young chicken (about 2 lbs.)
    ½ lb. chestnuts
    2 tablespoons sherry
    1 clove garlic
    A small piece of fresh ginger-root, say ½ oz.
    Salt, sugar, pepper
    1 dessertspoon lard

Boil the chestnuts for 10 minutes after slitting the skins. Peel and then steam for a quarter of an hour to finish cooking. Remove the meat from the chicken and cut into small pieces or chop with a sharp heavy knife into tiny joints, leaving the bones in. They should measure 1½ in. long by ½ in. wide.

Prepare the garlic (*see* GARLIC), add the ginger crushed and then the pieces of chicken. Cook till it begins to brown, stirring to prevent burning. This should take four or five minutes only. Then add sherry, salt, pepper to taste, and two lumps of sugar. If necessary add a little stock, cover the pan and simmer gently for half an hour or so. Add the chestnuts and allow them to become thoroughly hot through, then serve in a deep dish either as a main dish for lunch or with rice.

Before serving, a Chinese cook would probably add a little soya sauce and a few drops of sesamum oil.

CHICKEN WITH MUSHROOMS

> ½ lb. cooked chicken cut into dice
> 4 oz. fresh mushrooms, cut up
> 2 oz. diced carrot
> ½ oz. fresh ginger
> 1 clove of garlic
> 1 oz. lard

Prepare the garlic (*see* GARLIC). Add the carrots and cook for five minutes, being careful that they do not brown.

Add the ginger crushed and the mushrooms and cook five minutes longer. Add salt to taste, two lumps of sugar, a little sherry, and finally, the diced chicken and a cupful of stock. Stir for two minutes, then thicken (*see* THICKENING) and continue stirring for another minute. Serve very hot.

Runner beans or a dish of peas make this a good supper dish, or it can be eaten with rice, as part of a Chinese meal.

CHILIS

> 2 green chilis (skin only) cut small
> ½ lb. minced pork
> 1 medium-sized onion
> 2 shallotts

2 mushrooms
2 oz. cooked peas
2 medium-sized tomatoes skinned, and without seeds
1 clove garlic

Prepare the garlic (*see* GARLIC). Add the pork and cook for two minutes. Meanwhile cut up all the vegetables finely.

Add the onions to the pork and cook again for two minutes, then the chilis, mushrooms, tomatoes, and finally the peas, allowing each ingredient to cook for a minute or two before the next is added.

Season with salt, pepper, a lump of sugar, and if desired, a little Bovril instead of soya sauce. Thicken (*see* THICKENING) and stir in a piece of butter the size of a walnut.

CHOP SUEY

CHOP SUEY appears to be a Western version of Chinese food and not a Chinese dish at all. The principle of it is simple : a great variety of vegetables, all cut very finely, are cooked with one or more kinds of meat. The method of cooking is what we in the West term broiling ; the ingredients are first fried in a little hot oil or lard and then simmered in gravy. This method has some modifications, but that is the basic principle of it.

Some suggestions for the selection of ingredients are given here, and the method outlined for one of them.

1. *Chicken Chop Suey*
    ½ lb. chicken, in thin slices
    ½ lb. onions, chopped finely
    3 tomatoes, without skins and pips
    1 piece of celery cut up
    1 oz. mushrooms, sliced
    (If Chinese materials are available include ½ oz. bamboo-shoots, thinly sliced)
    ¼ lb. bean-sprouts

343

2. *Pork or Beef Chop Suey*

   ¼ lb. beef or pork in small thin slices
   6 mushrooms, sliced
   2 onions cut into tiny pieces
   ½ head of celery, diced
   2 tomatoes, without skin and seeds

3. *Lobster Chop Suey*

   4-6 oz. lobster meat
   ¼ lb. minced onions
   6 small mushrooms sliced
   ¼ head of celery
   2 tomatoes (if desired)
   (Bean-sprouts and/or bamboo-shoots as for Chicken Chop
   Suey, if available)

Skin the tomatoes and remove the seeds, and chop small. Heat a little lard and cook the lobster meat for half a minute, then add the vegetables and cook again for 2 minutes, putting in the tomatoes when the other ingredients are cooked, as tomato tends to hinder cooking.

Sprinkle a little sugar, salt and pepper, and add a very little Bovril (or some soya sauce) and thicken (*see* THICKENING).

Beat an egg and cook it for 1 minute in a very hot pan with no more lard than will serve to oil the pan ; turn over and cook for 1 minute on the other side.

When the egg is ready, dish the Chop Suey, lay the egg on top and serve.

DUCK

CHINESE cooks have many ways of cooking duck, some of them rather elaborate, but all excellent. A simple and unusual recipe is :

DUCK WITH CHESTNUTS

Joint a duck and cut 1 lb. of pork into small cubes. Put into a pan over a slow fire and extract some of the fat. Then add ½ lb. fresh mushrooms cut in pieces, an onion sliced, 1 oz. ginger-root crushed, and lastly 1 lb. of partly cooked, peeled chestnuts. Add stock to cover, and a little Bovril (as substitute for soya sauce). Simmer till the duck is thoroughly tender and serve very hot with rice.

DUCKLING

A GOOD way of preparing a small duckling of about two pounds' weight is to stew it with mushrooms.

Remove the backbone from the duck and then chop it, bones and all, into small strips not more than 1½ in. long and ¾ in. wide.

Prepare the garlic (*see* GARLIC), and then put the pieces of duck into the pan and cook for 3 minutes. Add salt, pepper, 2 lumps of sugar, half a glass of sherry (and if available, a little soya sauce). Stir well for a minute and then add the mushrooms, sliced, and cook for 2 minutes longer.

Cover with stock and simmer for three-quarters of an hour to an hour. Thicken (*see* THICKENING) very slightly, cook again for a minute and serve.

GARLIC

WHENEVER garlic is to be used, try this method : melt an ounce of butter (or lard) in a pan and cook one or two cloves of garlic, according to the quantity of the ingredients it is to flavour, without allowing it to brown. When quite soft it should be mashed into the butter and forgotten. If you treat it in this way you will not find that anyone will complain that you have used it ; they will merely wonder what it is in the dish that gives it that unusual flavour which they can't quite describe—a tribute to the cook's subtlety.

LOBSTER

HAVE you tried fried lobster ? Cooked as the Chinese cook it, lobster is excellent. Here is one recipe :

Cut up finely 6 oz. onions, 2 oz. celery, 4 oz. cucumber, two or three mushrooms and about 1 lb. of lobster meat.

Cook the vegetables for a minute or so in a tablespoonful of very hot lard, then cover with stock and cook again for three minutes.

While the vegetables are cooking take another pan and cook the lobster in hot lard for a minute, then add two tablespoonfuls of cooking sherry, and simmer for a few minutes longer.

Add the lobster to the vegetables in their pan and cook all together for three minutes. Thicken (*see* THICKENING) and add a piece of butter the size of a walnut, with salt and pepper to taste, stir briskly for two minutes and serve.

A Chinese cook would undoubtedly add a little soya sauce as well as bamboo-shoots to perfect this recipe, but try it without. Don't be afraid to vary your vegetables—a tomato skinned and de-pipped or a piece of carrot instead of the cucumber—and don't begrudge the seasonings.

Leave the vegetables, etc., ready before you go out and you will be able to prepare this dish in a quarter of an hour on your return. If you don't want rice with it, try really crisp toast.

MUSHROOMS

A NEW way with mushrooms may be worth trying, though I am not sure that a new way is ever called for while there are mushrooms with grilled bacon.

Take ½ lb. of fresh mushrooms, of the thick variety ; 1 clove of garlic ; 1 oz. of fresh ginger.

Melt 1 oz. of butter in a pan and fry the garlic till soft ; then mash it into the butter (*see* GARLIC). When the garlic has been well mixed into the butter put the mushrooms into the pan and cook for about five minutes.

Crush the ginger and put it with the mushrooms, then add three teacups of stock and simmer very slowly till soft, after which hunt the ginger and remove it.

Strain off the gravy and arrange the mushrooms in the dish in which they are to be served.

Return the gravy to the pan and add a piece of butter the size of a walnut, two lumps of sugar, salt to taste, and (since the store-cupboard does not contain soya sauce) a little gravy-browning or whatever you use instead, if anything. Bring to the boil and thicken (*see* THICKENING), stirring for one minute. Pour the gravy over the mushrooms and serve any way you like—as an accompaniment to a Chinese meal, or with a grilled steak, or even for breakfast, on toast.

MUSHROOMS AND MEAT-BALLS

½ lb. lean pork, minced, or chopped very finely
4 oz. fresh mushrooms cut in quarters
1 clove of garlic
2 oz. fresh ginger
A little cornflour

Prepare the garlic (*see* GARLIC), and cook the mushrooms in the pan for five minutes. Add a little salt to the minced pork, make it into balls about the size of a ping-pong ball, and roll each in cornflour.

Crush the ginger and put it with the mushrooms, then pour over them a teacup of stock and simmer gently for half an hour.

Cook the meat-balls separately for 25 minutes with just enough good gravy to cover them.

Remove the ginger from the mushrooms and serve them in the same dish with the meat-balls.

This dish may be eaten in the Chinese manner with rice, or it may be tried out with mashed potato and/or boiled Jerusalem artichokes, to atone for the absence of water-chestnuts which are usually an ingredient of the meat-balls.

NOODLES

NOODLES can be bought at Italian shops in Soho or in Chinese food-shops. Both are made of a fine flour-paste, with or without eggs, like macaroni. Noodles are finer than macaroni, and flat. They are best when freshly made, as they do not require so much boiling. Noodles made of rice-flour are also made by the Chinese. They may be eaten for a change in place of rice, with certain dishes, or they may be fried or broiled and served as a part of special meat and vegetable dishes. Crisply fried, they are delicious and quite unlike the soggy mass that is sometimes served boiled, with tomato sauce, in England.

However they are to be served, broiled or fried, crisp or soft, noodles must first be boiled. They should be dropped into fast-boiling water, and removed as soon as ready into a colander and cold water allowed to run on them. They should then be spread thinly on a damp cloth and left to cool and dry. If they are fresh the boiling process will not take more than 2 minutes.

For crisp fried noodles enough lard for deep frying is required. When thoroughly hot, so that a blue smoke is given off by the lard, put in all the noodles and let them cook till golden brown, then take them out and drain and they are ready to serve. Soft fried noodles are boiled noodles cooked for half a minute in a very hot pan just ' oily ' with lard. Plain boiled noodles are reheated after being cooled, but not in fat.

A sample dish with fried noodles is given opposite, and a few additional suggestions for other mixtures.

NOODLES WITH CHICKEN

¼ lb. chicken-meat, sliced
4 white mushrooms, sliced
1 onion, sliced finely
1 piece of celery, cut small
½–¾ lb. fresh noodles

Boil the noodles as directed above and fry till very crisp. Put the chicken in a hot pan with a little lard and add the other ingredients and a little salt. Cook all for two or three minutes. Thicken (*see* THICKENING) and flavour, and add (if possible) a very little soya sauce.

Serve in a bowl with the crisp noodles on top.

NOODLES WITH CRAB

4 oz. crab-meat
½ an onion, finely sliced
2 white mushrooms, sliced

Serve with soft fried noodles mixed at the last moment before serving.

NOODLES WITH PORK

Substitute 4 oz. shredded pork for the crab-meat in the recipe for Noodles with Crab.

Note.—Any or all of these dishes may need a very little thickening.

OMELETTES

Fish and Meat Omelette

3 eggs
6 prawns, cut small

1 oz. chopped cooked ham
1 oz. cooked chicken, finely diced
A little grated onion
2 small sliced mushrooms

Heat a little lard or butter in a pan and add all the ingredients with the exception of the eggs. Sprinkle with salt and pepper and stir round for two minutes.

Add the beaten eggs to the other ingredients, and cook quickly for 2 minutes, turning once or twice so that both sides are cooked and of a golden brown colour.

Lobster Omelette

For this omelette the only materials required are 3 eggs, ¼ lb. lobster meat cut small (less will do ; the smallest tin is enough to make a very tasty omelette if fresh lobster is not available ; crab or prawns may also be used). 1 small onion chopped very finely.

Cook the onion in a very little lard for a minute, adding salt to taste.

Add the lobster and cook for 3 minutes or a little less.

Add the eggs beaten and mix with the lobster. Cook on both sides over a quick flame.

PORK CHOPS

An English dish with a Chinese air is pork chops in batter.

Cut 1 lb. lean, fresh pork in cubes and let it steep for at least an hour in sherry. Sprinkle with salt.

Make a batter with 3 eggs and 3 tablespoonfuls of flour or rice-flour, adding a little water if needed. Let the batter stand till the pork is ready, then drop each cube of meat into the batter separately and fry in deep boiling lard till golden brown. Serve very hot with rice or potatoes.

PRAWNS FRIED IN BATTER

Follow the directions given for shrimps in batter. Tinned prawns are delicious and lose the flavour of the tin when cooked this way.

RICE

Chinese rice and Indian curry rice are the only kinds obtainable in this country, I believe, which you can boil with any confidence. Indian rice is expensive if it is good, but Chinese rice, bought at the Chinese food shops, is quite as cheap as the pudding-rice you get at any grocer's.

When properly cooked, rice is quite dry and every grain is quite distinct from the grain next door. Many Chinese cooks steam rice, but it can be put into a large saucepanful of cold or boiling water and boiled for 20 to 25 minutes and be turned out quite perfect. It is an easier method than steaming, really, as it is necessary to know the exact quantity of water and the variety of rice used and the relative proportions of each required in order to produce satisfactory steamed rice.

TO COOK RICE

Place the desired quantity of rice in a shallow vessel standing in a pan of water. Now add to the rice enough water to cover the open hand when laid on the rice. Cover the pan and boil till the water is all absorbed.

*

The following method, though more common in India than in China, is never known to fail :

Fill a very large saucepan with cold water and throw in a teacup of rice for every 2 persons. Cover with a lid till the water boils, remove lid and scum and allow to simmer for 17 minutes, or until no hard core can be felt when a grain of rice is squeezed between thumb and finger.

It should be unnecessary to add that all the kinds of rice sold in our stores are meant for rice puddings, and not for curry. So get Indian rice if you want to entertain Indian, Anglo-Indian, or Chinese guests—or anybody else who is out of the nursery—to curry.

FRIED RICE

As a change from boiled rice, fried rice is very good. This may be prepared without any additions or it may be made into an excellent dish with chicken, crab-meat, or a mixture of meat and fish.

Fried Rice with Crab

Take 6 oz. crab-meat (fresh or out of a jar) and 3 well-beaten eggs. Cook for a minute in a pan containing a very little hot lard (scarcely more than you would use in frying a pancake). Add 2 lb. of cooked rice, salt and pepper (at this stage the Chinese cook adds a very little soya sauce, but you could experiment with your favourite sauce if you cared to risk changing the flavour of the dish somewhat : you may have views on sauces !). Stir about and cook for 3 or 4 minutes, adding 2 spring onions very finely chopped if you care for them. These are not supposed to need more than a half minute's cooking.

Fried Rice with Chicken

Using 6 oz. of finely chopped cooked chicken in place of crab, proceed as above.

*

Other combinations with fried rice which suggest themselves are flaked Findon haddock (which is not Chinese but is worth trying), and a mixture consisting of ¼ lb. lean roast pork, 2 oz. ham, 2 oz.

shrimps, fresh or out of a jar, 4 oz. onions, with eggs and spring onions as before. The method in these cases is the same as the recipes already given, all the ingredients being cut very small and the same order followed in cooking.

These dishes are excellent, and help to make a very little meat go a long way.

SCRAMBLED EGGS

BEAT up as many eggs as you require, say 6 eggs for 3 or 4 people. Add to the beaten egg a little salt and pepper, a tablespoonful of sherry and a teacupful of picked shrimps.

Heat a dessertspoonful of butter in a pan and cook the mixture as if it were ordinary scrambled eggs.

Serve very hot, alone or with toast.

SHRIMPS FRIED IN BATTER

MANY excellent dishes with shrimps and prawns are eaten by the Chinese. Among the simplest and most delicious is shrimps fried in batter.

Allow half a pint of shrimps for each person if the dish is to be the main one of the meal. It is excellent for breakfast or as a savoury for lunch. It is not necessary to serve rice.

Shell and clean the shrimps carefully, then pour over them half a teacup of sherry and stand for an hour. Make a batter allowing 1 egg and 1 tablespoonful of flour to every half-pint of shrimps, adding a little water if necessary, and let it stand till the shrimps are ready. Dip each shrimp in the batter and drop into hot fat from which blue smoke is rising. Remove when golden brown and drain on kitchen-paper. Serve very hot and crisp.

SOLE

THIS is a quick and excellent way to serve a sole, preferably of the Dover variety.

Take ½ lb. of filleted sole and cut it into small strips. Slice 2 oz. white mushrooms and 2 oz. cucumber.

Cook the vegetables for about a minute in a shallow pan containing a very little hot lard, sprinkling over a little salt, pepper and sugar. Add a piece of butter the size of a walnut and enough stock to cover. Cook for 3 or 4 four minutes.

Rub the strips of sole in pepper, salt and flour, and cook for 2 minutes in boiling lard. Remove and drain, then add to the vegetables and cook together for a minute. Then thicken (*see* THICKENING) and add a little Bovril and another small piece of butter (in lieu of soya sauce and sesamum oil), stirring briskly for half a minute.

This dish is best served with rice, but it can be eaten alone, if desired.

SOUP

THE basis of most of the usual Chinese soups is the same—a small quantity of shredded pork, chicken or beef, fried for a minute or two in no more lard than is needed to make the pan oily, a few leaves of green vegetable (spinach or lettuce), a few sliced dried or fresh white mushrooms added, and the whole covered with water or stock to the desired quantity and allowed to simmer. Noodles are often added to soup, and these make it much more substantial.

Shark's fin and birds' nests soups require ingredients outside the range of composite cookery, but all Chinese cookery books include recipes for these.

SOYA SAUCE

MOST Europeans will agree that a good deal of the flavour of Chinese food comes from the soya sauce with which it is generally made.

Its manufacture is very simple and may be undertaken by anyone within reach of a shop where Chinese foodstuffs can be bought.

Take 2 lb. of soya beans and boil till soft, and then add an equal quantity of wheat or barley. After this has thoroughly fermented add salt, and 3 times as much water as the volume of the beans before boiling. Set aside for 2 or 3 months, then press and strain out the liquor. Good soya has an agreeable taste, and may be used in English cooking with satisfactory results, particularly for giving colour and flavour (it should be very salt) to soups and gravies. It improves much by age if kept tightly corked.

The sauce ready prepared can be bought at Chinese restaurants and food-stores in London.

STOCK

1. *Meat Stock*

THE quantity of meat used in Chinese dishes is small, but there is no doubt about the excellence of the stock which it is correct to use, and its nourishing qualities are considerable. It consists of equal quantities of chicken-meat and lean pork, in the proportion of about a pint of water to 6 oz. of each kind of meat. Bones may of course be used as well, but they should not be used as a substitute for the meat. Cut the meat into small pieces and simmer for three hours. The quantity of stock yielded should be about half the quantity of water. Strain, cool, and remove any fat, and the stock is ready for use as required.

2. *Vegetable Stock*

Although the first essential of Chinese cookery is to use stock instead of water, this need not present an insuperable barrier. Let us suppose that you find yourself without any meat stock, or anything with which to make it. Here is the way out of this difficulty.

Take a carrot, an onion, a piece of turnip, or a small new one, a leek, if you have it, or anything green (a few lettuce leaves, or pea-pods). Chop these, or cut them in strips.

Meanwhile put into a pan—a frying-pan or a shallow wide-mouthed saucepan is best for most Chinese cookery—a dessert-spoonful of lard (NOT dripping, please) and let it get quite hot. Add the chopped vegetables and fry them in the lard, without allowing them to brown. When they begin to look transparent and rather wilted pour over them 3 tea-cups of boiling water, and let them simmer for a little while. Strain off the liquid and you have a nourishing and tasty stock, made in a few minutes.

I have seen a Chinese scholar in an overall make a delicious soup by this method, adding to the strained stock a dozen circular shavings of carrot, a few fine strips of onion, and celery in proportion cooked in lard, and flavouring it with a tablespoonful of Chinese soya sauce, for which a little Bovril or other meat extract could be substituted. A leaf of spinach per plate was added a minute or so before serving, just to make it pretty. The cooking was done while the guests drank a preliminary glass of sherry.

SUKIYAKI

ALTHOUGH this is not a Chinese dish, it is so popular among those who enjoy Chinese food that it seems worth while to include it, particularly as it can be made with materials normally at hand. It can be prepared in the kitchen, but usually the raw ingredients are placed upon the table and the diners cook it as required, a bowl of rice being served to each person, or a large dish set on the table when the first ' round ' of sukiyaki is ready.

A chafing-dish, or an open pan over a gas-ring will serve equally well to cook it in. The raw ingredients are neatly arranged in separate piles upon one or more large meat-dishes and set before the cook. Whatever ingredients are selected the method of cooking is the same.

Wafer-thin strips of steak, about 1½ in. long by an inch wide, make a good sukiyaki ; chicken, duck and fish are equally good, but the slices must be of the thinnest possible. The selection of vegetables depends on the season of the year, but an appetizing and cheap sukiyaki, enough for 4 people, may be made as follows:

½ lb. steak sliced thinly

6 spring onions cut in pieces

1 large onion cut in very thin rings

1 large carrot cut in rings

The heart of a small cabbage cut into strips 2 in. long and ½ in. wide. The cabbage may be replaced by a lettuce separated and washed, or a handful of spinach leaves.

1 cup of mushrooms, sliced

2 oz. lard

2 dessertspoons sugar

A little salt

A little Bovril dissolved in a teacup of hot water. (This is a substitute for soya sauce, though inferior to it)

Heat the pan over a quick flame and put in the lard. When thoroughly hot add one-third of the onion and, allowing an interval of 2 or 3 minutes between each, one-third of the cabbage, carrot, and mushrooms. When all are beginning to look a little wilted, sprinkle over a little salt and a quarter of the sugar. Then pour over enough of the Bovril to keep from burning. Turn the flame low, simmer and stir, and when the vegetables appear to be almost cooked (this is only a matter of a few minutes) add some slices of meat and stir it well into the gravy at the bottom of the pan so that it cooks quickly to keep the juice in. A little water may be added if the mixture is too dry. (*Note.*—Some cooks put the meat in the pan first so that it is seared by the hot oil before the vegetables are added. Try both ways in turn.)

When the first round of sukiyaki has been served by placing a little upon the rice in each bowl, a fresh lot is prepared, adding more meat and vegetables to the gravy left in the pan and cooking as before.

When all has been cooked the gravy which remains in the pan can be used to flavour any rice remaining in the bowls.

If sukiyaki is made in the kitchen it can be cooked all at once and kept hot over a very low gas.

THICKENING

THE method given in most Chinese cookery-books for thickening is very simple. Mix $\frac{1}{2}$ oz. of cornflour into a smooth paste with a breakfast-cup of water, and add as much as is required to give the desired thickness to the dish, stirring smoothly all the time.

ARRACK

ARRACK, although not a native Chinese drink, used to be imported in considerable quantities a century and more ago, especially from Batavia, the arrack of Java being more highly esteemed than that from Goa or Colombo, where other varieties are produced.

Batavia arrack is the strongest, and is distilled from a mixture of 62 parts of molasses, 3 of toddy or palm-wine (a liquor distilled from the juice of the coco-nut tree) and 35 of rice. The process of manufacture is as follows :

Take the desired quantity of rice, boil well and add yeast. Press into baskets and set over a tub or other vessel and leave for 8 days, during which time a liquor will flow freely from the rice. This liquor should be distilled and then mixed in the proper porportion with toddy and molasses and left to ferment for a week in a large vat or jar. After the fermentation is complete, distil once, twice, or three times, according to the strength required.

' In its effects,' says an old writer, ' this spirit is like rum or gin, and is a source [*sic*] of much inebriation among all classes, accompanied with the disease and distress attendant upon intoxication in other countries. . . . It is sold in China at 40 cents a gallon for the best, and 27 or 30 cents for the poorest.'

The Epicure

BUTTER

SKIM the cream off cow's milk and simmer gently till it turns to butter.

Yin Shan Cheng Yao

GRILLED STEAK

TO make a grill, beat the beef and remove the skinny parts. Then lay it on a frame of reeds, sprinkle it with cinnamon and ginger, and add salt. Mutton may be treated in the same way, and also the flesh of deer and elk.

Li Chi

MUTTON-BONE BROTH

INGREDIENTS :

Mutton-bones broken in pieces, 1 carcass
Dried orange peel $\frac{1}{10}$ oz. (remove the white)
Ginger, $\frac{1}{10}$ oz.
Cardamons, 2
Green ginger, 1 oz.
A little salt

Simmer slowly in 30 pints of water and strain before sending to table.

A Recipe from the Imperial Kitchens of the Mongol (Yuan)
Dynasty, published in the 14th century A.D.

SOUP

TAKE mutton, venison, chicken and pork and put them in a cauldron with the bones. Boil all together until very rich. Remove the meat, add onions and ginger and flavour with the five seasonings. Pour the soup into a bowl and set it on a platter, placing in the bowl a silver ladle with a spout, holding about a pint. Then serve the soup, beginning generally with the host. Each diner should slowly imbibe a ladleful and pass on the ladle to his neighbour in the same way as wine is passed round. The soup should be followed by all kinds of meats.

A Recipe from Annam in the ninth century A.D.

SOUP BALLS

FOR soup balls take equal quantities of beef, mutton and pork and cut them small. Then mix boiled rice with the meat, in the proportion of two parts of rice to one of meat, form into cakes or balls, and fry.

Li Chi

STEEPED BEEF

TAKE a piece of newly-killed beef and cut it into small pieces. Steep it from one morning to the next in good wine, when it may be eaten with pickle, vinegar, or the juice of prunes.

Ibid.

SUCKING-PIG

To bake a sucking-pig cut it open and remove the entrails, then fill it with dates. It should then be wrapped round with straw and reeds, and plastered over with clay, and baked. When the clay is dry break it off. Having washed your hands, remove the crackling and macerate it along with rice-flour, so as to form a kind of gruel which is added to the pig. Then fry the whole in enough melted fat to cover it. Having prepared a large pan of hot water, place in it a small tripod, and fill with fragrant herbs, and slices of the pig. Take care that the hot water does not cover the tripod, but keep up the fire without intermission for three days and nights. The whole is then served with the addition of pickled meat and vinegar.

Ibid.

HOUSEHOLD HINTS

PORK of an especially delicate flavour is said to result from feeding selected pigs on oranges ; similarly crabs fed on sesamum seed are highly esteemed.

The Japanese offer as a congratulatory gift biscuits of flour mixed with powdered shrimps dried and long past their prime. However, they atone for this by eating yellow chrysanthemum petals as a salad, not because of their nutritive properties, but for purely æsthetic enjoyment.

CHINESE COOKING

CHINESE cookery has a much nearer resemblance to the French than the English, in the general use of ragouts and made-dishes as well as in the liberal introduction of vegetables into every preparation of meat. Some of the articles, however, which they esteem as delicacies would have few attractions for a European. Among others, the larvæ of the sphinx-moth, as well as a grub which is bred in the sugar-cane, are much relished.

DAVIS

A FEAST

THE following description of a Chinese feast, written by a Frenchman early in the nineteenth century and quoted at length by Langdon, includes some dishes familiar to all who have attended similar feasts, but also some which have, presumably, gone out of fashion :

' The first course was laid out in a great number of saucers of porcelain, and consisted of various relishes in a cold state, as salted earth-worms, prepared and dried, but so cut up that . . . . . I did not know what they were until I swallowed them ; salted or smoked fish and ham ; . . . . besides which there was what they called Japan leather, a sort of dark skin, hard and tough, with a strong and far from agreeable taste. . . . All these *etceteras*, including a liquor which I recognized to be soy . . . were used as seasoning to a great number of stews, which were contained in bowls and succeeded each other uninterruptedly. All the dishes, without exception, swam in soup ; on one side figured pigeons' eggs, cooked in gravy, together with ducks and fowls cut very small, and immersed in a dark-coloured sauce ; on the other, little balls made of sharks' fins, eggs prepared by heat (of which the smell and taste seemed equally repulsive), immense grubs, a peculiar kind of sea fish, crabs and pounded shrimps. . . . I contrived to eat, with tolerable propriety, a soup prepared from the famous birds' nests . . . a substance transparent as isinglass, and resembling vermicelli, with little or no taste. . . .

After all these good things . . . succeeded the second course. . . . The table was covered with articles in pastry and sugar ; in the midst of which was a salad composed of the tender shoots of the bamboo . . . pretty baskets, filled with flowers, were mixed with plates of delicious sweetmeats and fruit. . . . When all was finished we adjourned to another room to drink the tea which marked the close of the entertainment.'

LANGDON

ACKNOWLEDGMENTS

THE Editor desires to express her indebtedness to the late Mr. C. H. Brewitt-Taylor for permitting her to quote from *San Kuo, or Romance of the Three Kingdoms*. She also has to thank Mr. Arthur Waley for allowing her to include poems from *One Hundred and Seventy Chinese Poems*, *More Translations from the Chinese* and *The Temple, and Other Poems*.

Thanks are due to the following publishers for permission to include extracts from the books enumerated hereunder :

Messrs. George Allen and Unwin : *More Translations from the Chinese* and *The Temple, and Other Poems*, by Arthur Waley.

Messrs. Constable & Co. : *A Hundred and Seventy Chinese Poems*, by Arthur Waley.

Messrs. Kelly & Walsh : *San Kuo, or Romance of the Three Kingdoms*, by C. H. Brewitt-Taylor.

Mr. A. Probsthain : *Chinese Prose Literature of the T'ang Period*, by E. D. Edwards.

The Editor has endeavoured to trace all copyrights and to make correct acknowledgment of the sources of all the extracts appearing in *The Dragon Book*. If she has inadvertently been guilty of any error she tenders her apology.

INDEX OF SOURCES

(Unless otherwise stated translations from the Chinese are by the Editor)

Index of Sources

Davis, Sir J. F., *Chinese Moral Maxims* (Murray 1823), pp. 27–8, 202, 265–6 ; *The Fortunate Union* (Murray 1829), pp. 25, 60 ; ; *Sketches of China*, 2 vols. (London 1841), pp. 43, 159, 361.

Dennys, N. B., Ph.D., F.R.G.S. Extracts on pp. 29, 39, 40, 46, 55, 61, 70–1, 76, 82–3, 88, 149–50, 322 are adapted from *The Folklore of China* . . . . (London 1876). . . .

Doolittle, Rev. J., *Social Life of the Chinese* (1866), pp. 41–2.

Eight Factory Regulations, p. 34.

Eitel, E. J., *Folk Songs*, *China Review*, vol. i, 1872–1873, pp. 129–31.

Fang Ch'iu-yai, Sung dynasty (A.D. 960–1280), poet, p. 101.

Fortune, Robert, *Two Visits to the Tea Countries of China*, 2 vols., 3rd ed. (1853), pp. 31–2, 38, 64–8.

Gardner, G. T., pp. 128–9.

Giles, H. A. *See* Yuan Mei ; ; *see also* p. 124.

Han Yü (d. A.D. 874), scholar and official, pp. 25, 79–80, 212–3.

Hao Ch'iu Chuan (*The Fortunate Union*), pp. 197–201 (adapted).

Hsieh Yung-jo, 9th century, scholar, pp. 238, 255–6, 260–1.

Hsü Hsuan, See *Chi Shen Lu*.

Huang-fu Sung, T'ang dynasty (A.D. 618–906), prose writer, p. 87.

Huc, E. R., *The Chinese Empire*, 2 vols. (London 1855), pp. 20, 31, 61, 75, 81–2.

Imperial Cookery Book of the Mongol Dynasty, pp. 30–1, 359 ; see also *Yin Shan Cheng Yao*.

Kao, Emperor, reigned 202–195 B.C., p. 102.

Langdon, W. B., *Ten thousand things relating to China* (1842), pp. 26, 33, 45, 52, 59–60, 143, 361–2.

Lay, G. T., *The Chinese as they are* . . . . (London 1841), pp. 20, 325.

Li Chi (*Book of Rites*), pp. 35–6, 56, 58–9, 69, 70, 71, 72, 76, 81, 82, 325, 359, 360 ; adapted from Legge, *The Li Ki*, *Sacred Books of the East*, vol. xxvii, pp. 153–4.

Li Hou-chu, poet, pp. 102–4.

Li I-shan (Li Shang-yin), A.D. 813–858, poet and prose-writer, pp. 19, 44, 45, 58, 77, 86.

Li Li-weng, 17th century, poet and painter, p. 105.

Li Po (d. A.D. 762), poet, pp. 105–110.

Lieh Tzu, early Taoist philosophical writings, pp. 29, 236, 264, 283.

Lin Chi, Ming dynasty (A.D. 1368–1644), poet, p. 105.

Liu Hsun, 9th century, author of *Ling Piao Lu I*, a description of the region of Kuangtung and Kuangsi, pp. 157–9.

Liu Tsung-yuan, A.D. 773–819, poet and prose writer, pp. 20–1, 80, 185, 219, 229, 263–4.

Lo Ch'iu, 10th century, poet, p. 37.

Lu Fang-weng, Sung dynasty (A.D. 960–1280), poet, p. 111.

Lu Hsun, *Chih Kuai Lu*, a collection of marvels, pp. 255, 273.

Lu Kuei-meng, 9th century, recluse, pp. 220–1.

Lu Lun, T'ang dynasty (A.D. 618–906), poet, p. 111.

Marco Polo, *Travels*, pp. 22–3, 61–4.

Mateer, C. W., *Mandarin Lessons* (Shanghai 1900), pp. 26–7.

Mayers, F. The biographies on pp. 93–4 and 167–74 are adapted from the *Chinese Reader's Manual* (2nd ed., Shanghai 1910).

The Dragon Book